D1217190

# An American Saga

## William George Hughes
## 1859-1902

A Pioneer Texas Rancher
His Life ✦ His Times ✦ His Story

by Garland Perry

i

William George Hughes
(Circa 1900)

# AN AMERICAN SAGA

## William George Hughes

A Pioneer Texas Rancher

## FIRST EDITION

Copyright © 1994 by Garland Perry
Registration No. TXu 654-592

ALL RIGHTS RESERVED.  No part of this book may
be used or reproduced in any manner whatsoever
without written permission of the author.

Published in the United States of America
by Garland Perry
P.O. Box 200, Boerne, Texas 78006-0200

ISBN 0-9646196-1-1: $24.95

Library of Congress Cataloging-in-Publication

CIP 95-75913

Printed by LEBCO Graphics
31400 IH-10 West
Boerne, TX 78006

To Charlotte and Jerry Hughes
Thank you for being our special friends

Garland & Fran

# PREFACE

In mid-August of 1987, the postman delivered an unusual letter to me at the Kendall County Courthouse where I was beginning my first term as County Judge. The letter was from Gerard H. Hughes of New London, New Hampshire--a person whom I had never met. It was unusual in that the envelope didn't have a street nor box number on it and that the address was typed with an old manually operated typewriter.

Upon opening the letter, I was quickly struck with the impression that I was dealing with a very special person; a well educated, cultured gentleman of great character and wisdom. Mr. Hughes told me that he was born on a ranch at Hastings, Texas, about three to four miles west of Boerne. He stated that his "paradise on earth" was traumatically shattered when at eight years of age he had to move far away to a big city, never to return to the place of his boyhood dreams.

Mr. Hughes inquired about the availability of a photographic book HISTORIC IMAGES OF BOERNE that I authored in 1982. He said he was an old man of 93 years, and he too had a story that should be told--if I was interested. Of course, I was anxious to learn more about his connection with the turn-of-the-century Hastings community, and I told him so in my immediate reply.

Did Mr. Hughes ever have a story to tell! It was a real **blockbuster** about his father William George "Willy" Hughes, who came to Southwest Texas as an 18-year-old British immigrant in September 1878. A refugee from high-level English society in London, young Willy was intent upon becoming a sheep rancher when he purchased 160 acres of Kendall County land in March, 1879. Willy had no background for farming and ranching, and his chances of success on the terribly remote Texas frontier were essentially none. But Willy Hughes never seriously considered the possibility of failure. Nobody told him that he might not succeed; and he never asked that question.

Through seven years and some 200 letters to the writer, Gerard H. "Jerry" Hughes spun a remarkable story about his father, W. G. Hughes, and his spectacular successes, some disappointments, and tragic events during his time as a pioneer Texas rancher. Throughout the past seven years, Jerry has continuously provided the writer with books, photo albums, stories, records, and copies of letters that his father wrote to his family.  A selection of those exciting, fast-moving letters were published in a popular book, G.T.T.-GONE TO TEXAS, in 1884 by the MacMillan Company of London.

The saga of William George Hughes is a fascinating story about a bright, energetic young man who made remarkable contributions to the progress of pioneer Texas ranching and to his community at a crucial time in Texas history.  Jerry was right. His father's story is worth being told.

# ACKNOWLEDGEMENTS

It is with deepest gratitude that I thank the kind people and institutions whose assistance made it possible for me to assemble the research material and complete this work.

I am greatly indebted to Gerard H. Hughes of New London, New Hampshire, and members of the Hughes family for sharing pictures, letters, books, and documents about Mr. Hughes' father W. G. Hughes. Love and appreciation to my spouse, Fran, for her support and determination in sticking with me during the difficult phases of this project. She has the patience of Job, and with the help of her computer she keeps me organized. Neither she nor the computer ever complains. Fran is the stabilizing influence in our partnership.

Thanks to Jan Winebrenner for editing, evaluating, and suggesting changes for improving the manuscript. Without her professional expertise, completion of this challenging task would have been most difficult. Also, our good friend Mary Ullrich made a significant contribution by proofreading the story and making timely suggestions for its improvement. Both Fran and I are so very thankful to our friend Paul Porterfield for being Fran's resident mentor and teaching her the intricate computer commands for organizing and printing a manuscript. My deepest gratitude to young Amy Foster, a graduate student at the University of South Carolina for her final review of the manuscript. I'm indebted to Ms. Debbie Miller, librarian at the Belleville, Illinois, BELLEVILLE NEWS-DEMOCRAT, for her tremendous effort in researching the newspaper archives for articles about the 1902 accidental death of W. G. Hughes. Also, I'm so very grateful to descendants of the John C. Stout family for being so generous with their documentation and family stories about the Stout children's earlier experiences at Hughes Ranch. They were tremendously helpful with this and other events relating to their own families. I'm grateful to Marjorie Roberts Strayer of San Antonio and her brother, Bob Alan Roberts of Divine, who not only provided key information about their part of the Stout family, but they also put me in touch with their cousins in California, who filled in crucial details to the story. My most sincere thanks to Clay and Donald

Hughes Stout, Dorothy Candlish Winke, and Mrs. Barbara M. Finley for their timely assistance in this regard. Also, I wish to acknowledge my appreciation to Dr. John Willard Stout, Jr. and his sister Mrs. Beatrice S. Dooley for authorizing my use of material from their father, John Willard Stout Sr.'s memoirs.

Others who gave a helping hand with the W. G. "Willy" Hughes story were Mary Cartwright, noted historian of Boerne; M. A. Shumard, attorney and former Kendall County Judge; A. T. Wendler, Mrs. Crescentia Pechacek, Edgar Schwarz, Jr., Elizabeth Hudson, Vernon Norris, and Howard Calder of Boerne; Laurabelle Ullrich, a great-niece of Mr. Hughes, and Mr. George H. Spencer of San Antonio. I also thank Professor John M. Carroll, Department of History, Lamar University, for providing references on certain elements of the Hughes story. Thanks to Mr. David G. McComb, Professor, Department of History, Colorado State University, and Professor George Kirsch, Chairman, Department of History, Manhattan College, Riverdale, N.Y., for their input to my inquiries about the games of polo and cricket that were played in Kendall County by English immigrants in the late 19th century. Ms. Judith Moss Hawkins, Parish Secretary, St. Paul's Episcopal Church of San Antonio, was most gracious in providing information about the wedding of W. G. Hughes and Lucy Stephenson. Last but not least, I wish to express my thanks to Mrs. W. H. Maytum of Boerne for allowing me access to her property to take pictures of the old Hastings schoolhouse and of her home.

There are numerous libraries and research institutions whose professional staff members were most courteous and helpful with their time and support. Beginning at home, Louise Foster, librarian at the Boerne Library, and all of her employees and volunteers were extremely generous in locating necessary books and documents that I could not have done without; the nearby San Antonio Library personnel were helpful in lending their books and in faxing extracts of research material to the Boerne Library. I'm also thankful to the Boerne Area Historical Preservation Society for their assistance; and my thanks to Bob Bailey and Mac Gilliat, County Extension Service Agents, Agriculture, for Kendall and Real Counties, respectively. The late Tom Rogers and Mrs. Rogers of Montel, and Mr. Brooks Sweeten of Rocksprings, provided vital information concerning Angora goats and Mohair production in Texas. Special thanks to the

Rosenberg Library staff in Galveston--especially Judy Young, Office Manager, and Lisa Darst who helped me find my way around the archives and meet key people in the research departments.

At the Texas State General Land Office in Austin, Mrs. Susan Dorsey, supervisor of the Archive and Records Division, and her staff were highly efficient and courteous in providing requested records for research; the same positive attitude and efficiency was experienced at the prestigious Barker Library, at the LBJ Center in Austin. Special thanks to Ms. Rita L. Moroney, Research Administrator/Historian at the Office of the Postmaster General, for her personal assistance in obtaining historical information on the Hastings Post Office at Hughes Ranch. I greatly appreciate the cooperation of the libraries at University of North Texas at Denton and the University of Houston, Clear Lake, for their assistance. My thanks to management and employees of the ST. LOUIS POST-DISPATCH and the SAN ANTONIO EXPRESS-NEWS for making their research records available to me. My gratitude to Darlene Herrin and staff--Denise Pendley, Donna Stewart and Paula Pfeiffer--at the Kendall County Clerk's office for their expert assistance and cooperation.

Special thanks to Derrick Austin and Lauren Liljestrand, student employees at the Texas Tech University Southwest Collection Library in Lubbock. These two young people were a joy to work with, showing great interest and enthusiasm as they shuttled back and forth with books and other publications that were extremely useful. Ms. Kay Bost, curator of the research library at Southern Methodist University, was most cooperative in providing information requested.

My appreciation to Mr. Richard V. "Rick" Machen, Extension Livestock Specialist at Texas A&M University Agricultural Extension Service Center at Uvalde, Texas, for his update on current food preference research for sheep, goats, cattle and deer. The Mohair Council of America located in San Angelo was the source of much of the data relating to Angora goat and mohair production in Texas and the United States. Mr. Durey Menzies is the Executive Director of the Mohair Council. A unique and informative source of research familiarization came from The Angora Goat Museum at

Rock Springs, Texas. The American Angora Goat Breeders Association uses the museum for its base of operation, and both organizations are under the capable direction of Mrs. Mary Jane Glascock.

My heartfelt thanks to others who also made significant contributions to this work. I accept full responsibility for all errors and oversights.

# CONTENTS

## Chapter I

**BOY IMMIGRANT**

The British Cunard liner "Erin" glided into the placid waters of New York Harbor early Sunday afternoon, September 15, 1878. There, tugboats gently nudged the big ship into its docking slip on Manhattan Island's lower west side.

A clear Indian Summer day greeted the multitude of weary passengers who crowded the upper decks, straining against the side rails for a better view of the harbor and the surrounding area. They had spent several days--sometimes in rough seas-- crossing over from England. Now, their journey over, these salon, stateroom, and cabin passengers all gathered to peer at the city structures and watch the bustling activity on the streets of New York City. Families dressed in their Sunday best were taking afternoon drives in buggies, surreys, and fancy carriages--many drawn by classy, fast-stepping, matched horses. Some sightseers were on horseback and a few young couples were seen riding bicycles or walking in miniature parks and along streets, or just enjoying the waterfront scenery. Others rode city streetcars that moseyed along main thoroughfare lines with their warning bells constantly clanging.

As soon as the ship was safely anchored and docking lines secured, the gang planks were lowered and passengers from upper decks began their exit. At the terminal they made a short stop at customs before proceeding to their destinations. It was an exhilarating sensation for first time visitors to America, the land of opportunity and great expectations. Many first class passengers were American tourist returning home and Europeans with visas or visitation permits; others were immigrants who went by barge to the Immigration and Naturalization Service clearing facility a short distance away.

Steerage passengers were the last to leave the ship. In steerage people of all races, cultures, social status and religions were clustered together below deck. Living conditions in this compartment were characterized by poor lighting and ventilation, overcrowding, filth, and offensive odors emanating from numerous sources, including inadequate and poorly kept sanitary facilities. Many impoverished passengers had no eating utensils and were forced to eat food off the table with their hands. Steerage passengers opted for these less favorable accommodations only because of the much cheaper rates.[1]

Sheltered people who were getting their first exposure to this mass assortment of humanity were startled at what they saw. Young William George "Willy" Hughes at 18 years old was one of those shocked by the poverty of his shipmates in steerage. This handsome blue-eyed lad with impeccable English social credentials had severed connections with British Society and immigrated to America. Once there, this strong boy of medium height and 150 lbs was planning to settle in California territory or maybe tackle the Texas frontier.

William George Hughes
Before Leaving London

[1] Egerton, John, VISIONS OF UTOPIA, University of Tennessee Press, Knoxville, 1977-- London to Rugby, Tennessee by steamer and railroad: Third Class, $42.50; First class, $105.00

# His Heritage

No one could have been less suited to the squalor of a ship's steerage compartment than young Willy Hughes. Born in a wealthy district of London on May 29, 1859, he was a child of noble descent. His great-grandfather, the famous Reverend Thomas Hughes, was the vicar of Uffington Church and one of three cannons of St. Paul's Cathedral. A tutor in the court of King George III, he mingled with the most elite of British society. The reverend's wife, Willy's great-grandmother, was Mary Anne Watts Hughes. A woman of many talents, she was a gracious hostess, often entertaining the most notable celebrities in her home--among them, Sir Walter Scott, whom she considered a close friend. She authored his biography, LETTERS AND RECOLLECTIONS OF SIR WALTER SCOTT. Willy's grandfather, John Hughes, was the only child of the Reverend and Mrs. Hughes of Uffington. An author and artist, he traveled about Europe and mingled among highest social circles. While residing in France, he wrote AN ITINERARY OF PROVENCE AND THE RHINE which was published in 1819. John Hughes and his wife, Margaret Elizabeth Wilkinson, raised six children: George, Thomas, William Hastings (called Hastings), Walter Scott, Arthur, and Jeanie Elizabeth. Each found a place in London's society.

Jeanie Elizabeth was a leading English socialite and close friend of Alfred Tennyson, George Eliot and George Frederick Watts. A professionally trained vocalist, she sang at the Albert Hall[2] dedication in 1871. She was also a friend of popular Swedish soprano Genny Lend¹ and is said to have been invited to perform with her in concert. Jeanie married Nassau John Senior, son of famed political economist Nassau William Senior, in the late 1850s. Her brother Thomas Hughes distinguished himself as a scholar and a writer, gaining fame for his classic, TOM BROWN'S SCHOOL DAYS, based on his experiences at historic Rugby boys school. Later, he served as a

---

[2] An immense domed art and learning center with an 8,000 capacity auditorium, dedicated to the memory of Prince Albert, Queen Victoria's Prince Consort who died of typhoid fever in 1861.

× Jenny Lind

Queens Counselor, Circuit County Judge, and in 1880 he founded Rugby, Tennessee, a Christian Socialist-oriented community for middle to upper class British immigrants. Rugby, with its classic Victorian Library which Hughes established in 1882, stands today as a major tourist attraction on the Cumberland Plateau of Eastern Tennessee.

Hastings, the middle son of John Hughes, studied at Harrow and, with a mind for business, began importing sherry from Spain. It was into this prominent family that Willy was born, the first son of Hastings and his bride, Emily Clark. Two other sons were born of this union, Gerard and Henry (always known as Harry). Emily Clark was the daughter of a Welsh clergyman and niece of Nassau William Senior.

Hastings Hughes moved his young family to Port St. Mary's, Spain, in 1862 to establish closer ties with his budding import business. It was here that tragedy struck the Hughes home. When her fourth child and only daughter, Emily, was born on December 29, 1863, Mrs. Hughes contracted a fatal disease from her midwife. She died a few days later, in 1864.[3]

Following the burial of his wife, Hastings terminated his business relationship and booked passage on the next ship to England for himself and his four young children. Back in London, he arranged with his sister Jeanie to take charge of his boys; his mother, Elizabeth "Granny" Hughes, took his infant daughter to raise. Thus the Hastings Hughes children grew up in a very proper, aristocratic environment. Aunt Jeanie insured their proper cultural exposure. As a young man, Gerard started an apprenticeship in art under the tutelage of the great painter-sculptor G. F. Watts; Harry was tutored in the fields of botany and zoology. Beginning in her early childhood, Emily took piano lessons, and Willy showed exceptional talent as a violinist at a young age. Granny Hughes had a strong hand in the overall supervision of the children, although other relatives assisted in their upbringing. The bonding between Hastings' children and their grandmother was especially close and enduring.

---

[3] DeBruyn, John R., LETTERS TO OCTAVIUS WILKINSON: TOM HUGHES' LOST UNCLE, based on letters in the Morris L. Parrish Collection of Princeton University Library

At this point, one might reasonably ask what this Hughes family background and genealogy have to do with Willy Hughes' immigration to Texas. First, it is important to understand how a bright young man with Willy's refined social status could possibly humble himself to a peasant lifestyle somewhere on the American frontier. Secondly, "Primogeniture" was definitely a factor in causing Willy to emigrate. Primogeniture is a term that originated from English Common Law, whereby the oldest son inherited the family estate.

For many years, British society further refined primogeniture, by custom and social practice, to dictate that younger siblings of families with recognized social status must adhere to certain standards in order to remain acceptable at the same level of society. Careers that were approved for those listed in the social registry were selective government civil service employment, army and navy officers, lawyers, clergy, college professors, medical doctors, trade and commerce, and a few other positions of similar status. Hastings Hughes, who was the third son of John and Margaret Hughes, appears to have maintained the standards for acceptance in British society with his import business, through family connections, and because of his personal contact with diplomatic officials in the powerful British Empire.

Hastings established one important connection in American diplomatic circles through his friendship with John Murray Forbes[4], a rich and famous Boston railroad builder and financier. Forbes was dispatched to London as a special envoy for the U. S. government during the Civil War. His objective was to intercept and divert delivery of two ironclad warships, then under construction, that were about to fall into the hands of the Confederacy. While unobtrusively making his way through tedious private diplomatic channels, Forbes met and became friends with Nassau John and Jeanie Senior and her brothers, Hastings and Tom Hughes. In fact, the Seniors hosted a special social event in honor of Mr. Forbes.

After his mission was successfully completed through the purchase of the ships

---

[4] JOHN MURRAY FORBES, LETTERS AND RECOLLECTIONS, Edited by Sarah Forbes Hughes, Vol. II, pages 38, 39, 92, 93

by the British government, Forbes returned home, but he kept in touch with the Seniors and Hastings Hughes. In fact, when Forbes' youngest daughter, Sarah, went to London to establish an art gallery business in the early 1870s, she resided at the home of the Seniors where she met Hastings Hughes. Not only was he instrumental in helping her meet key people and get her business started, he also introduced her into appropriate social circles to further enhance her identity in the highly competitive art distribution system.

Eventually, however, the financial burden that comes with maintaining such a social position became too heavy for Hastings. In 1876, he suffered severe financial losses and was forced to withdraw his three sons from their respective schools. Willy was at Marlborough, Gerard at Cheltenham and Harry, the youngest, at Westminster. The older boys left school immediately, but Harry remained enrolled at Westminster because of a pending Queen's Scholarship, which was later awarded then declined.

Hastings moved the three boys to a small four-room house in the suburbs of London. In this new surrounding, the men had to do all housework for themselves, including cooking, which they did cheerfully and with enthusiasm.[5] The boys were told by their father that their status had changed and they would have to seek employment outside the learned and socially recognized professions.[6] Willy accepted employment as junior clerk to Mr. Allender, Managing Director of Aylesbury Dairy Company, at £50 (approximately $250.00) per year. His salary was raised twice in eighteen months, and he had saved £130 ($650.00) before he decided to seek his fortune in America. His father and Uncle Tom tried to discourage Willy from going to this rough and rugged country on his own, but to no avail. Realistically, they knew he had no future in England, with loss of his accustomed social status.

Most likely, Willy was influenced by colorful material published and distributed in London by Doctor W. G. Kingsbury of Boerne and San Antonio, Texas, who made

------

[5] Hughes, Thomas, G.T.T.--GONE TO TEXAS, MacMillan Co., London, 1884

[6] Ibid

6

a strong pitch for British subjects to settle in Texas.

Dr. Kingsbury was Immigration Agent for Texas and kept an office open in London for nine years, 1875 to 1884.[7] Willy had also read fascinating stories about California, and that was another option he was considering when he stopped momentarily in September, 1878 to view beautiful New York Harbor. Then he walked on down the gang plank to the waiting barge transporting immigrants to the Immigration and Naturalization Service processing center at Castle Garden.

## Letters Home

Before he left England, Willy Hughes agreed to write to his father regularly, giving his thoughts, impressions, and experiences in this new and sometimes awesome land. He did indeed write, and the letters later formed the basis for a book by Willy's uncle, Thomas Hughes, entitled G.T.T-GONE TO TEXAS. The book was published in 1884 by MacMillan and Company of London. Throughout the book, Willy Hughes' letters leave positive feelings about his character, intelligence, and ambitions, as he thinks, plans, and grows into maturity in a new world with its sometimes harsh environment. This was so totally different from anything he had ever anticipated, even in his wildest dreams. These exciting letters that follow were written over a four year period and even today they are just as fascinating as they were one-hundred-ten-years ago.[8]

In New York, Willy wrote about calling on Mr. A. Hewitt, M.C., a friend of Uncle Tom's, who tried to dissuade him from leaving the city at that time. He thought

---

[7] Perry, Garland, HISTORIC IMAGES OF BOERNE, LEBCO Graphics, Boerne, Texas, 1982

[8] With minor changes for clarity and ease of reading, the letters are repeated as they were used in 1884. Their excellent quality and distinctive English style and humor of that period are a treasure.--Author

Willy at least should stay with him until his cousin, Jim Hughes (Uncle Tom's oldest son), returned from Texas with a carload of mustang horses to sell on the New York market. But Willy was determined to proceed on his journey and left town in a couple of days.

Willy's letters reveal his innermost thoughts as he meets different people and observes the countryside on his first trip abroad. Through these letters, we learn of his day-to-day activities, how he lived, and what he planned to do. They also reveal his keen desire to learn about agricultural practices of that day, livestock management, and marketing principles, and to develop his analytical abilities. His letters home give evidence of his great sense of humor and his youthful tendency to be flighty. Above all, they show his character, his strong mental and physical capacity, his determination, and his willingness to work hard to achieve his goals.

This first letter to his father shows Willy's surprise and disbelief at the manners and customs of some steerage passengers. His association with "common" people was far removed from the elite society in which he grew up. This letter also confirmed that he was still vacillating about his final destination: California or Texas?

WILLY TO HIS FATHER                    Sweeny's Hotel, New York
                                       Sunday, Sept. 15, 1878.

Here I am at last, and have just been pitching into bacon and eggs, and stewed tomatoes, and coffee and iced water.

We had a splendid passage; they say it was the quickest the "Erin" has had. We got into dock at about 2 o'clock, and after the saloon passengers had gone off we were barged down to Castle Garden. What a farce the overhauling by U.S. Customs is. Whether because it is Sunday or not I don't know, but they just opened a few things, and put a very large signature on in chalk, and hurried you on. I was hardly sick at all, and enjoyed the voyage immensely, especially the awfully barbaric manner in which we were fed! Very few had plates; they used the table (or board with high edges which rejoiced in that name), and as for spoons-

8

-never heard of them, "Weren't hands good enough!"

Half the steerage were Irish, the rest all sorts of nations. Some of the Irish **could** eat. A quart of soup, a quart and a half of potatoes, about 4 lbs. of beans, and a gallon of "Plum duff" (or pudding) was what some of them seemed to stow. And at tea it was very interesting to watch them. I made a special study of one last night. He was the happy possessor of a soup plate and large cup, both of which he filled to overflowing with tea, and then divided his butter into two (they give you about half-a-pound) and put one lot in the cup, the other in the plate, and then divided his bread between them, and mopped it up with a spoon.

What a place this is! Nothing but the jingling of car-bells to be heard. I was very much struck with the white steamers on the river with the working contrivance at top. I could see ten all at once, scudding about between New York and Jersey City. They guide awfully well.

I cannot say what I am intending to do as yet. I have read those papers you gave me through, and fancy sheep-ranching, which they say is most profitable, and which I know a lot of young English fellows have gone in for, will be what I shall strike at. At all events, whatever it is, I know you can trust me to put my best foot foremost, and I will write as soon as I have anything to say.

I met an old mountain fellow on board. He comes from Utah, where, I believe, he gardens fruit, but he was very close on all subjects. He was very quaint. He had been visiting England for a few weeks, and so, as he had not seen his brother for twenty-three years, "just looked in for half-an-hour," as he told me. He explained all about "homesteading" and "preempting," &c. He became a citizen of the U.S., but is an Englishman by birth. I asked him if it were profitable to recant after becoming a citizen? So he says, "Well, it's just this-wise; when ye've once become a 'Merican citizen ye'll never want to go back again--No, SIR!"

9

He was a dumpy and broad little man, with a sort of wideawake twice as broad as himself, and always had his hands in his pockets and his legs apart.

I expect my next move will be to San Francisco, from whence I shall "look round."

## Gone To Texas

Willy must have enclosed a separate note in his letter dated September 19th from Philadelphia, because he obviously was on his way to Texas, but gave no explanation of his change in plans about San Francisco. He did comment in the letter about his share of small difficulties and his reluctance to discuss his problems with anyone else.

The cost of transportation to California might have been a factor in his making the decision to go to Texas. A ticket to San Antonio was $75.00,[9] and the distance was roughly a third less than to San Francisco (1,800 vs. 3,000 miles).

WILLY TO HIS FATHER                    Philadelphia Station,
                                       Thursday, Sept. 19, 1878

I seem to be blest with a very small share of difficulties, and if any block does occur it worries me to discuss it with any one, as it has always been an intense pleasure to me to do everything for myself without help....Mr. Hewitt was very kind. I had quite a fight to get away, and I expect he thought I was too young to go by myself, and wanted me to go into the country with him till he could hear where Jim was, which I suppose would have taken a month or so. My train starts in twenty-five minutes, so I am off to get some tea and my bag checked.

---

[9] Cousin Ted's letter from N.Y., Jan. 16, 1879

## Chapter II

**BASICS OF RANCHING**

Once Willy Hughes made his decision to go to Texas, he was unwavering in his determination to pursue a career in ranching.  Although his letter of September 27th gave a vivid description of his travel by train and observations of the great American countryside  and its people, there is no doubt that his interim thoughts were on getting a quick education in sheep production and management.

WILLY TO HIS FATHER                        Central Hotel, San Antonio

                                                          Sept. 27, 1878

Here I am at last, after an awfully hot dusty journey from New York.  I stayed a little time in Philadelphia, and am glad I did so.  They are building some new public buildings there, which are, I suppose, to answer much the same purpose as our Law Courts.  They are very fine. It is a tremendous block with a huge court in the middle, and is built of polished Scotch marble; and going into the court quite takes away your breath, it is so cool.

The Quarantine officers were awfully strict all the way; each large town sent out its officer to make every one sign and swear they had not been in any yellow fever district since July 20th.  They turned out three men at Waller, a small place between Hempstead and Houston.  I have since seen two of them, and they say they let them come on after airing their heels on the platform for twelve hours.  I got a health certificate at St. Louis without trouble, but every town after satisfied its conscience by making me sign as well; sometimes at night, when I was in the middle of a -- well, as sound a sleep as you can get with your head and body in a lump and your legs somewhere over the back of another seat.

We passed some very amusing "cities," Log City, and Lairetta City.  They were both in the middle of the prairie, and all the city was a small pile of logs thrown on the ground, and a sign-board with the name of the city on it; not a house, or an animal or a human being anywhere within ten miles!

I went to Mr. J. F. Lockwood's yesterday. He knows Jim intimately, and has given me the run of his rooms, and I have been introduced to a Capt. Turquand, an Englishman with a large ranche, and am going to be introduced to another man to-morrow. Jim is driving cattle North, and is not expected back here for some weeks.

It has been awfully hot here lately. Yesterday it was ninety in a "cool" room. I am in excellent health and spirits, and do not feel the heat so much as I did in Spain.

The chief amusement here seems to be getting up party squabbles of every and any kind, and they say in the papers "A rare good time may be expected," which means there will probably be plenty of row. They never seem to think of the business part of the concern....

One of the things the Yankees do well is boot-making; they do make comfortable boots and walking-shoes.

Mr. Lockwood is going to show me a place on the river where I may get a swim. He is very jolly and amusing. He says he riles old Jim by making fun of the English and their way of speaking. Jim is very popular here, every one in the town knows him.

## San Antonio Experience

Upon reaching San Antonio, young Hughes wasted no time in "putting his best foot foremost." He met key people associated with raising and marketing sheep and wool; he volunteered to work for a sheep rancher and livestock broker without pay, just to learn the skills, science, techniques and basic business management principles in sheep and general livestock husbandry.

As a mannerly, personable youngster, Willy gained extra attention and support from those successful ranchers and livestock dealers who admired his spunk and determination and his intelligence and enthusiasm for learning about ranching.

Willy first estimated that he would need two years of work on a good sheep ranch before venturing out on his own, but that was not the case. He worked approximately four months before declaring that he had learned **everything!** He was joking, of course, but he did learn something about plowing, harrowing, herding sheep, and human survival under the most stressful conditions.

WILLY TO HIS FATHER

A Brushwood Prairie,
2 miles from San Antonio,
October 4, 1878

Here I am, camping out with a lot of sheep. The brother of the landlord of my hotel introduced me to a man named Willis, who has been sheep-raising and selling for ten years, and has just made enough to live on comfortably. I think we shall work together very well.

There are a few men in the sheep business who have a **name**, and sell their sheep at $5 to $15; whereas men like Willis get only $1 to $2½, and they say, "Oh, it's just this a way y'know, **they** get a name, and then they get big prices, that's where it is!"

They casually admit that they (the big men) had some good rams from somewhere and improved their stock; but they utterly fail to see the connection between this and the "name" they "get."

For next season we are going to have a couple of rams out from England and just "fix" that missing link. Will you get all possible particulars for me as to shipping them in London, freight, etc.; and let me know whether they can be shipped to Galveston or Corpus Christi direct (I shall probably not be able to get to either place to find out for some time, and no one knows anything about anything a yard away from him in this part of the country).

We came out here the day before yesterday. Willis took me to the yard where his "buggy" was. It is the oddest old rattletrap I ever saw, and he ties a horse and a mule in. They are not nearly the same size or colour.  All the harness is made up of old bits of strap and rope, and I don't think any one could "fix" the horses but himself.  He throws all the harness down by the buggy, and if a buckle or anything gets lost it don't scare him; he says, "Oh, never mind, guess I'll fix it somehows."

Well, sir, we started off in this thing right for this place as the crow flies.  This is a large prairie overgrown with tall prickly bushes,[1] and Willis, whose ranche is 100 miles away South, has brought a few thousand sheep here to sell to the people of San Antonio.

If that buggy's wheels were only a yard or two nearer its body it would be better.  As it is, they get away amongst the bushes; you suddenly feel a heave, and see the two wheels on the left side riding over the top of a bush; you cling on to the rail for life, down comes that side, and the other (a plucky pair they are) sees if he can't go away higher than the first. And then you find half the harness has unhitched itself from the crooked nails and things.

I have now been out here two nights, and like it very much.  We shall start for his ranche as soon as all the sheep are sold, which may be a day or a week.  I am not going to take any wages, but then he keeps me and feeds me and teaches me, and I leave when I like, and of course the rams (which we shall want about next April) will come out at his expense.

The first night we had a run.  The moon went down about 11:00 o'clock, and at 11:30 the flock had started off on the rampage towards a Mexican flock a mile off, and we were afraid they would get mixed, so we had a run to round them up and get them back before they reached the others.  The next morning the Mexican came over to breakfast and lassoed a kid, which thirty seconds afterwards was airing six component parts on trees, and a seventh in a stew-pot on the fire, and we set to.

We have black coffee, and onions, and bread, which we bake

---

[1]  Prickly Pear Cactus -- Author

ourselves, and potatoes and bacon. Willis works himself, so I expect to learn lots under him. Sheep-men here are, for the most part, of two kinds: the men like Willis, who work, and who never make any improvements, and men who seldom see their ranche and have herders; and they could make improvements if they were only to attend to it themselves. The men who make it pay are the ones who combine the two kinds--so I guess we look like cutting up smart, anyways we'll try.

It is awfully hot still. I have a bathe in a creek just here, and am rigged out á la herd-boy. My coat and pants, which are briar and water proof, light, and cool, and look like brown silk, cost $3½ together! and hat, with two-mile brim, $1. One ought to come with **nothing** and get rigged out here: they know better what is needed, and one gets just the things one wants.

I am awfully well. I expect I shall work with Willis somewhere under two years; then I'll get across to England and get a few rams and come back and run second to none, or turn toes up. Of course I am reckoning that I don't get leaded by any of these shot which (they say) occasionally get about so thick you can't see the sun. Our camp here consists of the buggy and pair aforesaid, Willis' boy, a bright lad of twelve, three camp water-barrels, three stew-pans, which act as ovens, etc., etc., a few blankets, and a few odds and ends, viz. a knife and fork or two, and tin boxes of salt and sugar.

P.S. We shall want the rams about the end of March, and they will have to come to New York. We should like to know freight. I shall write to Allender[2] asking prices of rams, and telling him I want him to get one of his farmer friends to pick us two next Spring. And if you can get us freight particulars now, I will get you to start them from London for us when we want them.

---

[2] Manager of Dairy where Willy worked

WILLY TO HIS FATHER                    Brushwood Prairie,

                                            Oct. 10, 1878,

I expect English rams will cost too much for Willis by the time they get here, so I shan't bother Allender in the matter until I want mine. You might get the price of a good one for me that I may tell Willis, I haven't any idea. I suppose though they would come to £25, or more.

Willis' boy was taken very feverish a day or two ago, and I have been taking the flock out. There are 1500, and when out feeding they cover half-a-mile diameter, and they always go on walking, and by the time you get to the head the tail will have twiddled around and started. They licked me at first, but I can manage them now.

We had a storm the night before last. It was lightning half way round the horizon, and then blew up in a few minutes and just let us have it. I fixed up under the wagon. The animals started in the middle of it, and then it was a case of mackintosh and top-boots!

Some of the ewes are dropping lambs, and it's fine to see those kids trying to get through long grass when they are half-an-hour old. They jump, and spike themselves, and fall on their noses, and repeat the process until they are dog-gone tired, as Willis would say. I think his expression is a corruption of something worse. We get up about 5 o'clock and have breakfast, then the sheep start at 7 and are out till 12, then dinner; then start at 1.30 and in at 5.30; tea at 6, and "in bed" by 7.30, when Willis and I talk, and he tells me about the time they were "fighting and hoorawing and fussing about here," meaning the war between North and South.

We are very good cooks, and our greatest variation is in our bread, which we cook in different ways. It was awfully good this morning -- a liquid batter of flour and water and yeast and salt, and a few eggs, then set some oil boiling in a skillet and pour the batter in in doses. It makes a sort of crisp soufflé cake. You fry about four at the same time in a

16

skillet eight inches across, fish them out in about two minutes and pour four more in. They are light and wholesome. I ate about 200 or 250 I should say, that's about half a cwt.[3] I am now a mile away from camp looking after these sheep, and only started this letter to say that I wanted you to get me the price of good rams somewhere about, as I shan't bother Allender at all in the matter.

## All The Way To Mexico

Willy quickly established himself as an excellent correspondent. His crisp, fast-moving letters give a colorful account of what life was really like on the Texas frontier in the 1870s. His trip roaming through the brush land of South Texas, and a fascinating excursion into Mexico, were adventures that few people experience in a lifetime.

WILLY TO HIS FATHER                                   San Antonio
                                                       Oct. 24, 1878

We have not left here yet you see, but Willis has sold his sheep, and we expect to start for his ranche to-morrow. I think the open air suits me to a T. We slept in a room in town last night, and it seemed stuffy after sleeping out on the ground, so we camp out again to-night. The night I took your last letter to post I had a supper, after nine days bacon and flour and kid, and you bet I let in! They give you at all the "un-napkin" places here a grand meal for 25 cents, about six dishes. One never gets through them except under special circumstances, but I got through all mine that night, and two cups of coffee. I had a steak and two sorts of vegetables, and two poached eggs and a dish of stew, and another of mutton and some stewed prunes, and any amount of bread and butter! I had a fortnight's herding, and have mastered that and learnt a good deal

---

[3]  Hundredweight

17

about sheep. I employed my spare time in tarantulizing tarantula spiders out of their holes, and throwing stones at rabbits.

I was almost going with the three fellows who bought the sheep. They were going to Fort Worth, 200 miles, and neither knew how to drive properly, so they wanted me to help them; but they wouldn't give me my fee of 5 dollars per week besides grub, so I refused.

You people don't know what coffee is over there. We buy it in the green, and roast and grind it ourselves, and then **boil** the powder, which is ground about three times as coarsely as we used to grind it, so it all settles to the bottom of the pot and doesn't come off when you pour out the liquid, which is partly because the spout, or lip rather, is at the top of the pot.

I think I see my way to starting a good thing next spring. I find that the Northern sheep-men all come South to buy. The central market is San Antonio, and the Southern breeders bring their cattle there, and the Northerners (as those three we sold to) come there to buy. One of the three told me that some of the sheep they had just paid 1 dollar 25 cents for were worth 2 dollars 50 cents up North; and next spring I think I shall drive North with a few sheep, if I feel capable.

Please get my cash transferred to Lockwood's here, as I feel I can trust myself with some capital by the time that it is transferred. I am in no hurry though.

P.S.--We start at sunrise to-morrow, so I shan't see Jim till we return with sheep in a few weeks. Don't think I want any more than that money of mine--I couldn't do with any more.

WILLY TO HIS FATHER                    Concepcion, Texas[4]

Nov. 8, 1878

I have had tremendous fun since I wrote to you on 24th Oct. Willis and his boy, and the Mexican herder and myself, started next morning at sunrise for his ranche, 120 miles South, Willis and I leading in two-horse wagon with spare horse tied behind, and the nigger and boy in buggy and pair with two horses tied behind. It was tremendously hot all the way. We did it in three days, the last day starting at 1.30 a.m. and getting in at 6 p.m.

The first day the wagon nearly upset into a deep gully as we were going down one of the perpendicular creeks, of which we crossed thirty or so. Perhaps you know them--dry watercourses about twenty feet deep; you go straight down and then straight up. We rushed down, Willis putting on the break hard and throwing the reins into my lap, and the left horse almost went down the creek on the left.

The second day one of the horses behind the buggy kicked the other, which one bolted behind a tree, and as it was tied somewhere under the buggy it shot the hind part up, and out went the boy, who was driving, on to the mule's back; the reins dropped, and the horse and mule started off, taking the buggy over the legs and chest of the boy. (He wasn't hurt.) Willis and I heard the Mexican yelling behind, about 300 yards off, and we saw the buggy dash up in a cloud of dust, and it didn't stop till the pole had applied itself to the horse behind the wagon and sent it swinging to the side. No damage was done.

After this the Mexican funked and took to his horse, and I got into the buggy with the boy to help him. It is the rottenest old buggy you ever saw. Willis bought it second-hand and has had it five years, and has done the "repairing" himself, so you can imagine the result. It is **all** mendings,

---

[4] SE Duvall County--Author

19

especially as to the harness; and coming down we had to tie the tires on in several places with strips of goat-hide. All the wheels were rattling, and the left one was--well, "rolling"; and, as I was just beside it, I watched it with great interest as we went down the gullies or through ruts a foot deep. How it held together I don't know. The worst gully was an awful one, nearly perpendicular. The horse, although used to gullies, funked it, and reared; so the Mexican went to the head of the animals and pulled them. When a few yards down it was too much for him, and he sprang aside, and down we dashed and up the other side safely. I was driving, as the boy, like the horse, had funked, and got out at the top.

For miles and miles we went through burnt and burning grass. It doesn't flare, but smoulders; and we passed trees that were still flickering in places. One night in a forest we could see it smoking out west of us, and the wind was blowing our way, but it didn't reach us.

On the second day, in the evening, we passed a wagon by the roadside with two small girls in it, about six years old. It had camped there the night before and the horses had stampeded, and the father of the children had been out since daybreak after them, and had not returned. We asked them if they were frightened; "Oh, no," they said. "Have you any water?" (They were four miles from any.) "No." "Then what will you do for it?" "Starve, I guess," said the eldest; as much as to say, You ought to know that. Their father now came up after a fruitless search all day. His boots had been burnt up by the sun, and the soles were tied on with string. We left them water, and promised to send the horses back if we found them; but we didn't see them.

Willis' house is a log hut, with bedroom, and kitchen, and out-houses; one for children, of which there are nine, and other for corn, etc. The first night it rained hard, and I slept in his room, he and his wife in one bed, and I in the other. I wanted to sleep on the floor, but, as he remarked, "the floor gets covered with water sometimes." The floor, I may mention, is the earth, and, instead of being raised, is rather lower than outside, from being trodden on.

We were at his ranche for three days, and then he and I went on in the wagon to a friend's ranche, to sleep there. The ranche used to belong to two young Americans, who were murdered by their "pastores" for plunder.

Next day the rest of the sheep-buying party came up (we are down South, buying sheep to drive to San Antonio) in an ambulance belonging to Mr. Smith, one of the party. We consist of Mr. Smith, who was educated at Yale, is stout and merry; Judge Yarborough, who sings comic songs or tells comic stories all day, and prefers dabbling in sheep to lawyering; Jones, a young Northerner, who is in Texas for pleasure, is pretty rich, I fancy, and has come out with them for a lark; and Willis, myself, and the Mexican.

We started at once for Smith's ranche, the luggage and four of us in the ambulance, and two on horseback; stayed there for a day or two, and then started on down here. They are very great on card-playing and whiskey-drinking, and play poker at every stoppage, and at night, by the light of the moon, till 11 o'clock or so. They don't gamble, but bet imaginary sums, and owe each other thousands of dollars.

We were two and a half days coming down here, and stopped at a small town named Collins for stores, and laid in lamp-oil, flour and potatoes, bacon, whiskey, etc. Coming along the oil got into the flour and potatoes, and the whiskey got into "the crowd." It is not lawful to sell whiskey down here, but it is bottled under the name of "Stomach bitters," and sold in a square glass bottle with directions, about "two table spoonfuls, etc."

After every drink they get very talkative, and, as each is a perfect character without it, it is intensely interesting to listen to them. The nigger pretends not to like it, but says a little makes him "mucho bravo";

21

so it is as well that he takes some, as it is a pretty rough country down here, and we all carry arms (about twelve in number) loaded, and by our sides at night. We are now camping just outside Concepcion, a small Mexican town.

Willis and the nigger are out after some goats which the former lent a man on shares three years ago, and has not taken the trouble to look after (no wonder he doesn't get rich!); and the other three buying sheep in the wagon; and I am looking after camp, with the things scatter round and my coat hanging beside me with a loaded revolver sticking out of the pocket--one feels safer with one, though it is very seldom required--and for half-an-hour before I began writing I had been preparing a larded kidney for my dinner, and it is now roasting over some wood coals and tied up in grass and looks awfully good.

Just after passing Collins, Jones, who was riding (and had had some whiskey), let his six-shooter off by mistake, and it kicked into his face and cut him. He comes in for the wars whether tight or sober. Coming from San Antonio in the ambulance, with Smith and the judge, they stuck in a bog (Willis and I nearly stuck in the same place when we came down), and Jones being, well, the soberest of the party, had to get out, and, up to his waist in mud, unhitch the horses and hitch them to the back of the wagon, and so pull it out again.

9th Nov. Just off in ambulance for a drive over country after sheep.

WILLY TO HIS FATHER                                    Concepcion,
                                                      Nov. 19, 1878

Since I wrote to you we have been a week's trip after sheep. We camped seventeen miles from here or more, near a very large waterhole (they are very scarce here), and we were a mile or two from any ranche. That was our camp, and from there we scouted for sheep.

22

We had lots of shooting at antelope and deer, and wild turkeys, geese, cranes, ducks, partridges, etc. We have not bagged any venison yet. Though I have only had five shots, the first I got a bird, and the second and third rabbits; so I thought I was infallible I suppose, as I shot the last two carelessly and missed. They were both at a lot of curlews sitting by a pond.

From our camp by the waterhole, we all, except the Mexican, whom we left in camp, went after sheep, two of us riding and the other three in the ambulance. We didn't take any food, or cooking tricks as they call them, as one expects to be fed gratis at the few ranches one graces with one's presence, even though there are five mouths to feed.

The first of the two days we had dinner at a very clean little ranche off **café au lait** and batter cakes. That night we got to a wealthy stock-owner, whose "hall of reception" was a round space cut out of a thicket. We didn't do any business with him, but nevertheless, as usual, ate about a whole goat of his, and made free with his corn-meal. Next morning we had a light breakfast of coffee and corn-bread, and started for camp, getting a **little** corn-bread and coffee in the middle of the day at a ranche (the ranches are sometimes five or six miles apart or more), and when we got back that evening we were ravenous, and had a large supper off goat and bread and molasses and bacon and coffee--this is our larder in full; and then we started back here next day, stopping that night at a large horse ranche, where we invaded the house, and slept in one of the rooms, and monopolised a detached kitchen.

We saw Mexicans breaking in horses, and also cutting off the manes and tails of some wild ones. They drive them into a corral, and then lasso them, and tie their legs together after tripping them. The old stud horse gave them some trouble, but they at last lassoed his front legs as he was galloping round, which sent him on to his nose, and then of course they were on to him with ropes. When he got up he just was mad to find he was cropped.

We are now on our old camp ground here, and haven't got any sheep yet. It is splendid weather, and as I write (on the inside of the back of the ambulance) there is not a cloud to be seen, and it is as hot as a **hot** summer day over there; and it is cooler now than it was when we left, as there have been two nights of rain which has filled the creeks which were dry before.

I fancy these fellows don't mean much business, but I am learning a lot about stock and the country, and am having a very jolly time. I have no work to do except what all the others do, as the Mexican attends to the horses, etc., and the grub is very good for camp, and there's lots of it.

Oh, yes! by the bye, my special work is baker's. I can bake better than any of the others, and make better bread. You bet we have good flour bread--little rolls about as big as a hen's egg, and we have them hot for breakfast and cold the rest of the day. I have just hit the dodge for making them **au fait**, or whatever it is.

The man who keeps the store here had confidence enough to sell them a bottle of gin this morning, and a quarter of an hour after it appeared in camp those four and the Mexican had emptied the bottle. At this moment the only one who is overcome is the Judge, and he is asleep by the wagon; the other three are playing poker as usual.

I am picking up Mexican fast; every one as far south as this speaks it, and there are very few Americans here; I don't think we have come across **one** since we left Willis' ranche, and only two Mexicans who have been able to talk English; but the three bosses of our party all speak Mexican.

It is extraordinary the difference between English and the people down here in small expenses. Our Mexican servant invites any of his friends to eat with him at his master's expense, and no one says anything, and when we were camping near the waterhole, two Mexican herders

24

came twice every day merely for food, and just took what they wanted without being invited. But it is the regular thing out here to eat at any one else's expense, and consider it a piece of condescension. I have gained about 20 lbs. in weight, I believe, since I left England, and am in excellent health.

The ranches, or farms, down here are several miles apart, some of the owners owning as much as 180,000 acres; this is the case with one or two, the rest a paltry 500 or upwards! Some ranches own, besides other stock, 2000 or more horses, which roam about the country in herds.

The people about here live very simply, the richest have only wooden houses, and eat goat or mutton (very seldom beef), and although plenty of game can be had for the shooting, they very seldom take the trouble to kill it. There are quantities of wild turkey in the woods; they run about in flocks, and are so common that if a man shoots one he generally cooks the breast and throws away the rest.

WILLY TO HIS FATHER                        Laredo, Rio Grande,
                                                     Dec. 2, 1878

The day after I last wrote we bought 600 sheep, driving them into a large pen, and then catching each one and looking at his teeth, and branding him with a square tar mark, and chopping his tail off, and putting him through the gap. I was catching and bringing to the gap nearly all the time, and it is tremendous exercise, as some of the sheep are pretty strong.

Next day we met a buyer who wanted sheep in a hurry, and so took ours and paid us what we gave (or rather what Smith, Jones, and Yarborough gave), and $100 besides, which was a very good day's work.

We are now on the American side of Laredo, which is on both sides of the river, and are going to start into Mexico to-day or to-morrow, as sheep are very much cheaper there; and not only that, Mexican money is at a discount of 15%, so that a Mexican dollar, which is at par in Mexico, can be bought in America for 85 cents. We brought a box full (two or three thousand I expect) of Mexican dollars with us safely.

We passed some splendid scenery occasionally.[5] Most of the way is quite flat, but two days we came upon hills covered with all sorts of thorny bushes, cacti, etc. The scenery for the last five or six miles or more was lovely. A very hard north wind was blowing, and as we passed the mouths of Canyons we nearly got blown over, and had to put up the ambulance cover.

This is a very pretty little town;[6] it has sprung up within the last thirty years or so; there are the inevitable Mexican plazas, and a very well built church, and the houses are well built and painted in all sorts of brilliant designs outside--I am speaking of this side of the river, as I haven't been across yet; the other side seems to be as large. The river here is as broad as the Thames at London Bridge, but shallow; no navigation comes up as far as this, and the town is built on a sandy kind of soil and about 20 feet higher than the river, which is gradually working the sand away. We are having beautiful weather, very warm; I don't think there is a cloud on the sky at this moment.

Yesterday we washed in the Rio in the morning, and in the afternoon I went for a stroll along the shore and saw evening parade at the barracks;[7] and when returning saw a blaze in town. It was a large store on fire, and when I got there the church bells were being hammered, and Mexicans were rushing along the balcony of the first floor getting the furniture out. There is no fire-engine in the place, and we pulled buckets

---

[5] Speaking of trip to Laredo. -- Author

[6] Laredo

[7] Old Fort McIntosh, Laredo--Author

of water up by ropes on to the balcony at the back, and handed them up through a trap-door on to the roof, and got the fire out in about an hour after it began. The only serious damage done to the things was from the water, and crazy Mexicans who pulled down any woodwork they could; and after the fire was out there was still one crazy loon trying vainly to hack the wooden tiles off the roof with an axe.

We have been living like fighting-cocks, on beef and onions, and pickles, and oranges, besides the usual bacon and molasses, etc., and have hired a two-room house with a yard to it. We inhabit the former, and the five horses the latter. The atmosphere is so clear here in the country that, when six miles from Concepcion, we could hear the drum beating between the gusts of wind (which was blowing towards the town). Of course letters are not being forwarded to me from San Antonio, so do not expect to get answers to any that may be there, till I strike it again.

WILLY TO HIS FATHER                                    Laredo, Texas
                                                        Dec. 15, 1878

Since I wrote last we have been ninety miles into Mexico and back. We had a good deal of trouble getting a start, as none of the officials on the Mexican side seem to have any definite ideas with regard to the laws, and each one fingers around for a bribe instead of slapping out the law. We got across the river, wagon and horses, etc., on a barge, and, after making satisfactory arrangements with the officials in town, started; on the outside we were pulled up by another custom-house and taken back; "satisfactory arrangements" had to be gone through again, and a pass given us.

We then rolled out, and on the third day reached Lampazos, which is a small town amongst mountains; the latter were plainly visible from the Rio Grande. Going down we passed only about three ranches, and crossed a very pretty river (the Salado). All the Mexicans were very pleasant and hospitable. Going down we slept near a ranch each night. When we got into Lampazos we waited in the main plaza while the boss looked out for a house. The annual examination was just taking place; a seedy band was playing outside the schoolroom door, and some 150 or 200 girls marched in, in white dresses and red sashes, and then a few anxious parents marched in, as if they were taking each other down to dinner, and all dressed up to the nines.

We got a very jolly house, or stone-room, for storing wool or fodder; it was empty though, and outside was a yard with a small stream running through it: the river is tapped, and runs through nearly every yard in town. That night I had a bathe in it, while the others went with a party of cattle-men to see a performance by a strolling company of actors. We stopped in Lampazos about a week, and I think the other four cattle-men and ourselves were the only whites in town.

One of the others was an exact specimen of a Mark Twain hero; he had mined of course, and was a lump of wit and good humour. Someone asked him how much he had paid to go into the theatre. "Pay!" said he, "paid nothing. Our pistols were locked up, but I got hold of one and strapped it over my behind, and me and Johnson just walked through." The Mexicans are very funky of Americans if they have a pistol with them, and it's very seldom they haven't, and it was a very small piece of French leave.

The other four had been out after cattle (half the time or more on the spree) for six months, and they were getting irregular about their meals, got anything to eat anywhere, and they used to take us by storm and eat like giants. It is part of the fun to go and eat at another ranche's expense, and ask why the---- there isn't a better lay out in such a bully-looking crowd?

I had a tremendous walk one day. Lampazos is between two mountains. The one on the right looks as if it is about three miles, or not

28

so much, away; the other one is nearer; so I thought I'd walk to the furthest one. I started at 9 o'clock a.m. to walk, and walked across the prairie, and now and then the foot of the mountain would seem a mile off; but when I got there I found myself on the top of a small hill, with another mile of prairie, and so on; but I didn't stop, as I was going through cacti of all kinds, and various plants I had never seen before. At last, about 3 o'clock in the afternoon, I reached the foot of the mountain and went half-way up. I had a splendid view of an endless stretch of prairie, and away in the horizon one could see a stretch of about ten miles of prairie fire, which smoulders and flares along (this one burned for days); but the sun was rapidly going down, and I thought the sooner I got back the better, especially as I had to cross a river a mile or two from town. So I started back as quickly as I could.

The last half mile was so thick with cactus I could hardly get along, and when I was at last started pretty well the sun was disappearing. Luckily it was a full moon that night, or I should have had to bunk down and wait till sunrise; as it was I had no end of a bother and fun. I struck the river about a mile higher than where I had crossed it, and got mixed up in a jungle kind of a place, and could hardly get through, at last I got a place in the river, where I forded it; it was only about a foot deep there, and got into some corn-fields. At last I struck the road, and got back at 8 p.m., after eleven hours' walking. I wasn't tired, and only a little stiff next day. When I asked afterwards how far it was to the place, I was told fifteen miles! It is tremendously deceiving, as the atmosphere is so clear you could almost see a flea crawl over there. It nearly crazed two Mexicans when I told them I had been there, as they never walk more than half-a-mile at a stretch, and seldom that.

We found out that some large men had been around getting sheep to stock a ranche, and the price had gone up to as much as in Texas; and so we couldn't buy, as there would be two duties to pay, one out of the country, and another across the Rio Grande--so we returned.

We didn't strike ranches either of the nights coming back, and so camped miles away from anyone. Going down we had camped near a ranche each night for safety's sake. We are now back in Laredo, and, I think, are going down the bank of the Rio Grande, or somewhere.

I am quickly picking up Mexican. I go into stores and spout out for something, or jabber to an old woman who lives in a house looking on to the same yard that our horses are in.

Yesterday it was cold, but to-day it is hot again, and hardly a cloud anywhere. I am awfully well, but getting fat I'm afraid, in spite of riding eight hours a day. I fancy I shall get on swimmingly among stock, as I am learning about all the different kinds.

I shall know pretty well about all south-western Texas by the time we finish this trip. All the cattle-men one comes across are the very essence of good-humour and open-handedness; the great failing with them is that they can't keep out of the bar-rooms, and this is the reason why one hears such an account of the dangers about here. If they went about their business in a sober way, and didn't get into rows in gambling-halls and bar-rooms, they wouldn't be always getting killed.

The Mexicans have a very good kind of earthenware in which they cook almost entirely. It is red and thin but tough, and will stand any heat; but the handle, although the pot is on the fire, remains cold. They are used for coffee and frejoles (the beans they eat so much of), and a pot to hold three pints costs 12½ cents. They are the best things for cooking in I ever saw, and are made in all shapes and sizes.

16th. Just off to Rio Grande City.

WILLY TO HIS FATHER                          Guinagato Ranche,

20 miles from anywhere, Texas,

Jan. 2, 1879

A happy New Year to you all.

Since I wrote, we have been rolling about the country between
Laredo and Rio Grande City, and no post-office within 20 miles, the
nearest being at Roma (this side of Rio Grande). We were a few days at
Carrizo, and are now between there and Roma, and 15 miles inland from
the river (Grande). We have got three lots of sheep, about 1000, and
want 2000 or so more, which I expect we shall soon get.

When at Carrizo, Willis, and the Judge, and I crossed the river
again and went down to Guerrero, which is a picturesque little town on
a very beautiful river, the Salado. The only other American in town was
the American Consul, and so we were objects of great interest and
curiosity. We put up at a small café, and the first night when we entered
the small room (which opens on to the plaza) we found the bench opposite
the table full of expectant Mexicans, sitting like dolls, evidently specially
invited by our host to see the "curiosities."

When we left Laredo they had small-pox in town, and were
"packing around dead Mexicans considerable," as a cattle-driver informed
me; but that is the only unhealthy place we have passed.

We have been some days now at this ranche, which is like all the
others,--a lot of small log houses surrounded by a fence, and about five
or six large families, all related in some way, the men of which saunter
about doing nothing more than shooting a deer occasionally. This is
almost the only meat they eat, as they seldom kill a sheep, at least on this
ranche. They have no capital except a lot of land and some cattle which
they occasionally sell. They seldom buy anything but coffee and tobacco,
and their cash for this is what they receive from passers-by for corn and
for leave to water at their well. The only work I have seen done since we

31

have been here was by a party of six, one of whom was chiselling on a wooden plough and the other five were looking on!

We shan't strike a post-office for some days, so to-morrow I intend riding to Roma to post this, in case you should be getting at all anxious from my not writing. By the by, I hope you had a merrier Christmas then we had. It was most amusing. We had an awful day, and were out of provisions, and corn, and everything, and nearly got frozen. I will give you a list of that day's proceedings: 5 a.m., got up from under wagon and found icicles all about. It was raining, everything was wet, sheep had stampeded and were at last found in three different places some miles off, and brought back by three of the others nearly at night.

Smith and I started in the middle of the day on horse-back for the nearest ranche to get corn for the horses. It was awful cold and raining, and we thought we had lost our way, but at last we heard the roosters crowing and got to the ranche, where we thawed and had coffee and "muscal," or brandy made from cactus. Then we started back and dried the blankets and things as well as possible in a rain, before a fire enough to roast an ox. We had killed a wild pig, and had intended to have boar's head for Christmas dinner (only, as some one would remark, it was a sow), but unfortunately a dog ran off with the head. That day was the worst we have had, and no one is a bit the worse for it. It is now warm again, though it rains pretty often; but we got some more sheeting and have a tent fixed from the wagon, and so keep everything dry.

Jan. 3, 1879

P.S.--I hope my Christmas Day description don't frighten you; it exaggerates itself on paper, and taking all in all, we are having bully weather, and are as healthy and jolly as pot-boys. I can't ride to Roma to-day, after all, so this must wait a day or two, much as I wish to get it off.

<u>Oxfordshire Downs Sheep</u>

The arrival of the new year found Willy still deep in South Texas. He didn't know that his father had agreed to send him two Oxfordshire Downs rams and six ewes. Nor did he know that his cousin and best friend, Ted Hobson, was accompanying the sheep to Texas. Letters from his father in England lay in a stack in Mr. Lockwood's office in San Antonio, and when Willy finally returned to claim them, he learned that Ted and the sheep had already arrived.

FROM COUSIN TED

Smith and McNeill's Hotel,

Washington St., N. Y.,

Thursday afternoon, Jan. 16, 1879

I'm afraid you'll think I've been a long time before writing; but I have been waiting till I could report on the sheep. The "England" only arrived yesterday, owing to heavy weather, and the smashing of the steering apparatus. I went down to the dock where she's lying this morning, and saw the sheep: they are real beauties, and are in splendid health; indeed they ought to be, for they finished the last morsel of their grub this morning.

Mr. Page has had them taken to some stables where they will be well looked after, and will have them put on board my steamer (the "Rio Grande") by his own carman on Saturday. I find the run to Galveston takes about ten days, so I will provide about as much forage as they had before (I have got Mr. Howard's letter giving the quantities).

I had a glorious run in the "City of Brussels," eleven days from Queenstown, terribly rough weather part of the time, but once I got over the first feelings of qualmishness I enjoyed myself thoroughly, and my appetite was proverbial. There was a very rum lot on board, natives of all countries, but a great many very decent fellows. We divided into messes after we had been on board a bit; ours was the most select of the lot. It was composed of a 'Frisco artist, two diggers, and a Yankee

33

bo'sun (Jack Slack by name), and a widdy, one of the steerage belles, and your humble servant. Sometimes after a successful day's foraging in the cook's galley, we'd invite outsiders to supper as a great honor, but we were most particular as to their antecedents.

Foraging was one of the chief businesses of the day: after every cabin meal you'd be sure to see a dozen or so loafers hanging round the cook's galley offering to do any small job, such as peeling potatoes, or washing dishes--anything in fact that came first; and if it wasn't overdone, two square meals a day might easily be raised. There was one woman who excited all our indignation by the barefaced way she was always beating up our preserves. Her plan was to pretend she was always sick, and could only eat a little of something delicate. One morning she was seen to eat two rolls, a basin of porridge, and a lot of ham and eggs for breakfast, and at dinner time I heard her tell the chief steward she'd hardly tasted a morsel for days, and did he think he could get her something extra? I could stand it no longer; up I jumped, and said, "Well, ma'am, if you call what you had for breakfast fasting for days, how much **do** you get through when you **do** have a real square meal?"

She hated me ever after, and took every opportunity of alluding to **her** well-behaved children before me; but I was amply revenged, for all eyes were on her at meals, and if an unusally large loaf came on the table, it was always passed down to the "delicate Lady."

We had plenty of exercise, for the second officer used to come to the steerage every day and ask for volunteers to haul on ropes, or holystone the decks, or something of the sort; if it had been to be keel-hauled I think we'd have gone, we were so glad of something to do. For five days we shipped so many big seas, that it wasn't safe to go on deck. One of them swept me under a small signal gun, and barked my shins awfully. We had to have our soup and everything out of mess, she rolled about so. I was rather uncomfortable at first, because I had no bed, but

I soon got accustomed to the boards, and slept as well, in fact better, than most of the others. Some of them were awful restless beggars, and would get up at two in the morning and roam about all night, talking or playing seven up; the way they were cussed was highly gratifying to the disturbed ones.

The stewards were the decentest fellows I ever met; they were so popular on board, that we gave them three cheers when we left. I should never think of going cabin though; steerage is far too comfortable and jolly, and we had a deal more fun than the cabin passengers ever had aft.

They used to come and look on when we were dancing, nearly every evening. Our only musical instrument was a fiddle, which was played by the bar-keeper splendidly. Some of the fellows dressed as ladies, and would walk about arm in arm, on deck, amidst roars of laughter. There was one very amusing man on board, named Andrew Savage; he was just the shape of a barrel, pointed at each end; he was always going for something for his wife, about whose existence we were slightly skeptical; if there was such a person, her capacity for beer was something enormous.

It's very cold here, and there's a foot of snow on the ground. Traffic's almost entirely stopped, except with sleighs, of which there are any quantity. I like New York itself very much, and certainly think in time it will lick London all to nothing. I suppose you have seen their elevated railroads? They are far nicer than the Metropolitan Railway, and the carriages are better furnished, besides being able to go anywhere in the City for 5 cents.

I will write again from Key West, which is the only port we touch at. There's such a queer crowd here, Texan drovers, and all sorts of men. The fare to San Antonio by rail is $75, so it's an immense saving going by sea.

R.M.S. "Rio Grande," Off the coast of Florida,

Jan. 24, 1879

I am just writing a few lines to report on the sheep as I promised; but whether they'll ever reach you or not I'm very uncertain, as I am going to entrust them to an old boy on board who leaves us at Key West. The sheep are all right so far, and seem to me to be in very fair condition. They did not take very kindly to the forage provided for them in New York, as the American hay is so much coarser than the English, and they sent no turnips as I told them to do. However, they are getting used to it now, and eat it pretty well.

The weather here is awfully hot and sultry, very different to New York; but the ship is very well ventilated, so I don't feel it much. The sheep have been noticed a great deal by everybody on board, and several of the cabin passengers have asked for Mr. Howard's address, as they wanted to get some like them. The sailors are very fond of them, but seem to have strange ideas what's good for them in the way of food. I caught one of them the other day feeding them with a copy of the "Tribune," which he said was the best thing possible for them. The carpenter spends half his time playing with them; but he's under the impression that they bite, so he's very careful not to put his hands too near.

I am writing this in my shirt sleeves, and suppose in England you are all shivering in the wet. A little boat came off from a lighthouse this morning for papers and vegetables; there was only one man in it, and he very nearly upset himself standing up to take off his hat to the ladies.

The skipper's been fishing for barracoutas all day, but I've not seen him catch any yet. We are much better fed here than on the "City of Brussels"--beefsteaks, potatoes, rolls and coffee every morning for breakfast, and a very good dinner and tea. We get into Key West to-night about 8 o'clock, and leave again at 10. I believe there's nothing to be

36

seen but cigars, turtles, and sponges.

Galveston, Monday evening, Jan. 27, 1879

P.S. Sheep landed today, all in good condition; are going on by freight-train to-night. I accompany them in same van. This is an awful rum place.

WILLY TO HIS FATHER                    Mr. Lockwood's Office,
                                       San Antonio, Texas
                                       Jan. 30, 1879

Just back from our trip. Two of the bosses and self left Willis and the Mexican 160 or so miles off, to follow with the 1700 odd sheep, and we rolled up in the wagon. I am awful fat and jolly.

We got in here about 6:30 to-night, and after getting a room and some grub, I came round to the above's office, just in time to catch Mr. Lockwood before he went to the theatre, so I have got all my letters and his office to myself.

I have just got through my letters and will post this to-night, as owing to our not having struck a post-office for some weeks, I'm afraid you must have thought "a Bandito[8] had leaded me," as I see the doctor says in one of his letters; tell him though, it's not more than a 5-cent. business in some cases.

Thanks for all you've done about the sheep. It all comes in bully if they are all right. I will be after them and Ted early to-morrow, and will probably write you then or next day.

We had a bully time up from Mexico, and latterly awfully hot. We rode in the wagon without coats, and with sleeves tucked up. But more of this in the next as it is now considerably after 10 o'clock, and,

_____

[8] "Bandito," A substitute expression--Author

37

owing to its coming on to drizzle at 3 o'clock this morning, we had to turn out and get bedding, etc., into the wagon, eat breakfast, and roll out; especially as we had a 33 mile drive to make, and horses knocked up a bit, or rather a good deal.

P.S. I'm awfully glad Ted has come out. I often thought (lately) of writing to him about it, only I meant to get a little straight before doing so, so that it shouldn't be a case of the blind leading the blind; but I guess we'll make it somehow.

P.S. Seen sheep, apparently in fine condition. Just off after Ted and Jim.


WILLY TO HIS FATHER                    Jim's Hut, Allen's Pasture,
                                       4 miles out of San Antonio,
                                       Feb. 2, 1879

The sheep are very much admired, and are, apparently, in splendid condition. I do not at present feel capable of managing sheep on my own hook, and so have, after a long talk with Jim, seen Capt. Turquand, who is an Englishman with a ranche out here. He has been very kind to me, and has promised to take care of them till I want them, which will not be for eight or ten months I expect, that is till the season comes on in October. Capt. Turquand has been very fortunate with his sheep this winter, not having lost one. These will be safer with him than anyone else. They will be with his and receive the same attention therefore, and he is to use the rams this season if he wants to. I, in the meantime, shall study up the business on ranches, &c.

I hope, before October, to have taken up some land with Ted, and to know what I'm up to. Then these sheep, if they live (and they will have every chance to), will be acclimatized and will give us a fine beginning.

Nothing like "blowing" in this country! **They** are like a flock of

sheep, if one man damns or praises a thing the rest will follow.  So you
will see by the paper[9] I send you that I was determined to get people
running in the right direction at once.  They will now be praised higher
by each person who tells another about them, you bet!

SAN ANTONIO DAILY EXPRESS
Sunday morning, Feb. 2, 1879

**OXFORDSHIRE DOWNS**

"ARRIVAL OF A SUPERIOR BREED OF ENGLISH
SHEEP--A FORMIDABLE RIVAL OF THE FAMOUS
HAMPSHIRE AND SHROPSHIRES."

"Yesterday a reporter of the San Antonio Daily Express was shown
by Mr. W. Hughes a flock of sheep, consisting of two bucks and four
ewes, recently imported by him from England for breeding purposes.
These animals are, " &c., &c. (giving all that was claimed for the sheep
by their breeder, Mr. Howard).
"The sheep imported by Mr. Hughes, and to which particular
reference is now made, were purchased directly from Mr. Howard, and
were brought out under the immediate superintendence of Mr. T. Hobson.
They are splendid animals, and their magnificent fleeces will open the
eyes, " &c., &c.

Ted and I are living with Jim and his man.  It is quite a small hut,
but very comfortable.  We had five or six visitors to-day--cattle-men--they
are the jolliest fellows possible.  We all have been sitting in the huts as
it has been raining.  One fellow tried to get Jim's man to dine with him,
so as to leave Jim to do the cooking, but he couldn't do it.

Yesterday, Ted got some "overalls," or coarse brown trousers and
coat, and he is now wearing them.  The coat is like an Eton jacket, so you
may imagine what "six foot one" looks like in it.

Our visitors are now gone, and Jim's man is greasing some saddle

---

[9]  SAN ANTONIO DAILY EXPRESS

leathers, and Jim, who has just washed the dishes, is reading a paper, and so is Ted. Jim is looking very well. This is a most wonderful climate, I think, and seems to agree with every one...

That emigrant agent will be getting into pretty hot water very soon, if he hasn't done so already. Ted met several fellows as he came from New York, who were cursing him; and I read in a newspaper yesterday that he had sold a man 800 acres of land at Kingsbury, which is a place between Galveston and here, with a railway restaurant and four houses.[10]

He described it as a growing town, with five hotels and several good shops, and on one side of the 800 acres was said to be a stream, "which, although not quite a river, abounded in several kinds of fish."

Well, the man arrived at Kingsbury with his wife, to find the town as I describe it, and the stream a dry creek which never ran in its life, and the 800 acres of land in a high state of cultivation to be a piece of the prairie land, which is all round the place; so he went back to Galveston to wait till he could earn enough to take him back to England. Every one out here gives "that Emigrant man" a bad name, and if he came out I expect he would be shot. For a single man this country is all he describes it, or nearly so; but a married man expecting to settle down and make a living at once is badly sold, unless he has a lot of capital.

Flirt would be a great pet out here, as all the dogs are large and ugly, except one sort which the Mexicans have. They are hideously ugly, though small, and haven't a bit of hair on except a sort of narrow ridge of bristles along their backs.[11] They look as if they had been shaved, but are really born so.

---

[10] Kingsbury, located 9 miles east of Seguin in Guadalupe County, founded in 1874 by Southern Pacific RR and named for W. G. Kingsbury, Texas Immigration Officer, 1870s-1880s.

[11] Mexican Chihauhau breed. - Author

Cattle-men about here are just as Mark Twain paints them, and keep one roaring with their quaint sayings. Our party went up to the ranche of a fellow they knew as we were returning from Mexico. He suddenly recognized the Judge, and roared out his best welcome thus -- "Well, d___ your soul, **how** in THE H___ are you, any how?" his whole face beaming with pleasure. This is the sort of welcome one gets. They are so glad to see you that they sort of emphasize a bit.

We camped one night on the river coming up, about two weeks ago; it was awful hot, and we bathed in one of the pools, for at this time of year it is a series of pools and doesn't run; and then I went out turkey-shooting. I saw a flock of ten or so run behind a cow about fifteen yards off; so I stooped down behind a bush till the cow should go away. The cow thought I was serenading her and jumped about, and the turkeys got away in the brush and I couldn't track 'em. You bet, I felt inclined to pay that durned cow.

One day we caught a land turtle and baked it, and ate it and its eleven eggs, which were the same size as a yolk of an egg, and tasted just like one.

We have very strong north winds here, and they have blown Jim's hut a foot or two out of perpendicular.

FROM COUSIN TED                          Jim's Camp, San Antonio,
                                         Monday, Feb. 3, 1879

You will have heard from Willy before this that I arrived with the sheep all right. They (i.e. the sheep), I am glad to say, are in splendid condition, and could not have looked better the day they were put on board in Liverpool. You cannot imagine how they've been admired; every time I pass the stables where they are lying there is a small crowd looking on and asking questions. It was just the same at Galveston; everybody knew all about them half-an-hour after they were landed. I

41

assure you it would have required a couple of clerks and a principal to answer half the enquiries that were made of me. I got just mad at last and left.

I had rather a rough time of it in the freight train (of course I travelled with the sheep) coming up to San Antonio. The first night I slept on the floor of a cattle truck with half-an-inch of water in it, and the unfeeling brutes turned me out at four in the morning at a little out-of-the-way place called Harrisburg, and left me to wander about on the line looking for some human habitation. However, I met the watchman, and he took me in and gave me a chair to sleep on; I had to wait there till five in the evening, and it was just slow I can tell you.

That night I was a little more comfortable as I managed to get a couple of cushions, so I slept like a top till half-past four in the morning, when they turned me out again; it was just maddening. After abusing the Company for upwards of an hour, I started in search of water for the sheep with a lantern and a bucket, and after a lot of groping about in the dark found a well, and just as I was getting the water a great ugly black dog, a trifle smaller than a cow, hunted me off the premises. But I did get some at last out of a cistern, so I was happy.

Freight trains on these lines are about the slowest things in creation. I frequently used to jump off and cut cactus leaves for my charges, and catch her up again before she'd gone a hundred yards. In fact, I was cautioned about walking too fast in front in case I lost sight of her altogether.

At any rate here I am at last. I am sorry to say I was only able to give Willy five guineas change out of the cheque you sent, but there were a lot of little expenses that mounted up considerably. Jim's camp is a jolly place if the chimney would only draw; as it is, my eyes are watering so that I can hardly see to write.

I got rather frightened about the sheep off Key West, which is a regular West Indian place, populated almost entirely by Cubans and niggers: the steamer's side was so hot that you could not bear your hand on it, and they were all lying gasping for breath; however, with plenty of iced water they pulled through.

Did I tell you about the dead fish we passed through off the coast of Florida?  One of the steerage passengers happened to be looking over the side, and saw something white right ahead, which proved, when we got up to it, to be an immense shoal of dead fish, sixty-five miles long; in some places it was thicker than others, but there was always a large quantity round us for that distance.  Somebody said they were killed by an eruption in the Gulf, but I have not learnt whether that was the true reason or not...

P.S.  I've just got a gorgeous pair of top-boots, with "Hamilton Boot" printed in gold letters in front of them.  I expect they'd create a sensation in the Row!

WILLY TO HIS FATHER                          Jim's Hut, San Antonio
                                                    Feb. 10, 1879

My mind is at last easy with regard to the sheep.  I started with them on Wednesday, the 5th, with a man, and a wagon in which we had the animals.  We had a wet norther that night and next day up to about 2 p.m., when we reached Capt. Turquand's ranche.  He was very jolly, and made me stay that night, and in about two weeks, I am going to spend a week or so there.  He has got a lovely place amongst hills, with lots of ever-green oaks.  He has about 9 x 6 miles, half of which is fenced; and his house is in the middle of the fenced part.  It stands on a rise above a small stream, and you cannot see it till within a few hundred yards.  He has several English fellows there.  Ted and I just off down country.

43

WILLY TO HIS FATHER    Buck's Ranche, near Beeville, Bee Co.,

Feb. 22, 1879

This just to say that I'm well and flourishing. Went with Ted to Pleasanton, and for a week or so since that have been paying visits to several ranches down here 100 or so miles from San Antonio. I ride about, and camp under a tree. At present I am staying with two English brothers of the name of Buck, very jolly fellows. They've got over 10,000 acres here of the prettiest country I've seen. I'm pumping everyone about sheep. Going to start for San Antonio on the 24th, I think; and then going to visit Capt. Turquand. It's awful hot--not a drop of rain for weeks.

FROM WILLY    San Antonio, Texas,

March 4, 1879

Just back from my rambles down South. I have been over lots of land, and at lots of ranches, and have learnt everything almost,--ploughing, and harrowing, and all the rest of it.

I got the quinine all right, thanks; they use it a great deal out here. Since I have been here, however, I haven't needed any medicine, and don't feel like wanting it.

Thanks for your advice about sheep. The best sheep can be bought for $3½ now; though, after the losses in the winter, I expect they'll go up. About half the sheep died, I think. I am just off up to Capt. Turquand's, and will write from there.

COUSIN TED TO HIS BROTHER General Mason's Ranche, Leon Springs,

March 4, 1879

Here I am, settled at last; and I'm going to tell you all about it. When I left Jim's camp near San Antonio, as I told you in my last, I went straight to Capt. Turquand's, to see if I could get on his ranche; but he

44

was already overstocked with hands. However, he recommended me to try at General Mason's: so next morning I came here, and saw the general's son-in-law, Major Ellison, and after a little talking, agreed with him to come and take entire charge of his flock of Angora goats; for which he pays me a pound a month, with board, and a tent to sleep in. Of course this is not much; but it's better than nothing to start with, for you see I know nothing whatever about them, and have to have a good deal of help at first, and he has promised to give me something better, if I get on well, after a bit.

My work consists of driving them out to pasture during the day, and seeing to the kids in the evening, when I get home. His ranche is about 3000 acres, and I take them pretty well all over it. This would be pretty hard if I had to walk, as goats travel very fast; but as I'm allowed two horses it's not so very difficult, though it's a little monotonous at times, as I seldom see a soul all day.

I hope you will be able to read this; but if you knew the difficulties I've had, you'd excuse me. First of all I bought a bottle of ink, and got ready to write to you, three days ago, and when everything was ready, I discovered that the bottle had fallen out of my pocket. Next day I borrowed a bottle from the major, and prepared again, but whilst I was getting ready the cork slipped out; so did the ink; so I was stopped for that night. To-night I borrowed another bottle, and then discovered I'd got no pen. I was ashamed to go up to the house to borrow one, so I caught an old turkey, and pulled some feathers out of her tail, and tried to make a pen. Hence the bad writing.

There are three other men employed on the place, all of whom are Mexicans, and the house-servants are, too, so I hear very little but Spanish spoken, and am picking up a little. The Major is a remarkably nice man, and is very good to me. He does all the real working of the estate; the General only coming once a fortnight to see how things are getting on.

My tent, where I am writing this, is such a snug little place. I've fenced it all in with brushwood to keep the cows out. I'm glad to say I've not got to cook for myself, but get all my meals up at the house; and very good ones they are, too, so I'm very comfortable. There is a good deal of game round here, mostly deer and turkeys. I had a capital run after the latter some days ago, but did not succeed in getting one, as my coat fell off my saddle just when I was getting near enough for a shot, and I had to go back for it. The deer are generally very shy and hard to get at. I got within 70 yards of some yesterday, but I had no fire-arms with me.

The greatest trouble we have here is the want of water. There is none fit to drink within two miles, and even then it's as muddy as pea-soup. There has been no rain for four months, so all the creeks and waterholes are quite dry. Sheep-raising appears to be the most profitable business in Texas, if they are well looked after. To start in a small way you want a capital of about £250. With this, and taking good care of his sheep, a man ought to do well out here; better, I think, than in cattle, as the country is too dry for them. A number of the sheep-ranchers who come out here, after they have once got started, leave their flock entirely to the care of their shepherds, and they themselves loaf around town, smoking and drinking, and naturally enough soon lose all their money.

I had intended to make this a long letter, but it's miserable work writing with this beastly pen, so I'll say, Good night...

P.S. I'll buy a decent pen next week, and write a good letter. Old Graphics would be most acceptable.

WILLY TO MADGE[12]                              Captain Turquand's

                                                March 7, 1879

My sheep are getting on very well; they run in the same field as some Cotswold sheep. These have white faces, and the others scorn them, as they are very proud of their black faces; and when eating out of a trough, budge the others away with disdain.

I have just been riding all over the country on horseback, camping wherever I happened to be at sundown--sometimes under a tree, sometimes at a ranche, where they always welcome one. Once I had an awfully fine camping place. I had just laid in a nose-bag full of grub (as I hadn't struck a store for some time), and was peckish. It was nearly sundown, and I rode out of the village to find a good tree to enjoy my repast under. I passed a house where there was a well and a small enclosure with half a small haystack in it; and I went up to the house to ask if I might draw water. The house was bang empty; evidently deserted some time back; so I jumped for joy, turned my horse into the enclosure with the hay, and took possession of the well (which had very good water) and house; made a good hay-bed; and announced that dinner was ready. Then I let into tinned pigs' feet and bread; second course, cheese and bread; desert, dried apples; drink, water; salt served with each course; and had a splendid sleep afterwards.

Taking possession in this way would be rum in England, but here it's all right; probably the house will rot (they are of wood) before anyone uses the land again.


WILLY TO FATHER                                 Captain Turquand's

                                                March 7, 1879

I got here the day before yesterday, and found all the sheep in

---

12  Willy's sister Emily; often referred to as Madge by her family--Author

excellent condition. I have very sanguine hopes with regard to the offspring when crossed with some Merino bred sheep, if they can only stand the heat.

In a day or two I am going up North to look at land. It is healthier up there than South of San Antonio; and down in the South it is almost or quite impossible to find land at a moderate price with good water on it. Capt. Turquand's land is the best watered in the country I fancy; he has thirteen springs on his 6000 acres, and the creek that runs below his house has a rock bed, and he is building a dam some way down which will fill the bed of the creek, which is deep and broad, with water; so he will have a running lake, about 10 to 20 yards broad by 400 yards long, or more, in front of his house.

Yesterday one of his pupils and I went out hunting up cattle and horses. I rode one of the best horses I was ever on; he never seemed to get blown, and just enjoyed running in as much as I did. He has been trained to it, and is awfully quick. Some of the horses were pretty wild, and would dart about all over the place; but "Pat" (my horse) seemed to see which way they were going to go, and sometimes swung round nearly a complete double when going full tilt; so, of course, if you don't watch the movements of the horse you're after pretty closely, "you've got to swing off."

Ted tells me that Bob is coming out; if he is, will you get him to bring me out a small packet of the following seeds--turnip, mangold wurzel, clover, and meadow-grass. I want to try them on a small scale. Also, if Bob can bring it, "SHEEP; THEIR BREEDS, MANAGEMENT, AND DISEASES," by William Youatt, published by Simpkin, Marshall, and Co., Stationers' Hall Court, if it is not out of print. It costs 8s.,[13] and I presume that the half-yearly dividend on the bond which you speak of

---

[13] Eight shillings (about $2.00) - Author

will cover this and the seeds.

As soon as I can find a suitable piece of land, I shall buy it, and grow corn and millet. There is a very good sale for both. Good land will grow 50 to 100 bushels of corn to an acre, which corn sells at 45cts. to $1 per bushel, according to the market.

I shall begin with only enough sheep for these two bucks, and in a very few years I shall have a very valuable flock all of one kind, which is a great thing.

I shall keep fowls, pigs, and turkeys; so all the food I shall have to buy will be flour and coffee, sugar and salt, as I shall probably rear a few goats for meat purposes. All of these can be bought very cheap, and I can make more money this way than by working for any one; and besides, of course my stock increases and ranche improves, and becomes more valuable.

The only difficulty I see is land. The $500 I have will **well** cover small stock, and horses, and wagon, provisions, etc. I have been carefully into it and know it. Land may cost me $250; I don't intend that it shall cost me more, as I can get what I want for this, so that if Uncle Tom would let me lay out £50 or under of the money you mention in land, it would help me a good deal. I can begin making money directly I get started, and would pay this back with five per cent interest, as soon as possible.

I should like to know by return if there is really the least objection to this, as, if there is, I will make arrangements to run my sheep on a ranche and work there; but this does not pay so well, as I should have to work for nothing, for running my sheep on the ranche-owner's ground.

WILLY TO HIS FATHER                              San Antonio,

March 13, 1879

...With regard to the Oxfordshire Down sheep being a white

49

elephant, you can't upset us any out here; you may **send** a white elephant if you like, we'll make him pay, grow wool on him if necessary!

Ted is working on a farm and gets awfully well fed. I went to see him on my way back from Turquand's, and caught him up, driving back cattle from water. He sleeps in a tent, where he has plenty of company in the shape of--well, not fleas; they are animals Townsend calls red bugs in one of his Field letters, in which he says he had to get up in the middle of the night and go and get a bathe in a stream, they worried him so.

There is a beetle out here, called the tumblebug in polite society, that rolls a ball five times as big as itself. A green English fellow, just out the other day, asked "why was that ball pushing that bug about[14]?"

P.S. $484 received: as soon as I can find the land I want, we'll go booming.

WILLY TO MADGE                                        San Antonio,
                                                      March 13, 1879

I'm trying to sell my pony to-day as he only carries me thirty-five miles a-day, which won't suit yours, etc.

Jim starts on the trail in a few days now; he is awfully glad, as he says hanging around puts him out of temper and gets away with the needful.

Ted has a very jolly place and master--looking after cattle, horses, and pigs. He was herding goats, but they are kidding now, and so have been put under an experienced man. He used to employ his time in chasing rabbits into hollow trees (they don't have holes in the ground) and then burning them out; then he took them home in the evening and ate them.

---

[14] Tumblebugs march stern foremost, pushing the lumps with their hind legs.

It's a lovely day, but not too hot, as the wind's blowing.

FROM TED

General Mason's Ranche,

March 21, 1879

Willy has bought a place of 160 acres of good land, lying about fourteen miles from here, and thirty from San Antonio. A few days ago he called here and offered me the chance of working it with him for half the profits, deducting for what my share of the provisions cost, he supplying everything in the shape of horses, wagons, farm implements, &c. I join him at the end of the month, and we intend to raise corn, fruit, and vegetables, for all of which there is a good demand.

You needn't have been afraid of troubling the bankers by sending too many letters to their care. There are several hundred addressed there every day, and the partners themselves never see them. They're put into a large box with pigeon-holes for each letter in the alphabet, and the owners simply walk in and take them out...I gave up minding the goats, after a week of it, to the old goatherd again, and the Major made me cowboy instead. My work now consists of hunting for lost cattle, and taking large herds to the waterholes about twelve miles from here. I am writing this lying out in the woods, looking after a lot of fine bulls, which are too valuable to be left alone, to turn up some day or another, as is done by all our neighbours. Some of them simply live in the saddle, keeping their cattle from going too far. I have been doing so for the last week, as we lost no end of animals.

One day, sixty goats broke out of the pen, and got some miles from here. It took me a whole day to find them, and since then I've been riding after lost stock nearly every day. I'm glad to say that I am always fortunate enough to find them, but it's very tiring work, and knocks up no end of horses. I have to have two fresh ones every day, and both are dead beat at night. However, I've learnt to drive wild cattle, which is

51

something. The first time I tried I could do nothing whatever with them, and had to go back for help, but now I can steer them through another herd without mixing them, with anyone round here. It's very exciting when you're driving twenty or thirty head of cattle through a large herd of the scrub brutes, preventing them from getting mixed, and cutting them out if they do. I can tell you it's considerably harder than driving a quill in Mark Lane, but I wouldn't exchange lives for a good deal.

This ranche is a very fine one, though it's only 3000 acres. Most of the land is good, and there's been $12,000 spent, in the last year, in improvements. All the stock is well bred, from the cows to the very ducks, which are Muscovy; but I can't see how the money is to be returned for years to come, and if the stock can't stand the climate there will be a great deal lost. This winter four heifers died, which cost $375 apiece, in Illinois, in the autumn. For the Major's sake I hope the rest will be able to stand the heat of the summer, but I should very much doubt it.

I had a narrow shave of being stung by a scorpion the last time I was at Jim's camp. Dave and I were sleeping together in his little shanty, and had rolled up an overcoat to serve as a pillow, and in the morning when I woke there was one of the brutes lying on it, right between our heads. He had crawled there for warmth, I suppose. If either of us had turned he must have been nipped. There are any amount of snakes around here, principally the gentlemen with rattles. We killed one a few days ago six feet long. He had nineteen rattles in his tail. I generally use a little Scotch terrier to kill them. He just seizes them by the middle of the body and shakes the life out of them, and then eats 'em. He seems to know as well as possible that, if he's bitten, it's all up with him, and goes hopping about, keeping his legs out of the way till they're dead.

## Land In Kendall County

In a letter to his father dated March 7, 1879, Willy speaks of going up North to look at land. Two weeks later, he followed with another letter stating that he indeed had purchased 160 acres of land between headwaters of the Menger and Frederick Creeks, three and one-half miles west of Boerne in Kendall County.

So what did young Willy Hughes learn from his approximately five months of ranching apprenticeship in San Antonio and South Texas? His accomplishments in such a short period of time were remarkable. In just a few months (not the two years he had expected it to take), this bright, energetic and often optimistic young man met the right people and accumulated a wealth of information covering a broad spectrum of subjects relating to pioneer ranching.

Of course, Willy Hughes didn't learn **everything** about farming and ranching. But he did pick up many basic skills and techniques of livestock management; he became acclimated to the harsh weather and learned something about survival in very basic and difficult circumstances. Most important of all, Willy gained confidence, and through his association with successful businessmen and ranchers he was able to see the "big picture" of profitable ranching practices. He remembered that men with a **name** just happened to raise quality livestock that brought better prices. On the more basic side he learned how to build a thatched roof from the Mexican herdsman, and he was taught by sheep buyers and traders to look at a sheep's mouth and teeth to determine its age and general health.

Chapter III                    **A "REAL LIFE" FARMER/RANCHER**

Willy's letters of 1879 and 1880 continue to disclose this ambitious young man's thoughts as he cautiously plans and implements programs designed to insure his survival as a farmer and sheep rancher. For instance, Willy speaks of dividing different ranch enterprises into separate areas of responsibility--putting his cousin Ted in charge of gardening and vegetable production. His brother, Harry, who joined him in July, 1879, was given control of the sheep operation; and Willy himself acted as general manager while caring for other projects, such as purchasing land and livestock and preparing fields for planting. He also indicated that it would be wise for him to start his ranching venture on a small scale with emphasis on diversification. Lack of money required him to keep operations small.

Willy quickly learned from experience that his five months of observation and indoctrination at the hands of sheep buyers and ranch managers did not make him a skilled farmer. On March 7, 1879, Willy wrote to his father asking him to send the book, SHEEP; THEIR BREEDS, MANAGEMENT, AND DISEASES, by William Youatt. A few weeks later, he asked for THE BOOK OF THE FARM, by H. F. Stephens, F.R.S.E. W. Blackwood and Sons, 1871.

Willy was also beginning to salivate over prospects of increasing the size of his ranch. His intuition and logic led him to anticipate growth and expansion. He told his father that he could easily acquire some 2,000 adjoining acres of land through a lease arrangement with the option to buy later. While undergoing "real life" experiences at small-scale farming, he was thinking of space to expand his sheep ranching operation in the near future.

In some instances, Willy was overly optimistic. For example, he predicted he could produce up to 100 bushels of corn per acre. His estimate was too high for Hill Country dry-land farming. Also, young Willy had no idea how much crop damage to expect from wild deer, turkeys, stray livestock, and varmints. But he did have courage, determination, and a natural affinity for manual labor.

WILLY TO HIS FATHER San Antonio

March 20, 1879

I'm just watery hot, and I've been rushing about all day getting my team and baggage, as I've bought 160 acres near Boerne; it's an awfully hilly country, but fine grass, and healthy. There is unlocated land next door to me, not such good land, which will only cost me under $100 per 640 acres(!), and I can preempt eighty acres more for a small fee, and, if I want to fence, have the privilege of fencing in the 640 which I lay out for the State, next to my 640 acres. Of course, when the State can sell the land I have to take my fence off its 640 acres (if I **do** fence it), but, as all State land is reserved at $1.50c, it will be years before this is bought.

I am going to try and get some sheep "on shares," i.e. I take care of them for the owner, and we divide profits and increase. Jim started after cattle yesterday. I met him as I came from Boerne.

The American and friend haven't turned up yet; when they do I am going to try and get them to come and help me get ship-shape at my place, as Ted can't join me till after his month is out, which is on the 31st inst. I will tell you more about the place afterwards, when I have taken stock of it more.

I traded my pony and got a good horse; cost me $40 though. His name is "Billy," and he runs in the wagon with a mare whose name is "Bet": she cost me $25. They are both large horses, and about the same size, and go well. Bet is a grey, and Billy a dun.

The $500 covered everything; 160 acres, wagon, harness, horses, plough, corn, and hosts of cooking things, etc., and grub for a tremendous time.

I am off to collect the various parcels which are waiting for me. When the $100 come, I shall locate the 640 acres. The 160 acres tract has a hut on it, and a field, and more land which can be ploughed;

55

whereas the unlocated land is hilly and only good for stock. I paid (or rather shall pay when I get to Boerne) $225 for the 160 acres. I shall be on the safe side for provisions for over a year, and before that Ted and I will be making money. The only provisions we shall have to buy will be coffee, molasses, sugar, salt, flour, and pepper, as we shall raise vegetables, bacon, meat, eggs, and honey. There are two fellows here, one English and one American, that I know personally, who want to go into cattle; so I am going to have a consultation with some one about the unlocated land, and if they think it will raise cattle well I shall try and get one of them to go into it with me, he buying and owning 100 cows and a bull or two, and I finding land, houses, winter-fodder, etc., on half profits. I can fence the 640 acres and pens, &c. for about £100, and of course raising cattle is a good thing. Cows can be bought for $5 or $10, and their male calves when two years old would be worth that.

My address in future will be--Post Office, Boerne, Texas

## Getting Organized

Hughes Ranch was a beehive of activity from the day Willy arrived on the scene.

First, there was a matter of food, shelter, and livestock feed and pens. Then there was the clearing and fencing of land for a garden and grain crops. Willy was already late for planting, and he was badly in need of additional manpower.

He had previously made cousin Ted Hobson an offer to work and share in any profits, but Ted couldn't report until April first. Willy had talked with an Englishman and an American about working as "students," much as he had done with Mr. Willis. When they didn't show up the day they were expected, Willy went for help and returned bringing a Scotchman with no farming experience. His name was Grady.

Unfortunately, the one shanty that Willy acquired with his land was used for storage of barrels and containers of food provisions, flour, cornmeal, beans, rice, coffee, sugar, molasses. So putting "first things first," Willy and his associates had to sleep outside--usually under his wagon--until he could build a temporary lean-to thatched roof shelter.

WILLY TO HIS FATHER                                    The Shanty,
                                                       March 30, 1879

My letters have been so full of small commissions, you must almost dread opening them; but I think I am straight now.

I have been working like a nigger for the last seven or eight days. My man and I got here on the 22nd, and we have nearly cleared three acres of stones (some of which are as big as a man's body), and we are well on with tying up grass for thatching. I cut the grass, which is a kind used here for thatching, in the creek, not 100 yards from the door. We should have finished thatching probably, only I wasted three days in going to San Antonio, to see if that money had arrived, as I am very anxious to secure the 640 acres next to me before anyone else. However I am daily expecting to hear from Lockwood of its arrival, and hope the land will wait for me.

A large creek runs by here, about twenty yards in front of the door, but the water only runs half the year or so, during the rainy season.

In front of the house, there are 100 or more yards of level rock-bed, with steep sides about six feet high, and I am going to dam this up, and if it holds water, we shall have a lake.

Inquisitive neighbours came in at first, like grandmothers around a daughter's first-born, to give all sorts of opinions and advice; but they have found out they're not wanted. Ted joins me on April 1. He and I are going into partnership with regard to all products of the field, corn, &c. I find land, and tools, and camp necessaries, which of course remain my property, and we each pay our share of the grub-bill. We ought to make a good thing of it, not only in corn, and perhaps cotton, but in vegetables.

Boerne is cram full of sick people; there are three **large** hotels,[1] and numbers of boarding houses. In short, it is only a large consumption hospital: and yet I haven't seen a fresh vegetable in town! We are near enough (5 Miles) to run a van in everyday, if necessary, and I expect we should sell all we could raise.

You ought to see me now; squatted on the floor, leaning against a plough, barrels of flour and corn-meal, bags of beans and rice, kegs of molasses, frying-pans, skillets and coffee pot, spades, &c., &c., all around; chickens just going to roost in the trees outside, over the wagon.

Grub is awful cheap, I will give you a few items of the only necessaries. Beef 4 cents and 5 cents per lb.; bacon 8 cents (this one can cure oneself); flour $7 per barrel, or in small quantities $3 per 100 lbs.; beans 35 lbs. for $1; sugar 10 lbs. and 12 lbs. for $1; Molasses, $4 per 8 gal. keg; salt, $2 per cwt.; coffee, in the green bean, 6 lbs. for $1; rice, 15 lbs. for $1. Apropos of coffee, Capt. Turquand tells an amusing story of himself. When he and Mrs. Turquand came out, about a year ago, they went shopping; and amongst other things, he asked to be shown some coffee. The man of course brought the green beans--it is seldom sold anyhow else here-- "That's not coffee" says Capt. Turquand, "coffee's brown stuff, like snuff, you can't fool me!" It has been a standing joke against him ever since, in San Antonio.

To-day has been almost suffocatingly hot, and very little breeze for a wonder. I had a bathe, and couldn't lean against the rock, it was so hot. I hadn't **much** of a bathe though, only a splash; coming back from town, I came across a splendid hole and stripped, and was just going in, when I saw a snake swimming about with his head out of water. This was enough, I splashed in the shallow water near the hole. I don't mind

---

[1] Boerne hotels in operation in 1879 were the Phillip House, O'Grady Inn and the Boerne Hotel (Ye Kendall Inn) -- Author

bathing where there **may** be snakes, as they seldom if ever touch one, but after seeing one one doesn't exactly like to take a bath with it.

I have got a Scotchman working with me. He came to me with tears in his eyes, just before I left San Antonio, and asked if I knew where he could get a job, as he hadn't a cent, and had slept and eaten just where he could for some days; so I have taken him on for a short time, till he gets stronger. I left him in charge here while I returned to San Antonio, and on my return, found his work well got forward. He never did manual work before, having tried to get a school, as he is well educated. He is about twenty-six or twenty-seven I should say, and came out five years ago, as his father, who is a Scotch clergyman, wasn't well off, and had a large family, of which he is the eldest. He had saved up money in New York, for a visit home last year, but was taken ill, and it went to the doctor. He is to be pitied, but there are many more like him out here. He is getting stronger, and I expect will drop the idea of a school, and work out of doors, which will be much better for him.

I wish you could see this place. You ought to come and live here! It is in a tremendously long valley, and the healthiest locality in Texas.

I must cook our supper now, so goodbye.

FROM COUSIN TED                                      Willy's Shanty,
                                               Sunday, April 6, 1879

Here I am at last, permanently settled, I hope, for some time to come. I got here last Tuesday morning, having come straight from the General's the day my month was up, and found Willy hard at work thatching the roof, after a fashion he learned in Mexico. It takes a long while to do, but makes a capital roof when you do get it up: we have been hard at work at it ever since, and it's not finished yet.

We are all in great confusion, and shall be till we get the roof on and make a table. At present we eat all our meals sitting on the floor.

I tried my hand at making bread a few days ago, for the first time, and succeeded to perfection. It just rose beautifully, and since then I've always done it, and never had a failure. It's almost exactly similar to that used in the Irish cabins, except where we use Indian meal, which is a little cheaper but not so nice.

Our hours at present are from 5 a.m. to 7 p.m., but I expect they will be earlier after a bit. This is a gloriously healthy place, and much cooler than farther South. The town near us is a great resort for invalids in summer: people are ordered there much the same as they are to the hills in India....Our stock consists of three horses, six sheep, twelve hens, and a few tame turkeys which I bought from our nearest neighbour, a Cumberland man.

I'm afraid you'd hardly own us if you saw us now: we look so disreputable in our old canvas trousers and flannel shirts, and **such** seedy hats. But nobody here dresses respectably except the store-keepers. I meet no end of snakes whilst I'm at work; principally harmless ones. I killed four in less than an hour a few days ago. I just slice off their heads and bring them home for the chickens, who are very fond of them. One of the vicious ones gave me a great start. I was sitting in the grass, under a bush, and felt something tickling the back of my neck: at first I took no notice, thinking it was a straw, but after a bit I put up my hand to pull it away, and just as I touched it a lively snake about three feet long glided over my shoulder on to my knees. I can tell you I just jumped and cleared out!

Young Adams, with three more young Englishmen, arrived in San Antonio about a week ago. We have asked them to come up here for a bit to help with the clearing and fencing, but we have not had an answer yet. Probably some of them will turn up in a day or two. If they do, we shall get on like wild-fire: but it will be an awful squash, as our house is only 12 feet by 9, and at present it's filled with ploughs, boxes, &c. The next thing we are going to do is to build a storeroom for them.

I think we shall have lots of fruit this summer, principally wild grapes, which grow in huge quantities here and are very good eating, and make very fair wine, for which you get 6s. a gallon in San Antonio.

WILLY TO HIS BROTHERS                                        April 8, 1879

I have at last had the surveyor out, and located my 640 acres of land; so I have now 800 acres of my own, and on one side of me there are 640 acres of school land, and on the other 640 acres of State land; so we shall have plenty of breathing room.

There is over a mile of creek on my land, which is running now, although this is an unusually dry season. It does not run in all parts of the creek, but every hundred yards or so there is a long hole of running water; it then sinks under till it comes to the next hole....We are awfully hilly here, but it is a good grass country....The last time I came from San Antonio I started at 2 p.m., stopped at Capt. Turquand's an hour, and over half an hour in Boerne, seeing the surveyor, and got home at 9 p.m. Going round by Turquand's made the distance 37 miles. This was on Bet, the mare, who is a very good riding nag. We broke Ted's horse into the wagon with Billy yesterday. He bucked at first, but went very well afterwards, and didn't smash anything.

I must go to bed now, I'm so tired, and it's nearly eight.

If you fellows get tired of England, come on out, and bring Granny with you. It's an awfully unworrying life, and no weekly bills!

FROM WILLY TO THE DOCTOR[2]                    My hut, near Boerne
                                               April 9, 1879

You bet! We don't get too much literature out here to think letters

_____

[2] Family nickname for brother Harry;  "Chico" is the middle brother, Gerard.

are "boshy," so scrawl away all you know, and bring yourself out if you like. This is just the place for you if you get seedy, as it is awfully healthy.

I am just going into town for our weekly beef, five pounds of which will cost me twenty-five cents.

We are nearly eaten up with ticks; it's just awful; I look as if I had the measles bad, but the hens are getting away with a good many I think. " They are little flat red animals, about the size of a ladybird, and live in the trees; but if they can get fresh meat they prefer it.

FROM WILLY TO MADGE                    April 15, 1879

...I expect my poultry yard will increase rapidly, as I intend to make all the hens that want to sit bring out young ones, as they are not likely to find my 800 acres too small for them for some time to come.

I have a half-tailed rooster; the hens pecked the other half off the first day I brought him here. He was a very inferior cock where he came from, but since he has been here he has been swaggering around, and sitting on the fence, and crowing with all his might. He was the first cock I bought, and has bullied the second cock out of the yard; and the latter and his hens go into the field behind all day, and only come up at night to roost in the trees.

There are deer and wild turkeys about, but we haven't seen any yet, as we have hardly left the ranche. But there are rabbits around. Ted saw four to-night, and I shot one the other night with my pistol. I saw him by the creek, so I watched him, and yelled to Ted for the pistol. I held out my hands behind my back and Ted shoved the pistol into them, saying, "Look out, it's cocked!" So I upped the pistol at that rabbit and shot him through the head, and in five minutes he and his skin had parted company, the latter buried in the garden, and he hanging up outside the door; and we stewed him for breakfast, and wasn't he good, oh my!...I am generally cook, and turn out some fine concoctions; but Grady and Ted are rapidly learning.

FROM WILLY TO HIS FATHER                 April 15, 1879

We are getting along grandly. We have a fence about 40 yards by 20 round the hut, and a gateway opposite the hut that we put bars across at night to keep cows, &c., out; and we have fenced in a garden next to us about the same size as the yard, and have got lettuces, tomatoes, onions, carrots, radishes, potatoes, and standard and climbing beans in, and I shall put some melons in shortly ....We have plenty of live stock around us of our own, not to speak of every one else's animals, which seem to prefer us to their owners.

The German's cows and pigs pay us visits, also one of Stephenson's dogs, and his geese come and stay all day sometimes, and one of his gobblers has apparently taken up his abode here permanently.

Our greatest worry is our German neighbour. He is a rummy little old man, who seems to do nothing all day but hunt for his four oxen which he turns out every night. He comes by, and asks if we have seen them, and talks for some time, and then goes after them; then, in an hour or so he comes back and talks again, after saying that he saw his boy had found the oxen, and was driving them home. His boy is the only one whoever finds them, though Clouse always hunts too; and how the boy finds them among these hills I don't know, unless it is by instinct, as he has done nothing but hunt those oxen all his life, I expect.

We had a thunderstorm this morning for about an hour, and it poured like anything, and part of the time huge hailstones, some nearly as big as hens eggs, came down. It moistened the ground a bit, and I think I shall start some ploughing to-morrow, after I have been to Boerne for mail matter, which I fetch every Sunday and Wednesday morning.

63

FROM COUSIN TED                                    The Log Hut,
                                                  April 20, 1879

I'm working outside all day, cutting down trees and clearing out roots, or ploughing; and in the evening there's just time for supper, mending my clothes, or cooking, and then turn into bed, for which I'm always ready. We all sleep on the floor, one rug over, and one under us. I've got so accustomed to the hard floor that it seems as comfortable as ever a soft mattress did. The only one I've slept on since I've been out was at Capt. Turquand's.

It's getting to be very hot now. When we're working with iron tools we have to put them in the shade, or they blister our hands.


                                                  The Shanty,
                                                  April 27, 1879

Thank heaven the rain's come at last; as Willy says, "oodles of it!" You can almost hear the grass growing; and the creek's running again for the first time since last July. Willy's gone into San Antonio to buy some more grub, and a wagon and horse for hauling cedar-posts and lumber for the new fence. I've been left in charge with a man to help me, and have been trying to plough this morning, but the rain prevented me from doing much, I'm sorry to say, though I've managed to get wet to the skin twice this morning already, and am now steaming away before a big log fire. This hut just lets the water in everywhere. It's worse than my tent was at the Major's, and there it was positively dangerous to go to sleep without a life-buoy, on a rainy night! All the fowls keep coming in; it's impossible to keep them out. If Willy doesn't make a door soon, they'll ruin our Brussels carpet! The beasts have already eaten all my bacon; so I've got nothing to eat till Willy comes back in three days' time, but corn bread and beans. I think I'll slay the ring-leader of the bacon-eaters.

It's very amusing here at night sometimes. The part of the floor

64

where we sleep slopes in the middle.  Willy and I sleep on either side, and Grady in the centre.  He keeps continually rolling down on to one of us, and whoever he comes down on drives him back to the other side.  I wedged him up one night with large stones on each side, but he said they weren't exactly comfortable!

The Mater told me in her last that you were coming to the States this summer, and going to bring Chico and the Doctor with you.  You may guess I was delighted to hear it; but don't leave those youngsters in New York; bring 'em on here.  There's a sulphur spring within half-a-mile, and the Doctor can poison himself as much as he pleases!

FROM WILLY TO HIS FATHER                    April 30, 1879

...My finger does not pain me now, but puts a stop to my work.  It began with inflammation, and I think I made it worse by trying to go on with the ploughing, and it turned into an abscess.

We have a hard-working young fellow working for us, and have got an acre of corn in, and are preparing (clearing bushes, roots, &c.) for more.  Grady turned lazy, so he had to go, but I promised to let him work for his board if he hadn't found anything else in San Antonio when I went in to haul provisions.  He didn't turn up, so I suppose he has got a clerkship, or something.

There are some rum specimens of British subjects out here.  One of them, in San Antonio, belongs to a titled family, and I think his name is in the blue-book.  He hasn't a cent, and won't work, but just gets what he can out of everyone.  I mentioned his name to a fellow the other day, and he said, "Oh, you know him, do you?"  "Yes," I said, "I met him to-day."  "Did you?  How much did he get out of you?"

He has a most gentlemanly face, but his light London suit is beginning to look shabby, and matches the dirty white shirt with no tie or collar, very well.  He got into a scrape in England, I suppose, and got kicked out.

The ticks still rage furiously. (Aunt Maud sent Ted a packet of insect powder, telling him to put it on the bed and sheets!) Ted used to fill pins with them; but as we hadn't any statistics of the number of pins in the U.S., we gave that up; and now we crack them with our front teeth. They are harder than fleas, and won't be squashed between two nails.

Our German neighbour came round raging the other day to where we were burning some bushes, and tried to prevent us, saying we would "set his land on fire!" So we told him to go to the devil.

Then there was a scene of a German in all his majestic fury. He swore, and stamped, and shouted around; but we didn't take any notice of him. He has now cooled down, and was round here yesterday as affable as usual. Ted brought a letter for me to-day, from Momo or the Doctor, I think, and it blew in the fire before I opened it. I was just going to enjoy it and my dinner together, so it was very riling. I hope there wasn't anything of very great importance in it.

...I met old Willis in San Antonio the other day. He was in buying a pony, as he was still holding sheep outside town, and had let someone get away with his two horses and all his clothes.

Since I last saw them Smith has become bankrupt, and the great Jones got on a royal old drunk one night, which cost him $250.

I had a long ride to San Antonio the last time. My horses were hard at work in the field, so I rode Ted's pony, and he just knew I couldn't use my right hand to lick him, and walked nearly all the way. If I dropped the bridle and took up the rope with my left hand to whack him, he'd go off at right angles to the left like lightning, so I had to catch up the bridle again, and pull him straight.

I saw a very good surgeon about my finger in San Antonio; he is a Scotchman, just like the London type of doctor, and not like the man in Boerne, whom I should probably have addressed with "Is your master in?"

66

if someone hadn't previously told me that "That is Dr. Blank, sir, standing in his doorway."

WILLY TO THE DOCTOR                                    May 5, 1879

...Ted shot a red bird the other day.  The breast is brilliant scarlet, and I was going to send it to you for fish flies, only it got wormy before I had time to skin it.  We will shoot another soon, probably, and I'll skin him sooner.

Some wild turkeys come on to the field to get the corn, but we haven't shot any yet.  The pigs from the neighbouring ranches also come and root it up, and Ted says he shall sleep in the field to-night and shoot them, but I expect he'll weaken on sleeping out when it comes to the point.

FROM WILLY TO HIS FATHER                              May 20, 1879

...Ted is now out, trying to make a contract for cedar posts for fencing our thirty acres or so of pasture.  He started yesterday morning, and was to bring back a cow and calf if possible, so I expect the cow has been amusing herself at his expense.

I have been into San Antonio two or three times lately, after shingles for roofing.  The time before last I bought a horse for $13, said to have worked in a wagon, though from the way he "worked" I should say he never had.  I drove him and Ted's horse (which we've only had once or twice in a wagon), and I had just a bother with them.  After I got out of town I got them into going order, and they go splendidly now, especially my $13 animal "Tracy"; but I had to lead them all through town, and whenever I stopped for anything there was a circus to make them start again.  I had to get a man every time to saw Tracy's front legs with a rope, and this took some minutes, by which time a small crowd would assemble to see the fun.

Ted was hauling water in the wagon the other day and the axle broke, through a flaw (which of course I had mended for nothing), and the forty-eight gallons of water, or part of it, gave him a shower-bath.

We have had no rain for some time, and every day is almost cloudless and very hot, but there is always a cool gulf breeze blowing.

Ted found a wild turkey's nest with eleven eggs, and I have been vainly trying to get two hens to sit on them. I'll have to glue them to 'em I guess.

Why don't you people pack up and come out here right away? I am going to get a portable two-roomed hut, as our hut is so full of tools, harness, and grub, that there would not be room if Bob came out. Then, if his family comes, he can have the portable and build a kitchen off it, and Ted and I can rig up a box.

A neighbour of ours has a raised two-roomed house, with front verandah and large stone chimney, which cost him $230, hauling, and building, and materials and all ....People out here are mighty calm about their land. I went to a lawyer in San Antonio, about a piece I wanted in Boerne, which belonged to him. He said he'd never seen it, and didn't know when he should be able to, though he believed it **did** belong to him....I don't think that I shall ever smoke, as I know it hurts one's ability to think to a certain extent, and is also a beastly waste of time....Raspberries, currants, gooseberries, and strawberries are almost unheard of here. Think what a sensation we shall make when we raise them! I suppose, even if Bob hasn't started yet, it would be impossible to send a plant or two of each at this time of year for cuttings?....Yes, I think Texas horses and ponies are stronger than English ones. They generally run wild till four or five years old, so get plenty of exercise. I expect Ted every minute with a cow. I hope she gives four quarts. This is about the maximum at a milking here. Some only give one quart.

I have no pigs yet, as they grub up so. Our neighbours' pigs are quite nuisance enough.

COUSIN TED TO HASTINGS            Saturday, sometime in May, 1879

I made a great effort to write last Sunday, but it was so intensely hot indoors that my ideas seemed to melt away. It's a curious thing, that as long as I am out of doors I can do any sort of work, and don't mind the heat a bit, but the instant I get inside I'm fit for nothing.

Willy, I'm sorry to say, has had a very bad abscess on his little finger for the last three weeks, and has been able to do no work except cooking, so I've been pretty busy. We have now got a nice long straight field of about four acres cleared and ploughed. Part of it was also planted with corn and melons, but the wild turkeys ate them all up. I dusted one gobbler's jacket with a couple of charges of buck shot, but they've been coming to it all the same nearly every day since. We are not going to plant it again with corn. I wish we had some cabbages ready now, they are worth ls.[3] each at San Antonio, and more still at Boerne.

I expect I shall commence cutting cedar posts next week, for the fence. The cedar brake is about fifteen miles from here, so I think I shall have to camp there for one night each load. We shall, by cutting and hauling ourselves, save three and a-half cents a post, which will make a great difference in a two-mile fence. I intend some time this year to take a few wagon loads to San Antonio. You can always get $10 a hundred for them there, and sometimes $12, and as it only cost $1 for the privilege of cutting them, it's pretty good pay for your three days' work.

I dare say you will have wondered what the enclosure was. It's a rattlesnake's rattle, that I shot a few days ago. He was making such a row that I heard him a long way off, and came up and killed him. He

_____

[3]  One shilling (approximately 25 cents)--Author

69

was only about four feet long, but was as thick as your arm.

The chicken snakes are the greatest nuisance of all. They don't leave us a single egg. One of them ate seventeen out of a nest one day, and the same brute ate ten turkey's eggs that the old hen was sitting on. I will poison an egg or two for them. If I don't we shall never see the ghost of a chicken.

FROM WILLY TO HIS FATHER                                    May 26, 1879

....I think Chico and the Dr. had better come straight here, as we have lots for them to help us in.

The water in the creek runs through and over rock and gravel, and is splendid. It is the water down South, below San Antonio, that is so bad. I don't think I tasted any really good water all that trip.

I went to see Capt. Turquand yesterday, and while I was there one of the ewes dropped a lamb. This is the first. The Captain sings out, "Hulloa, Willy! there's another hundred dollars."

I have made some pretty good stock purchases lately. I ride about and hear where there are animals I want, for sale cheap. Yesterday I bought three milch cows (one with a three week old calf) for $30. This is the stock that pays here, and small settlers **won't** sell a cow except at a high figure, until they are hard up, which occurs pretty often, then they come down to a reasonable figure.

The other day we had such a hunt after those cussed horses. We were three days after them about the country, as they had a wild fit, that is, Billy and Tracy had. At last Ted got them into a high pen the other side of Boerne, but Billy cleared the gate and Tracy tried to follow, only Ted had hold of his rope. At last we got them here, and now they go about crestfallen with hobbles round their forelegs, the beggars!

...Horse-doctoring isn't of much use here. They never seem to be ill. The only ailing out of the thousands I have seen was a swollen nose, which was cured by lancing. If a horse does get ill, it's ten to one it's a $15 one, and the owner wouldn't pay 50 cts. to cure it. Now **sheep** doctoring **would** be useful. They very often die for want of proper care and knowledge, and raisers are not nearly careful enough with them....Bring a few shirts and socks, and as **little else** as possible. Beware of sharpers on trains and at stations. Go to the Central Hotel in San Antonio. Let me know when you expect to arrive in San Antonio, and I will meet you with wagon; or wire from thence to Boerne (cost 25c). We've plenty of horses for you.

Finger still bad. Dr. in Boerne said I should lose it if I wasn't careful.

WILLY TO THE DOCTOR                    May 30, 1879

...Just off with wagon and two yoke of steers to fetch the four ewes. The lamb was premature rather, and died.

I had six or seven attempts to get our first $11 cow and calf here, and at last had to haul her in the wagon.

Will I take a pupil? why yes; and the fee, $300 per ann., if he's a hanger on. If he'll work, and take an interest in what he does, he may stop as long as he likes for nothing!

I wish you would bring out my ENQUIRE WITHIN UPON EVERYTHING book. It's in my room.

Also, if you have time to get them made, a one pound and a half-pound butter print, with a "fleur-de-lis" on them. Get Chico to draw it carefully on paper, as the man will want a good copy. This is my brand. I'll pay you for the prints when you come out.

Bring comb, brush, tooth-brush, and sponge, of course, and look in my chest of drawers and bring all the light evening neck-chokers, if any.  They are very useful in the sun.

I mean those things you wear when on your way to a party at night.  You'd better bring the worn-outest old coat you've got, with the old trowsers, on board ship, as salt water spoils clothes awful.

## Building A Ranch

Ted and Willy were getting their ranching education through the "school of hard knocks."  Fortunately, and to Willy's credit, the operation was diversified in order to spread the risk and to maximize their chances for balanced cash-flow at the beginning of their business venture.  Of course, there were disappointments and minor failures, such as wild turkeys and neighbors' hogs eating his freshly planted corn, but Willy took these temporary set-backs in stride and concentrated on things that worked.  His letters continued to speak of his terribly important learning experiences.

Willy's one-hundred-year-old son, Gerard H. Hughes of New London, New Hampshire, told the writer in July 1992 that his father was a perfectionist who was known to react strenuously when things didn't go as planned.  This competitiveness and determination to do things right were traits that served Willy well throughout his lifetime. He quickly learned how to properly balance good land-use practices with the best quality livestock production.  His letters home continued to stress that ranchers who had a **name** just happened to have better quality livestock that sold for better prices.

Willy's flair for salesmanship and innovative marketing stand out among his other talents, but his early recognition of the need to manage his money well was an important factor in his future success.  From the very beginning of his ranching endeavor, Willy sought to purchase or temporarily lease land to avoid working on shares for someone else. He diversified small crop production for human and livestock consumption and sold surplus commodities at local markets as a supplemental source of cash.  This practice of being self-sufficient enabled him to support his ranch operation without incurring large debts.

His letters also indicated that Willy understood the importance of delegating different responsibilities to key associates. This allowed him more time to concentrate on overall ranch development and management.

## Help Arrives

In his introduction to Part III of G.T.T.--GONE TO TEXAS, Hastings Hughes tells of his plans to stop at the ranch with his two youngest sons, Gerard and Harry, before he journeyed on to New York in pursuit of a new business venture. Harry, the youngest son, had developed eye strain from studying by gas light and was planning to take a year off before going to New York or Philadelphia to medical school; and the middle son, Gerard, intended to spend three months with Willy before returning to his art internship with Mr. Watts.

Hastings and "the Doctor" could not leave England until after July 4th, but Chico left a month earlier, as they were all concerned about Willy's infected finger, and traveled overland from New York. Hastings and Doc traveled steerage to New York, where they obtained passage on a smaller boat to Galveston. They were accompanied by Ted's older brother, Bob Hobson, and a young friend, Lennie Windale, both of whom intended to settle in Texas. In Galveston they met Ted, who was returning to England to join another brother for a trip to New Zealand.

Hastings said he had a "real good time" at the ranch, helping build fences, digging a well, and doing other chores. He and Bob left for New York in October with a load of horses that Bob had broken at the ranch to sell in New York. Chico returned to his art studies in November, leaving Doc and Lennie with Willy at the ranch.

Prior to Bob and Hastings' departure, Willy bought 200 common ewes to cross with his Oxfordshire Downs rams, and Doc took charge of this very busy phase of the ranch's sheep operation.

Oxfordshire Downs Sheep, Hughes Ranch (circa 1890)

Willy Hughes' arrival in Kendall County in 1879 was well timed; he missed the most excruciating phase of the economic collapse that occurred during the Civil War and continued under the restraints of the Reconstruction Act until its termination in 1874. He also missed the terrorizing Indian raids that were a constant threat on the Texas frontier throughout the war years of 1861-65 and until the remnants of the Comanche, Kiowa, and Cheyenne tribes were soundly defeated at the battles of Palo Dura Canyon and Adobe Wall in 1874.[1]   In 1878, there was a minor Indian raid in Kendall County by a group of renegade Indians.  They terrorized farmers from the Bergheim area up the Cibolo valley to the outskirts of Boerne.  It was reported that several people were killed, and some horses and cattle were stolen.[2]

While Willy Hughes didn't encounter any Indians, he did acquire first-hand experience at roughing it on the rugged Texas frontier.  But even during the most hectic period of his early ranching days, Willy saw a glimmer of light at the end of the economic tunnel.  He obviously read and heard that the sawmill and lumber industry was expanding in East Texas; cotton farming and shipment of baled cotton through Galveston and other coastal ports was on the rise in the 1870s; longhorn cattle drives up western trails to railheads at Dodge City and Abilene, Kansas, brought an infusion of "Yankee" dollars to Southwest, West, and Central Texas.  Also, immigration of additional people from Europe (especially England) to the Texas Hill Country encouraged young Willy to go forward with his ranching plans.  But it was never easy.

### Food and Shelter

In his letters, Willy spoke of the romance of sleeping under the stars at night on

---

[1] Webb, Prescott, Editor in Chief, THE HANDBOOK OF TEXAS, Texas State Historical Association, Austin, Texas, 1952.

[2] Herff, Ferdinand Peter, THE DOCTORS HERFF, Vol. I, Trinity University Press, San Antonio, Texas, P. 102

a blanket and seeking shelter beneath a wagon during cold, rainy nights.

In due time, Willy acquired a large tent that was used for billeting purposes, then he moved a small house to ranch headquarters from another property he bought. It was nothing more than a "shack" or "shanty," but it was more comfortable than sleeping outside. It was not until October, 1882 that Willy built a better house at his new location.

Initially, water for household use was hauled from nearby streams in a wagon tank. Then two wells were hand-dug on tracts of land Willy bought in 1879, and a cistern was installed next to the two story-house he built in 1887. He added a windmill-powered water system in the late 1880s when well drillers were first active in his area.

Staple foods that Willy bought in bulk and kept in storage were: cornmeal, flour, coffee, potatoes, and molasses. He also bought dried fruit, peas, beans, and rice in substantial quantities. Dried meat--such as jerky, bacon, and sausage, and sometimes smoke-cured ham--was kept hanging in cellars or family smokehouses. Willy's two-story home had a large basement where fresh and cured meat was hung on metal hooks. Sugar, salt and pepper, and an assortment of condiments were also mentioned from time to time.

Most frontier settlers were good foragers. They were always alert for edible wild fruit and seasonal plants indigenous to their area. Hill Country residents knew about polk salad, dewberries, blackberries, wild cherries, and plums. Native pecans that grew in local creek bottoms and river basins were tasty and retained their delicious flavor for several months in the shell.

Wild game, especially deer and turkey, was abundant in the Hill Country. Bee hives were often found in hollow trees and cliff cavities. Honey was considered a delicacy. It was often used as a substitute for sugar in making desserts, or served in place of molasses or syrup. Occasionally, early settlers were fortunate enough to kill a black bear, but Willy never mentioned shooting one. In addition to the excellent taste of its meat, a bear provided an acceptable quality of fat that was used for cooking purposes. Bear hides were often used for rugs and chair cushions.

Willy's letters commented on different foods he ate while riding with sheep buyers in South Texas and Mexico in 1878-79 and at his ranch from 1879 to 1884. Meat came from both wild and domestic animals, but goat meat and mutton seem to have been a favored source of protein. Bread was a term used interchangeably for wheat bread or cornbread in Southwest Texas, where both wheat and corn were grown. Willy took pride in his skills at baking flour bread, but he never mentioned how he made cornbread.

Hughes followed the practice of other pioneer settlers and quickly cleared land for a garden and orchard. He recognized an opportunity to generate some income by marketing surplus vegetables and fruit in Boerne, a flourishing health resort for people suffering from consumption. By June 1879 he had bought a cow and calf and was planning to sell excess milk and butter.

In his letter of April 9, 1879 to Doc, Willy said he was just going into Boerne for his weekly purchase of five pounds of beef that would cost him twenty-five cents. That purchase was likely made at Fabra's Meat Market at 202 S. Main. This was a well-known business that served citizens of Boerne for over 100 years, through three generations of Fabras--Julius, Ludwig, and Henry--1857-1962. The "state of the art" 1887 two-story Fabra Smokehouse remains at the back of the old Fabra market site, and was awarded a Texas State Historical Commission Marker in 1981.

## Neighbors

The G.T.T-GONE TO TEXAS book omitted surnames of people mentioned in Willy's correspondence. Instead, it contained only the first letter of family names and of people living in the vicinity of Hughes ranch. Old school records, deed records, and a survey map available for viewing at Kendall County Courthouse give some clues as to who Willy Hughes' neighbors were. Also, correct names were sometimes found in copies of Willy's unedited letters and other research materials.

John Stephenson was his closest and most helpful neighbor. Mr. Stephenson actually served as Willy's mentor in matters relating to row-crop farming and gardening. He also was skilled at blasting rock with dynamite, and he was working in that capacity for Willy when the Hughes boys and their father were digging a water well in the summer of 1879.

John and Ann Stephenson had seven children when Willy Hughes moved to their neighborhood. They were James, 26; Jennie, 24; Henry; Joseph; Frances; Lucy, 12; and Ella at age nine.

Other families who lived in that locality were J. M. Swisher, R. B. Hugman, Jacob Remmick, C. E. Cole, A. Schultz, Chas. Klemme, Adam Hemphill, J. Dedeker, Henry Clark, I. Minnich, Rad Spencer, and Dr. J. F. Nooe.

Ten years later, in 1889, Willy Hughes certified in his application to the U.S. Postal Service that sixty people would be served by his proposed Hastings Post Office to be established at Hughes Ranch headquarters.


## Time For Pleasures

The 1880s brought significant changes in the economy and lifestyle of pioneer settlers living in the Texas Hill Country. Leisure time--at least on weekends--was something that citizens were beginning to enjoy for the first time in many years. Fancy dress clothing and shoes could be bought in San Antonio and sometimes in Boerne stores.

In his letter of May 30, 1879, Willy had something in mind when he asked his father to bring his comb, brush, toothbrush, sponge, and neck-chokers (ties) on his trip to Texas in July. No doubt he planned to show his father, brothers, and cousins some social highlights of Boerne and the Hill Country.

Old newspaper stories, postcard collections, beautifully colored and embossed birthday cards, autograph books, and letters indicate that writing, exchange of poetry, and social events must have been on the rise at that time.[3] A horse and buggy could be rented at Homer's livery stable in Boerne for $1.00 per day. (One old timer, with a twinkle in his eyes, confided to the writer in 1980 that for $1.25 a fellow could rent a horse that would stay in the road without reining, freeing up both hands when out on a date--whatever that meant). Thus picnic outings and Sunday drives to the Guadalupe River and nearby settlements were common events. But there were certain hazards to being out after dark in a horse-drawn vehicle. One night Willy Hughes ran the wheels on one side of his buckboard up the back of a cow that was bedded down in the middle

---

[3]  Perry, Garland, HISTORIC IMAGES OF BOERNE, LEBCO Graphics, 1982

of Main Street, Boerne. The cow jumped up, flipping the buckboard over, and sent Willy flying through the air before landing in a prone position on the ground.

The Boerne Village Band of 1860 vintage frequently gave outdoor performances on the Commons Plaza, and the German Gesangverein (singing club) dating back to 1860[4] often gave public concerts. A German slogan of that day was, "Wer nicht liebt Wein, Weibund Gesang, Der bleibt ein Narrsein lebelang" (the one who does not love wine, women and song will remain a fool all his life). Willy Hughes was no fool, but work and business were his priorities. He attended some celebrations, but not often. He likely did take his father and brothers to some of the German public events--at least as spectators.

Most English settlers who came to Kendall County in the 1870s and 1880s no doubt had their own social functions but there is little documentation of such events. Willy was a talented violin player as a young man, but his violin stayed in New York with his father until Willy had a place to keep it.


## Recreation

During his first two or three years in Kendall County, Willy Hughes faced a "sink or swim" situation with his ranching enterprise. His work schedule was daylight to dark, and his evenings were spent reading and writing by candlelight or kerosene lamp and planning his next business move.

Little time was left for recreational activity, but in one of his earlier letters[5] Willy did make reference to neighborhood boys coming over at night for wrestling matches, games, and pranks.

Horseback riding, fishing, and swimming were other activities that young men engaged in at that time. Perhaps British immigrants played chess and card games, but this is not referenced in G. T. T. However, during the 1880s some German-speaking

---

[4] Perry, Garland, HISTORIC IMAGES OF BOERNE, LEBCO Graphics, Boerne, Texas, 1982

[5] G. T. T. - page 109

men of Boerne spent much of their leisure time playing a popular card game called "Keno."[6]

The British ranchers living on the outskirts of Boerne are credited with having first introduced a number of English sports into Texas--perhaps the entire United States--during the early 1880s.

On the Upper Balcones Road, before crossing Balcones Creek into Bexar County, a level pasture is well known locally as the frequently used playing field for games of cricket, polo, and soccer by British immigrants.  Willy Hughes is shown in an 1886 picture as a member of the Boerne Cricket Team.[7]  Of 22 players on the team, 15 are identified and several of those were friends  of Willy Hughes.

The Boerne Cricket Team (circa 1886): Front row, left to right: J. S. Howard, Horace Hugman, W. Howard, J. Bright, G. W. Calrow, unknown, J. Howard: Second row, left to right: Buttersworth, unknown, King, King, A. G. Gilliat, W. Wright, "Deaf" Cooner, Cooper S. Hughes, Billy Hughes, "Toot" Homer, unknown, unknown, Fred Homer.

---

[6] Perry, Garland, HISTORIC IMAGES OF BOERNE, LEBCO Graphics, Boerne, Texas, 1982

[7] Ibid., page 33

## G.T.T.-GONE TO TEXAS Letters

### (Jan. 8, 1880--March 17, 1881)

Willy's letters from January 8, 1880 through March 17, 1881, continue to describe his struggle to keep the budding ranch afloat durings its beginning stage. Despite the many challenges and disappointments, there are definite signs of progress.

WILLY TO HIS FATHER                                    ....Ranche,

Jan. 8, 1880

....We have just had a tremendous rain, and our 2½ acres of oats are coming up well.

The roads between this and San Antonio are black land for the most part, and they got as sticky as "butter-scotch." I passed the stagecoach as I went down. It had clogged up with mud, and luckily had only three passengers, all men, who were in their shirt sleeves out on the road with sticks, knocking the mud from between the spokes, as the coach couldn't move!

I have not planted out the fruit trees, as I shall leave them for you to say where they are to be put.

The rain has put water into the creek, and the frogs make a tremendous noise all night, squealing. I have a muff of a Texan working for me. He's been hunting for my two work-oxen for two days now, and hasn't returned. Just fancy having to hunt one's cattle for miles and miles round! It takes more time than anything else almost.

We had a plum-pudding on Christmas Day. The Doctor made it. It was a great success, and we bought some whiskey and set the pudding alight in good old style. We didn't do any decorating, as we hadn't any holly, and mistletoe would have been out of place among such a lot of old bachelors as we are.

WILLY TO HIS FATHER                                    The Ranche

                                                       Jan. 19, 1880

.....We are awfully busy now ploughing up the field.  It is
exceedingly rich, and we turn furrow after furrow without turning up a
single stone.  There are about ten acres which we haven't got to clear at
all, and after ploughing I shall begin fencing, to begin to put in cotton in
Spring.

We plough with six oxen.  I plough, and another man drives.
Sometimes we come upon a root, and all the chains clink as the oxen
strain on them, but they generally burst it.  The field is a mile and a-
quarter from here, and it seems a long walk coming back at night after
ploughing all day....

I sold nearly half my sheep the other day.  They were a lot of sixty
that I bought first.  I bought a lot of a hundred afterwards that suited me
better (I got $2.00 per head for them, and paid $1.75 per head when I
bought them); so now I have only the hundred ewes left, and they are
doing very well....

We have decorated our hut with pictures from "The Illustrated,"
&c., and with a huge map of America.  I believe we know every name on
the latter almost, as it's just at the head of the table, and we study it at
supper time....


WILLY TO HIS FATHER                                    The Ranche

                                                       Feb. 3, 1880

....What a dreadful accident that Tay Bridge seems to have been.
We have just had a few days cold weather, the first since Christmas, but
I think it is blowing off again now....

We have been feasting lately on a sort of gourd, which some of the
farmers grow here.  They are very good eating, are as large as one's
head, with a thin neck.  I hope to grow a good many this year.  They are

very easily raised, and keep through the winter.

We had to stop ploughing for a few days, owing to the "Norther," but we are going at it again now for some days....

WILLY TO HIS FATHER                                     The Ranche,

Feb. 15, 1880

We have been working like steam engines lately, and things couldn't be going better to my mind than at present. Our general mode of proceeding for the past month has been as follows: The Doctor takes sole care of the sheep, and a better shepherd I couldn't have if I went all over the world. The sheep look splendidly.

An Englishman, at whose ranche, south of San Antonio, I stayed last year, visited us this day week on his way to his ranche, after a visit to England, and he said he only wished he could find his sheep looking as well as ours when he got to the ranche.

Windale is housekeeper, and looks after the horses, and cows, and calves. To-day I have turned out of the pasture, with their mothers, the last seven or eight calves; so now we shan't have any milk at all. We have two young bulls still in the pasture, and these we feed regularly, with the two English rams. The four English ewes run outside the pasture, and all are doing first-rate.

I have been working on the big field. For the last few days we have been seven strong. I plough, and another man drives the steers, two men grubbing out the bushes that are in the way, another man getting up stones for the rock fence, and two more cutting wood on contract.

The land is in places very heavily timbered with live oak. I pay a man $1.00 per cord for cutting up the wood, and I am going to cart it into Boerne, where I can get $2.25 for it. The wood does not hurt for keeping, so I am having it stacked up in cords to keep, as, if this year turns out well, wood will probably be again worth $2.50 and $2.75 per cord; but I am having it cut now, as labour is cheap. Of course, if the wood becomes worth $2.50 again, cutting it will, with everything else, "go up," and probably cost $1.50 or $1.75.

We have been camping on the field. At the beginning of the week we put two yoke of steers to the wagon containing provisions, tools, &c., and one yoke to the water-cart (which holds 96 gallons), and march up to the field; then on Saturday night we come down again.

Sometimes some of the "boys" from neighbouring ranches come up to the camp at night, and have games and wrestling, and play jokes on one another. On Friday night they took a green hand out "quail hunting." They all went into the brush, about half-a-mile from camp, down the creek, and set him at the end of a trail or cattle-path, with an empty sack, which he had to keep open in front of him, to catch the quail which they were going to drive up the trail into it. After sundry questions from him, as to whether they would bite, what size and color they were, &c., they came back along the trail to "drive the quail"; which consists of going back to the camp fire and waiting till the fellow with the sack has had enough of waiting. In half-an-hour or so the sack man was heard on the top of a neighbouring hill, about a mile from camp. From there he saw the camp fire, and struck out for it.

Another game is "donkey-riding."--Two fellows are tied back to back, and a saddle is put on them and girthed, and then another fellow gets on the saddle, and they pitch and pitch until they pitch him off.

Then there is "leg-wrestling."--Two fellows lie on their backs next to each other, but the feet of one at the head of the other; and each clutches the other one's shoulder with his inside hand; then each lifts up his inside leg three times while they count, and the third time they lock their legs, and one of them turns a sudden somersault backwards, and he is conquered. It is generally a very short combat unless they are evenly matched; but one or the other, anyhow, ends in going heels over head

84

backwards.[8]

I have opened the seeds, which are beautifully packed. Many thanks for them. The grass seeds I shall put in a spot in the pasture, but I hardly like to venture with the garden seeds, as my cotton field will take up all my time.

Windale has the comfreys in hand, and is preparing beds for them. With regard to silkworms; there are quantities of wild mulberries here, but it will be a long time before I can do anything in that line, I think, as there are such numberless paying things more immediately connected with the general ranche business....We have every prospect of unusually good prices for our wool this year.

FROM WILLY TO HIS FATHER                                    The Ranche,
                                                          March 21, 1880

Bob will, as you propose, start for New York about the 22nd proximo. We've got all the horses now, including one racer, a mare, from Dane's....

To come to an important question straight. I asked the Doctor the other day how he liked this life, and whether he would like to stop, and go halves in the whole concern, and he evidently thinks it would be just the thing he would like. He said, "Well, up to the present this life has been exceedingly fascinating, but of course I must ask father before giving any answer; and I think I would rather wait till I see him, if you don't mind, instead of writing about it."

I fancy from the interest he takes in everything, that it would suit him internally and ex-ditto better than sweating in a city; and as to his health, it couldn't be better. I can't palaver like Kingsbury and Co., but

--------------------------

[8] I am bound to say, though used to such matters from my youth up, that "leg wrestling" puzzles me.--Editor (Thomas Hughes)

85

those are the main facts, and we can study the question further when you are down here.

On the 29th inst. I shall have been here a year, and I fancy a small change may be noticed, if one looks closely enough. By the way, Bob says that McNeal used to can tomatoes in Virginia very simply, but used to keep it dark, and make good cash at it. If you know anyone in a canning business, could you get the main points, as to the length of time boiling, whether put into cans hot or cold, and whether they get all air-tight before soldering the last hole, &c.

I hope Bob makes a good thing of the horse business this time; if so, I'm going to invest in a few promising young horses, to hold till they mature....

WILLY TO HIS FATHER                                    The Ranche,
                                                    March 28, 1880

....All the horses are doing well; Bob says they are a much better lot than last. Windale is becoming a very good rider; he has plenty of pluck. On the 22nd inst. we began to break a big four-year-old horse. He broke easily, and Windale rode into Boerne for mail on him on the 26th. Coming out, his love of news got the better of his discretion, so, dropping the reins on the neck of the mustang of five days' riding, he took out the ILLUSTRATED, and began reading; and so off went the horse pitching **á la mode** with head down, and over his head went Master Windale.

He followed him for a mile or so, and caught him, but led him back! He "went for" that horse, though, on returning. He put a "bucking stick" on the saddle, and got on and raced round the field, and the horse couldn't get him off again.

The bucking stick is about two feet long, and tied across the horn of the saddle, just above your legs, and it's next to impossible for a horse to buck you out....

WILLY TO HIS FATHER                              The Ranche,

April 25, 1880

....Bob left for New York a week ago with the horses. There were twenty-one splendid little animals. Most of them he tamed here himself. We have been shearing at odd intervals lately, and have only about thirty more to shear. The main work has been on the cotton-field. We are now preparing for planting....Two of the English ewes have lambed twins, a third has lambed one, and a fourth will lamb shortly, I think.

To-day, as we were ploughing, a swarm of bees flew across the field and came all around the Doctor and myself. I thought they were going to settle on us, but they buzzed around and then went off. I followed them, but couldn't keep up with them.

This spring seems entirely different from the last one, which was so unusually dry. Now everything looks green and nice. A lot of humming birds are up in the valley behind the field, but I have never seen their nests. They feed on the honeysuckle. I never saw any live ones before this spring.

WILLY TO UNCLE TOM                              The Ranche,
Dear Uncle,                                      May 1, 1880

As there is such a thing as scab amongst sheep here, and it is pretty common, I didn't like to whistle till I was out of the wood, and so didn't write about the favorable condition of the flock before. I'm now glad to be able to tell you that our sheep are perfectly healthy, and doing well. We are nearly through with shearing, and in a few days I hope to take the wool down to San Antonio.

Our lambs, which are from the English rams, are unusually fine, and as the climate seems to suit the thoroughbreds admirably, and as they grow much heavier fleeces, and the wool is as valuable as that which is at present grown in the country, I have decided to go on with the breed, and hope to make a big thing of it.

I have had several applications for half-bred rams, and I hope to be able to sell a few next tupping season.

I started without experience, and without anyone to give me any very reliable advice. As it was, of course I made a few mistakes at starting; though now I feel as if I'd been in the business all my life.

I am going to divide my business here into different departments. The Doctor is, and has been, boss of sheep department. Windale is starting a market-garden, in which he is to have shares. I am going to take the farming department on the Schultz land, which is the best and prettiest piece of land round here. This, with superintending the other departments, will take up all my time.

I am, **pro tem**. (and it may lead to be permanent), in the horse business with Bob, who has just gone up to New York with a carload of horses, which he has been breaking at the ranche, since he returned from taking up the last carload....It is a profitable business if carefully attended to.

Do you know of one or two fellows with £250 or so between them, who would like to go into the stock business here, in a small way? As I said, I want to take up farming properly; and, if I could get some fellows to run cattle here, would give up this ranche and range, and put up another shanty for the Doctor, Windale, and myself, on the Schultz field. There is a good shanty here, including bed-room, kitchen, and store-room, with large bins, &c., a fifty-acre pasture, and a field in which to raise horse feed, vegetables for own consumption, &c., and a **good well**.

I have invested about $1100 in the whole place, including range of 1440 acres; and I want some one to put about the same amount into stock (about 100 odd head), of cows with calves, and heifers, I taking a quarter of the increase, and he doing the main work of attending to the stock. Yearling heifers, which as a rule begin calving at three years old, cost $5; two-year-old $7.50 cents; three-year-old (without calves) $9; and young cows (with calves) $12 to $14. There is always a ready sale for yearling oxen at $5.50 cents (this year as high as $6 has been paid), and when a cow gets old, she is allowed to fatten, and fetches $10 to $12; and as we are near a town, there is always a market for such.

It is a very good opening for a couple of fellows who **mean business**. I said £250 or so, as this would be the smallest it would be worth any one's while to invest with any expectation of good returns; but there is plenty of room here for stock, if the amount invested were twice the size, or even larger; as, besides my own range, there are over 6400 acres held by the State at half-a-dollar per acre, for School funds, and this land will not be sold for many years to come.


FROM WILLY TO MADGE                                        May 15, 1880

I would rather not have any books out yet, as they would get so dirty in our hut. As soon as I can afford to put up a small house I should very much like to have the books out; but I don't want to get them spoilt before that.


FROM WILLY TO MADGE                                        San Antonio,
                                                    Col. Lockwood, his office
                                                            May 25, 1880

Col. Lockwood wants to know if you don't think the enclosed[9] is a good likeness of me! You want a photo of me, so I let him send it,

---

[9] A caricature by Col. Lockwood, showing the change effected in personal appearance by twenty months of ranche life.

especially as he says he'll pay the postage, and so make me one letter ahead. Col. Lockwood says he wants you to let him know if it is like me as I was when I left England. I think you will agree with me that it exactly resembles the photo I had taken just before I left!

FROM WILLY TO HIS GRANDMOTHER                     The Ranche,
                                                                      May 27, 1880

I am so glad to see by the heading of your letter that you are away from smoky London for a bit, and to hear that you are going down to Longcott this summer.

Many thanks for your good wishes, apropos of my coming of age. Father won't be here on the 29th, his birthday, as the horses are not all sold; but I expect him and Bob early in June.

Everything here is flourishing. I have just returned from San Antonio, where I have been with my wool. I have stored it there, to sell in a week or two, when I expect prices will be higher. All the crops are coming on splendidly, and everything promises to be exactly the reverse of last year.

Our bees are working like anything. My best hive is a box about twenty-eight inches high by fourteen inches square, and the upper six inches inside has a floor with two holes in it, and above each hole is a super. The two exactly fill the top of the hive above the floor, and have glass windows, as also has the lower part of the hive, so one can see the bees working. Both supers are filled with comb already, and are being filled with honey very fast.

Bees are very plentiful out here, in hollow trees and holes in bluffs; and the farmers' sons are very fond of cutting them out and hiving them, when they find them. This year they will do splendidly, but last year the extraordinary drought killed nearly all the hived bees. One neighbour of ours had thirty-six hives, and all were killed but four!

You can't conceive the quantity of wool there is now in San Antonio. All the store houses are almost cram full, and the marketplaces are daily full of wagon loads just arrived; and the roads into town are lined with wagons-full.

My love to Madge, and ask her if she got that photo. which Col. Lockwood (Jim's friend) of San Antonio gave me. He is always fond of his "little joke," and is a very jolly fellow. I hope Chico managed to get a few days at Longcott with you.

P.S. Many thanks for "Good Words," which come regularly, and are very welcome.


## COMMENTS FROM HASTINGS HUGHES

I was unable to leave my New York business for the proposed trip with Bob to the ranche, and he found work in New York, which he preferred to breaking and "shipping" mustangs. In August, 1880, important business took me to Tennessee, and detained me there most of the time for more than a year. In June it had been settled by correspondence that the Dr. should stick to the ranche, instead of coming up to New York to study medicine. In December, 1880, Willy came at my desire to prospect in Tennessee, but found that part of it which he saw unsuited for sheep-raising, which branch of his business had gradually become by far the most important. He had given up the plan of starting a store for the sale of vegetables in Boerne, and had found some other plans, referred to in his early letters, also impracticable.

Here I ought to mention that the letters do not show the main troubles and disappointments met with, such as the failure of the cotton crop, death of thoroughbred lambs, &c., all of which were kept to themselves by the boys, lest they (the letters) should give a gloomier impression of life and prospects in that part of Texas than would be justified by facts. The letters were all written to near relatives of the

91

boys, who were of course anxious about them, and it was natural therefore that they should make light of whatever might from time to time be troubling them.

In making the extracts I have purposely omitted anything referring to the "profit and loss account," my object being to retain only such parts as show what everyday life is like on a ranche in Texas, such as theirs; but it will be sufficiently apparent that they have in the main "got on."-- Hastings Hughes

WILLY TO HIS FATHER IN TENNESSEE                    The Ranche,
                                                    Feb 23,1881

Dear old Gov.[10]

We are having the most glorious weather imaginable, in our shirt-sleeves from before sunrise to when we go to bed; but during the day a delicious south wind. The new grass has started up three inches, and Spring has evidently set in for good, bar occasional frost probably.

Our oats are doing well, and we set out several fruit-trees the other day, and all our early vegetable seeds are in. The comfreys are doing splendidly, and we are going to plant out a pretty big patch. Sheep are all doing first-rate and getting awfully heavy.

We have occasional bathes in the creek, which runs as hard as ever. I am glad you are thinking of giving us a look up....

WILLY TO HIS GRANDMOTHER IN ENGLAND               The Ranche
                                                   March 7, 1881

....The first Spring I was here was the drought, when nobody raised anything, which was discouraging. Last year we did fairly for our first year of farming and sheep; but this year finds us **well** ahead of our

---

[10]  Family name for Hastings

92

business.

Our sheep couldn't be doing better; last year's experience in the lambing season taught us what it was necessary to have for the proper management of the lambs. These are dropping like hail now (eight to-day!), and they are at once drafted off into the pasture, where they remain for a few days till the ewes "take" properly to them.

Each lamb is marked with a red spot or line on a part of its body, and the ewe marked in the same way, so that we know exactly which lamb belongs to which ewe; and a record is kept of the date the lamb is born, and of its mark, so as to know when it can with safety be allowed to run with the flock. When a few days old, and the ewe has taken properly to the lamb, they are turned into the field, where the oats are coming up splendidly; this brings a flush of milk on the ewe, and gives the lamb a good start. The last lamb born to-day made our fiftieth.

We have about four acres of oats as I told you, growing well; and two days ago I put in about an acre of corn, and to-day I hauled up the "camp tricks" to the tent at the Schultz field, as I am going to camp up there and plough up for corn. Our spring onions are coming up splendidly; and this morning I put in our seed sweet potatoes, from which grow the vines which are planted out later on--the vines "produce" the potatoes, so to speak. I have a seed-bed with beets, cabbages, lettuces, squashes, and cauliflowers in it, and some of them are beginning to come up; and I have a bed of very early corn in, and I expect we shall be the first round here to have roasting ears; and my ground for beans, melons, tomatoes, &c., is all ploughed, and ready to be planted, as soon as Spring has regularly set in, at least as soon as all chance of cold is gone, for Spring has set in some time; the grass is growing up green, and the wild flowers and bushes are all opening, and the nights are getting quite warm.

We planted out sixteen fruit-trees, apples and peaches, and they are all doing well; and the comfreys have been green for weeks, and we are planting out a large patch of them this Spring.  You have no idea how useful they are in case of a sick ewe.

I forget whether I told you that the grass seeds did not come to anything, but that the clover is all coming up, and looking well; I think it is going to prove a very valuable addition to the herbage here.  We planted it on about half-an-acre in the pasture, and have fenced off a little patch to keep off the sheep and calves, and let it run to seed.

We are still getting plenty of milk from old Gentle, and within a few weeks we shall have more milk than we shall know what to do with, unless we get a pig, as we have several good cows going to calve.

The English ewes begin to lamb the day after to-morrow, and Flora, the collie that Mr. Hewitt sent me, pups tomorrow, and we have two hens hard at work setting, and the whole boiling of them are cackling and laying, so we are increasing to a great extent.  And lastly, I forgot old Molly, the mare, she has gone off to her old range preparatory to foaling; and another mare of ours, who runs between here and Boerne, is also going to have a foal.  Oh! and then the cat; she's going to have kittens.  I think I've told you about everything now.

We have all had a fit of letter-writing to-night;  at this time of year I'm afraid we neglect it a good deal.  From daylight to late at night we are kept "a-going," I assure you:  first it's cooking breakfast and milking, and separating newly-born lambs and their ewes from the flock, then turning out the flock and drafting the older lambs with their ewes into the field, and holding refractory ewes for the lambs to suck; then there's ploughing or planting all day; then the flock comes in, and more new lambs to "fix," and more suckling and feeding; then supper to cook and washing-up to do, and by the time one has finished supper, one feels as though one could fall to sleep at the table.

It's glorious fun though; and we enjoy the life immensely.  I have to shave now!  It is my Sunday morning's job generally.  The Doctor is just off (11 p.m.) to his tent by the sheep-pen, where he has his cot, and sleeps every night now.  You've no idea how well he is looking; you would hardly know him.

WILLY TO GRANDMOTHER

March 17, 1881

The collie has pupped; she only had two puppies, but they are doing well.  All the country is green now, and the grass is everywhere splendid, and the creeks here and at the Schultz field running hard.

The beginning years of the 1880s found Willy Hughes immersed in the economic complexities and day-to-day reality of his active ranch/farm enterprise. He'd learned a lot from the hardships of earlier months. Eighteen seventy-nine had not been a good year. Rainfall was poor, and the tenderfoot rancher faced the challenges of nature. Ewes have a tendency to abandon infant lambs when giving birth on open range with their flock. The first lambs from Hughes' Oxfordshire Downs ewes were lost through abandonment. Competing with experienced family gardeners while attempting to grow vegetables for local markets on his own ranch without sufficient rainfall or irrigation proved to be a struggle for him.

Willy was quick to learn, however, and decided to concentrate on the sheep and wool business and leave commercial gardening, sale of firewood, cedar posts, etc., as side interests. He discovered he had other methods of supplementing cash-flow for which he was better suited.

By studying the books on farming and sheep husbandry sent from England, and by listening to counsel of his ranching mentors, Willy not only became skilled at the technical aspects of raising and caring for farm animals, but soon became adept at buying, trading, and selling livestock, especially sheep, cattle, and horses. In fact, marketing was surfacing as one of his better talents; but raising sheep was his forte.

Fortunately, sheep were readily adaptable to the Texas Hill Country climate[1], and they thrived on nutritious native grasses, which included buffalo grass, gamma, fescue, side oats, Indian grass, blue stem, mesquite, and others. So with a favorable climate that permitted two wool clippings per year, and the availability of accessible cheap land and

---

[1] (1) U. S. Dept. of Commerce, Natl. Oceanic and Atmospheric Adm. Environmental Data Service, 1941-74: Kendall County Annual rainfall 30 inches; average temp. 65°F.

(2) TEXAS ALMANAC, 1986-87 issue: Jan. Avg. Min. Temp. 38°F-- July Avg. Max. Temp. 94°F

excellent grazing range, Willy focused on developing the best sheep and wool management practices possible in order to maximize the return on his investment.

Willy demonstrated that he was familiar with such key management factors as acres of land required per animal unit; cost per head for seed stock; cost per animal unit for feed, medicine, and operating expenses; ratio of offspring per 100 head of breeding ewes; percentage of newborn survival; attrition through predators, disease, and old age; annual pounds of fleece per animal; market value of wool; optimum size of flock for best control; separation of rams and ewes, except for selected breeding dates, to insure most favorable lambing dates; and grouping of old and frail sheep to balance competitiveness for food and shelter, with the same principle, of course, applying to young sheep, cripples, etc.

Willy was very much aware of the importance of providing shelter for animals during severe weather and of supplemental feeding (mostly hay) during extreme winter weather conditions.

### Kendall Connection

The famous George Kendall, noted statesman, author, and owner of the New Orleans Picayune, brought Merino sheep to his Post Oak Spring Ranch four miles east of Boerne in 1855.[2]

When he died in 1867, the South's foremost authority on sheep husbandry left a treasure-trove of written material on sheep care and management. His articles were published by TEXAS ALMANAC 1858-61, and after the Civil War, in 1886 and 1887. Because there were only three public libraries in Texas at this time,[3] the TEXAS ALMANAC was eagerly sought by farmers and ranchers who often used it as an

---

[2] Brown, James, LETTERS FROM A TEXAS SHEEP RANCH, - University of Illinois Press, Urbana, Ill., 1959

[3] Perry, Garland, TEXAS LIBRARIES, Vol. 46 No. I, Spring/Summer 1985, Texas Library and Archive Commission, p. 23 -- Galveston Mercantile Library (1871), Galveston; Houston Lyceum Library (1855), Houston; and The Texas State Library (1839), Austin.

agriculture handbook. It was more like a Bible to sheep ranchers of pre- and post-Civil War periods, with contributing writers such as George Kendall and his friend, Henry S. Randall of Cortland Village, N.Y., sharing their wisdom on sheep culture.

No written evidence proves that Willy Hughes read Kendall-era issues of the TEXAS ALMANAC, but it is reasonable to believe that he did. In a letter dated May 15, 1880, he told his grandmother that he had exhausted all ranche literature. In addition to reading all available material, it is noted that Hughes quickly adopted most of the previously mentioned management principles that were introduced to Kendall County by Mr. Kendall.[4] Even if Willy had learned his ranch management terminology and expertise from other knowledgeable sheep ranchers, most of them knew about Kendall's sheep management teachings, and consequently, he benefitted from the great man's expert knowledge in this field.

In his own ranch operation, Kendall grazed 5,000 sheep on 15,000 acres of land, or one animal per three acres; he provided shelter and nearby shocks of hay for his sheep during cold, rainy weather; he kept his rams penned separately and turned them with ewes in increments between October 20th to November 1st so the ewes would drop their lambs between March 20th and April 1st, the gestation period being five months. Kendall once wrote, "A lamb dropped April 1st will be larger and better formed the day it is three months old than will a lamb dropped July 1st when it is six months old."[5]

Willy constantly sought to improve quality and quantity of his sheep/wool enterprise through better breeding and management practices. Unfortunately, adequate public records of sheep and wool statistics were not kept by the state government during the Civil War period, but the following chart indicates the degree of improvement in sheep and wool production in Texas during a 124-year span.[6]

---

[4] Kendall County was named for George W. Kendall when it was organized in 1862.

[5] TEXAS ALMANAC, 1860, p. 158

[6] TEXAS ALMANAC, Sesquicentennial Edition, 1986-87

# TEXAS SHEEP AND WOOL PRODUCTION[7]

| YEAR | SHEEP INVENTORY | TOTAL $ VALUE | VALUE PER HEAD | WOOL LBS.* PRODUCTION | AVG. CLIP PER HEAD | WOOL VALUE | VALUE PER POUND |
|---|---|---|---|---|---|---|---|
| 1860 | 753,363 | NA | NA | 1,493,363 | 1.98lbs | NA | NA |
| 1880 | 6,024,000 | 12,048,000 | $ 2.00 | NA | NA | NA | NA** |
| 1900 | 2,416,000 | 4,590,000 | 1.89 | 9,630,000 | 3.98 | NA | NA |
| 1930 | 6,304,000 | 44,758,000 | 7.09 | 48,262,000 | 7.65 | $10,135,000 | $0.20 |
| 1984 | 1,970,000 | 76,830,000 | 39.00 | 17,500,000 | 8.88 | 16,100,000 | 0.92 |

\* Incl. twice yearly shearing.

\*\* In 1880, W. G. Hughes took 3,100 lbs. of wool to market in San Antonio that sold for $821.50, or $0.265 per pound.[8]

7 TEXAS ALMANAC, Sesquicentennial Edition, 1986-87

8 G.T.T., Letter to Willy's grandmother, dated 5-21-1882.

## Land Acquisition

For a profitable sheep and wool operation, Willy needed more ranch land to increase the size of his flock and consequently, wool production.

In a letter to his brothers dated April 8, 1879, he said, "I have at last had the surveyor out, and located my 640 acres of land; so I now have 800 acres of my own, and on one side of me there are 640 acres of school land, and on the other 640 acres of State land; so we shall have plenty of breathing room."

Approximately one year later, May 1, 1880, in a letter to his Uncle Thomas Hughes, Willy said, "I now have 1440 acres of land and a total investment of $1,100 in the whole place."

In an unedited copy of this same letter, Willy tells his uncle that he will send 5% interest on the (100) sheep account at the end of 12 months from the date of his loan. This information puts to rest a mystery that has prevailed for years regarding Willy's earlier source of financial assistance upon entering the sheep business.[9] However, Uncle Tom wasn't involved to any great extent with financing Willy's activities because of a gigantic conglomerate investment he was making in Northeastern Tennessee. But his minimal help to Willy was crucial at the beginning. And, of course, Willy's father provided some support when he could.

Willy bought a second 160-acre tract, the Leopold Schultz place, Survey No. 442, on August 2, 1879 for $400., financing it with a note through the Scottish American Mortgage Company, Limited, of San Antonio.[10]

As with learning about buying, selling, and trading livestock, Willy spent considerable time studying quality and potential productivity of land during his first years in Texas. Much of that time was also devoted to learning intricate details for purchasing

---

[9] In an unedited letter to his father dated March 4, 1879, Willy asked if Uncle Tom meant what he said about lending him money at five percent interest?

[10] Deed Records, Kendall County Clerks' Office, Vol. 4, P. 699

public domain land, especially State school land, which began selling publicly in 1874.[11]

Laws pertaining to sale of State land were passed by the Legislature, and the Commissioner of the General Land Office was given responsibility of carrying out the law. The basic statutes were changed or amended from time to time, but the Act of February 23, 1900, published in the 1904 Texas Almanac, describes general procedures that Willy Hughes followed in purchasing school land.

Amount of Land: Limit of four sections per person or 2,560 acres.

Price: Grazing land, $1.00/Ac. minimum; Farm land, $1.50/Ac minimum. (Land was cheaper in earlier years.)

Terms: One-fortieth down and 3% interest on unpaid balance each November 1st. for 40 years, or until principle is paid in full. Purchaser must live on land for three years.

Other Conditions: Purchaser could sell all or part of the land at any time, but vendee had to complete three years' occupancy. He was also required to record his deed with the county clerk and send the original deed to the Land Office with his note payable to the State. The owner could buy other State land within five miles of his original tract, but not more than four sections.

It was with these generous terms that Willy Hughes became highly proficient as a land investor. The State's method of selling with 1/40th down payment and 3% interest paid annually fitted Willy's thin pocketbook.

Today, purchasing with a low down payment, favorable terms, and no penalty for early payment of principle, or acquiring land with the least personal investment, is called "leveraging." This particular word, "leveraging," may not have been in Willy Hughes' vocabulary at that time, but he quickly mastered the mathematical aspects of the leveraging equation. For instance, he bought a 640-acre tract of school land (Survey 233) on November 4, 1880 for $320. His down payment was $8.00 (1/40th of purchase price), plus a $1.00 filing fee. He sold that same 640 acres on July 20, 1881, for $600.

---

[11] Categories of Land Grants in Texas, Reference Sheet #1, Texas General Land Office, Archives and Records Division.

With revenue produced by this sale, Willy paid off his $312 balance on the principal and received a letter patent from the State for the land, which he conveyed to his buyer. Willy's personal expenses had been an $8.00 down payment, $7.22 for eight months' interest at 3% on the principal, and a $1.00 filing fee, or a total of $16.22 invested. His net return on the $320 investment was $303.78. Not a bad return for his out-of-pocket expense of $16.22.

The Deed Records of Willy's first few land transactions show his exact purchase and sales price. Later he used less revealing terms in the Warranty Deed, such as, "for one dollar and other considerations." But at least there are some early records showing that he made generous profits on most of those early land trades.

Willy's unedited letter of May 1, 1880 to Uncle Tom also said the new County maps for the previous year (1879) had come out recently and showed that there was just room to lay another certificate for 640 acres joining his property, so he collared it at once. Willy further stated he had planted 10 acres of cotton. His father wrote in his Introduction to Part IV of G.T.T. that the cotton raising experiment was a failure, along with several other ventures. But the greenhorn farmer never mentioned giving up.

In another unedited letter from Harry Hughes to his sister, Emily, dated May 2, 1880, he said Willy was plowing land for planting sugar cane.[12] Harry finished his letter on May 7th and enclosed a sketch of a surveyor's map he made showing that Willy had bought land strategically located adjacent to five tracts of State school land. This was a brilliant move because it gave Hughes free grazing access to open, unleased school land without crossing private property. Most of the land shown on this sketch later became a part of Hughes Ranch.

---

[12] Experienced farmers would have planted cotton and sugar cane in early April, but that was also lambing time--Author

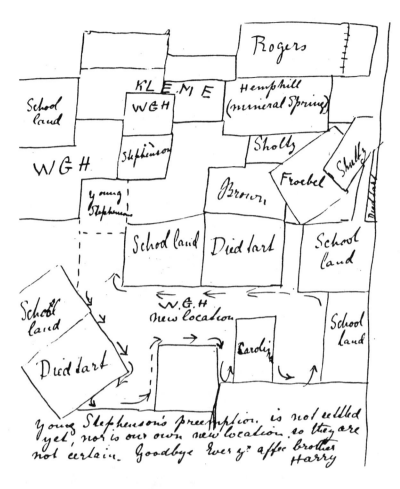

A freehand drawing by Harry Hughes of tracts of land
3 1/2 miles West of Boerne where Hughes Ranch was located

According to his letters published in G.T.T.-GONE TO TEXAS, Willy acquired 1,440 acres of land during his first two years in Kendall County (1879-1880).[13] In 1881, Willy bought equity in two larger undivided tracts and purchased 26.5 acres at a public tax sale. He sold his first 160-acre place, Survey No. 731, along with his second 640-acre school tract for $1,400. At end of 1881, he had 1,424.5 acres of land, which included one section of preempted acreage. Willy also acquired access to more grazing land by purchasing equity in a larger tract that joined unfenced school land.

---

[13]  The first 640-acre tract must have been preempted through a five year state lease, or some other arrangement, as County Deed Records do not show it as having been recorded in 1879.

103

## Livestock Transactions

While Willy's land ownership was easy to estimate on an annual basis by reconciling sales and purchases shown in deed records at the end of each year, it was not nearly so easy to determine his sheep and other livestock holdings at any specific time. This was especially true after the G.T.T.-GONE TO TEXAS letters were discontinued at the end of 1883.

The Part III introduction of G.T.T. by Hastings Hughes said that Willy bought 200 ewes of the country to cross with his thoroughbred Oxfordshire Downs rams. That happened before Hastings left the ranch in October 1879 to start work in New York as a sherry importer. In a letter to his grandmother dated January 19, 1880, Willy said he sold nearly half his sheep, a lot of 60 that he bought first, and replaced them with a lot of 100 afterward. It appears that he then had approximately 250 ewes.

Willy also had told his grandmother in a letter of December 31, 1879, that he was feeding cottonseed to twenty or so calves, indicating that he was establishing a small herd of cattle. He made no reference to horses at that time, but he and his brother Harry had previously commented on their having four to six horses between them.

However, it was the visits to the ranch by cousins Jim Hughes and Bob Hobson that triggered Willy's interest in breeding and training horses for commercial purposes. Both of these cousins were accomplished horsemen--Jim as a rider who bought and drove Texas longhorns up the Western cattle trails to Abilene and Dodge City, Kansas, and Bob as a veteran of three years' service in the Royal Horse Guard Blues[14] before coming to America. Hobson was especially fascinated with the wild mustangs and their potential for racing and use as polo ponies.

Willy Hughes was also an excellent horseman, and through association with his cousins he began thinking more about selecting and improving a breed of horse to meet future market potential and for use on his own ranch.

---

[14] DeBruyn, John R., LETTERS TO OCTAVIUS WILKINSON: TOM HUGHES' LOST UNCLE, narrative based on letters in the Morris L. Parrish Collection of the Princeton University Library.

Willy's Uncle Thomas Hughes came to New York and Boston several times on business during the 1870s and 1880s, and for a time he leased pasture space in the Garden City area of New York for his sons and their cousins to use when shipping horses from Texas to the New York market. Willy Hughes' only surviving child, Gerard H. "Jerry" Hughes of New London, New Hampshire, shared copies of two 1880 newspaper clippings telling about horses cousin Bob Hobson took from Willy's Texas ranch to Uncle Tom's New York holding facility. These stories encouraged Willy to ship his own horses to the New York market.

NEW YORK SPORTSMAN
May 29, 1880

## POLO PONIES FROM TEXAS

"I ride as good a galloway
As any man in Town;
He'll trot you sixteen miles an hour,
I'll bet you half a crown;
He's such a one to bend the knee,
And tuck his haunches in;
And to throw the dirt into your face,
He never deems a sin."

**Editor Sportsman:** The introduction of the game of polo in 1876 also introduced to us the pony of Texas. Originally brought North for the sole purpose of polo playing, these beautiful little animals have won their way into favor for saddle and even harness purposes, and still more recently for racing among the younger members of the American Jockey Club, until the increasing demand has made them a profitable article of traffic to Texas parties.

Some two weeks since twenty-four head of these ponies arrived from Texas in charge of Mr. Hobson, who in November last brought North a number of extra quality, among which was the pony called Thunderer, which had carried Mr. Hobson many miles in Texas and in

Mexico, and recently won the race at Jerome Park for Mr. Belmont Purdy, his present owner. The ponies are from "Uffington Ranche," property of Mr. W. G. Hughes, who is a nephew of the Hon. Thomas Hughes, of "Tom Brown's Schooldays" fame, for whom Mr. Hobson is herdsman. The ponies are now located on the O'Brien pastures, near Reed's Hotel, on Central avenue and One Hundred and Sixty-ninth street. They are of every conceivable color, many of them pied. To enumerate them would involve considerable space, but among the choicest ones is a chestnut mare of fine size, form, and action, a couple of grays of fine appearance, and a roan of the smaller type, which struck us as a particularly nice one. They are turned out and ramble the fields and woods at will. As may be imagined, they are looking very rough after the long journey, but are on the whole a remarkably well-formed, good-sized, and hardy lot, and gentlemen desiring a pony for polo playing, racing, or other purposes, would do well to make an early visit of inspection to O'Brien's, where Mr. Hobson will show them with all the pride of a true Englishman.

Pony racing will, at no late day, become as popular here as in England, where for years the sport has flourished, and where, from time to time, thoroughbred crosses have been resorted to, which gave greater ambition and speed--some of the smaller, quick-footed horses of the Whalebone family having been tried with excellent results. Notwithstanding all this, Mr. Hobson informed us that among the lot first arrived was a little mare from Texas, which it was his desire to have shipped to England, for she had shown him speed superior to that of any pony he had seen in the old country. But fate was against him, for at Pittsburgh "Hobson's choice" broke her back while in the car. Had she lived, it is likely a match would have been made with the English pony Silly, which is matched to run Mr. Purdy's Texan during the summer.

Dime-novel literature and Peralto's riding feats had conveyed an impression that the Texan pony is a hard-mouthed, wild, untameable animal. This is all wrong, though there are exceptional cases, which would confirm it. Mr. Hobson's are, as a rule, well used to seeing people, and many as kind as the ordinary saddle horse. During our visit we played and patted a number of them, who seemed well pleased with the attention paid them, and though some are quite unbroken to saddle Mr. Hobson had no use for the Mexican bit with those he was breaking.

Yours,     VIGILANT.

NEW YORK HERALD

June 14, 1880

EXTRAORDINARY ESCAPE OF POLO HORSES.

A few weeks ago the HERALD referred in an article on polo to a lot of ponies and horses which Mr. Hobson had just brought up from the ranche of Mr. Thomas Hughes, in Texas.[15] The public may be interested to hear of the narrow escape that three of them had yesterday afternoon. The Hughes party are putting up at O'Brien's ranche on Central avenue, about a mile from Macomb's Dam. The house stands on the highest ground for half a mile around, about four hundred yards to the east of the avenue. Thirty yards to the northeast of the house there stood, till between four and five o'clock yesterday afternoon, a three storied barn, with stables on the ground and second floors and a loft above. Some days ago a gray mare and a black stud had been stabled on the second floor, and a roan stud underneath them. These were fortunately the only animals either in the barn or the adjoining corral yesterday afternoon. The party had dined early, and were taking their ease on the stoop with a friend who had come to see them, looking at the thunderclouds over the Hudson and wondering whether the pasture was to get its much needed rain, when

_____

[15]   Error; Thomas Hughes never owned an interest in Willy's ranch.--Author

107

there came up from Central avenue a mighty rushing wind. In a few seconds the table and chairs--everything on the stoop, in fact, except a heavy Texan saddle and a bucket of water, with a bottle of sherry in it-- were blown off the stoop, and Mr. Hughes found himself running, laughing, after his straw hat and tobacco tin which had been carried round the corner of the house. He caught them and was still picking up some cigarettes, hearing nothing but the rush of the hurricane, when he looked toward the house and there stood his cousin, with a look on his face which said that something was very wrong, shouting and looking in the direction of the barn. Mr. Hughes turned and saw that it was now a mass of broken timber spread all over the corral. There on the top of it stood the gray mare, trembling in every limb, tied to her post without a scratch. The roof and loft had been blown right away from her, and she had come down from the second floor standing on the boards. But poor little Sylvius, the black stud who had stood beside her, was not so fortunate. He had been caught by the rafters and floor of the loft and was lying on his back among the ruins, with his neck doubled up. They could not suppose that he would ever come out alive; but Miss O'Brien found an axe and a saw in a trice, and they were soon at work in the driving rain and the dust of the old barn, with the lightning playing round them, tearing up the planks and hacking and sawing away at the rafters, and in a minute or so Sylvius struggled up and stood beside them, but with a good deal of the devil-may-care, for which he is famous, taken out of him for the moment. They had only time to see that he was unhurt. Then it was, "How about Comanche?" said one of the party. "Oh, he must be crushed." "Never mind: up with those planks: he must be under them," and up they came, and in a few seconds part of his breathing body could be seen, then his head, both between two of the rafters. Up came the rest of the boards at it again with saw and axe on the rafters, and presently the plucky little Indian was on his sturdy little legs again looking round as if nothing had happened and at once beginning to munch a great handful of hay which Mr. Hughes handed him from a tumbled up truss hard by. Then he stepped carefully in and out and over the smashed planks and rafters and shingles and was safe with the other two in the only clear corner of the corral. "Thrue," said Mr. Hughes, as he turned to look at the wreck which they had been treating in this unceremonious way. "How those ponies got out of it without being crushed or torn to pieces I cannot tell, for besides the jagged ends of rafters and planks there were sleighs, a light wagon, a chaff cutter and I know not what goods and chattels belonging to our landlord sticking out in every direction."

----------

Courtesy, Historic Rugby, Inc.
Margaret Elizabeth Hughes and Her Granddaughter Emily

## Granny Immigrates To America

Margaret Elizabeth Wilkinson Hughes was 84 years old when she immigrated to America in 1881. Her decision to leave England was not a frivolous one. She considered many factors before making the long voyage to the new land. Concerned about the health aspects of living in foggy, smoke-filled London, Granny was also tired of the hustle-bustle lifestyle of English society at that time. Earlier, in 1874, she had packed up Hastings' four children and moved with them to the Isle of Wight, where they lived for a year before returning to London.

Two years later, in 1877, Granny's daughter Jeanie Senior died of an unknown illness. Five years earlier, her oldest son, George, had also died. These losses, in addition to grandson Willy's departure for America in 1878--followed by Hastings and his youngest son, Harry, in 1879--caused Granny to decide to leave her homeland and emigrate.

Granny Hughes was like a mother to Hastings' children. She had had complete responsibility for Emily from early infancy and had lived in the home of John and Jeanie Senior, where she also cared for the young Hughes boys for several years prior to her move to the Isle of Wight in 1874.

Granny named her home on Wight "Uffington House." Perhaps it was because of his love for his grandmother that Willy initially called his place in Kendall County "Uffington Ranche." In an effort to entice Granny to come to Texas, he stated in his letter of December 31, 1879, "It would be pleasanter for you to have a temporary wooden house on the ranche until the house is built. It can be made exceedingly comfortable, and its cost, altogether, is £60."[16]

It appeared that Granny was all set to drop anchor in Boerne, Texas, until she learned that her second son, Thomas Hughes, a noted author and popular celebrity in England and the United States, was preparing to announce the founding of an English Colony on 75,000 acres of wilderness land on the Cumberland Plateau of Northeastern Tennessee.

Ever the social reformer and a disciple of Christian Socialism, this was Thomas Hughes' altruistic dream of a haven for "second sons" of middle-to-upper class English families who, without social constraints, could make an honest living from the sweat of their brows in agricultural pursuits.

The colony project had substantial financial backers from both sides of the Atlantic, but this was an enormous undertaking. From its inception, the colony idea received most favorable English and American press coverage; however, most of this attention was due to Thomas Hughes' extreme popularity throughout America and England. He was the Chairman of the Board and chief spokesman for the British Board of Aid to Land Ownership, Limited.

---

[16]  A British pound at that time was worth approximately $5.00 U.S. currency-- Author

Residing at his leased property on Manhattan Island during the summer of 1880, Thomas wrote news releases and lectured around the country to raise money for his pet colonization adventure.

In August, Tom summoned his brother Hastings to go to the colony site in Tennessee and look after administrative matters on his behalf. Hastings encountered numerous difficulties and didn't get back to his New York import business for nearly a year. Among other things, construction of residential and some public buildings was already behind schedule. In fact, the Tabard Hotel was not yet completed.[17] This, and other inconveniences were a source of concern to new land owners coming to this strange and desolate primeval setting.

On October 5, 1880, Thomas Hughes gave the formal dedication address for his unique English settlement which he named "Rugby" after the historic English school he attended before going to Oriel College, Oxford. He gave an eloquent speech which was said to have temporarily alleviated some misgivings that residents had about their utopian community. Even Hastings Hughes showed considerable enthusiasm for Rugby's prospects in a letter to his Uncle "Oct" Wilkinson the day after the dedication ceremony.[18] He wrote "--And if dear Mother comes--and she is talking about it seriously--I shall make it my permanent headquarters."

Any such change in Granny's plans would have been a terrible disappointment to Willy and Harry Hughes in Texas. But Hastings and Tom had obviously talked about the situation and the possibility of bringing their own American family members together at Rugby.

In December 1880, Hastings invited Willy to come "prospecting" in Rugby. Willy, who probably knew more about soil types and grazing land than his father and

---

[17] DeBruyn, John R., LETTERS TO OCTAVIUS WILKINSON: TOM HUGHES' LOST UNCLE, narrative based on letters in the Morris L. Parrish Collection of the Princeton University Library.

[18] DeBruyn, John R., LETTERS TO OCTAVIUS WILKINSON: TOM HUGHES' LOST UNCLE, P. 46 - "Hastings was never a deep believer in the (Rugby) venture."

Uncle Tom combined, quickly determined that both the poor post oak clay soil in the Rugby area and the Cumberland Plateau climate were no match for the ideal climate and excellent grazing land in the Texas Hill Country where he had planted his roots two years earlier. He declined to accept the invitation and returned to Boerne. The same thing happened in Thomas Hughes' situation. As devoted as their sons were to their parents, none of the Hughes boys nor their Hobson cousins could be persuaded to participate in the Rugby colonization endeavor.[19]

Nevertheless, Granny opted to emigrate to Rugby rather than Boerne, for two reasons. First, her most famous son desperately needed her stabilizing influence and her show of support in this, his greatest humanitarian and business undertaking. Secondly and equally as important, she wanted to move her granddaughter Emily closer to her father.[20] On May 23, 1881, Margaret "Granny" Hughes and 17-year-old Emily arrived in Philadelphia, twelve days out of Liverpool on American Line steamer Illinois, on their way to Rugby.[21]

Granny's pending arrival was well publicized in both New York and Philadelphia newspapers. This sedate, regal lady had received excellent press coverage that attracted enthusiastic public support all along the U.S. East Coast. A large crowd of reporters and local citizens gathered at dockside to cheer and get a glimpse of the courageous Mrs. Hughes as she and her granddaughter disembarked with their party of travelers and domestic help, the Dyer family who accompanied her to America. The courage and determination of this aged matriarch in support of her son Tom's colony became a popular news item of that day.

Hastings Hughes met his mother and his daughter Emily aboard ship. He then

---

[19] Willy also recognized the economic advantages he had in Texas: cheaper land with most favorable terms and a climate that permitted two wool clippings per year.

[20] DeBruyn, John R., DISSIPATIONS AT UFFINGTON HOUSE, Memphis State University, Memphis, Tennessee, 1975

[21] DeBruyn, John R., LETTERS TO OCTAVIUS WILKINSON: TOM HUGHES' LOST UNCLE

took the entire Hughes entourage for a day's rest outside of Philadelphia, at the home of Mr. George Childs, the editor of THE PHILADELPHIA LEDGER,[22] before proceeding by train through Cincinnati, Ohio, where they spent two or three more days at the home of W. W. Scarborough, a banker and philanthropist who owned stock in the Rugby development.[23] On May 31st, they moved on to Sedgemoor Station, a remote, isolated stop in Morgan County, Tenn., where they transferred to a waiting wagon for the last seven miles over a rough and muddy wagon trail through the wilderness to Rugby.

Granny and Emily arrived at Rugby's Tabard Hotel about 7:30 p.m., where they were greeted by a very excited group of Rugbeians who were anxious to see them and hear the latest news from England. Before turning in for the night, Hastings produced letters for Granny and Emily (Madge, as the family called her) from the Hughes boys in Texas. Emily was ecstatic. She had not seen her brother Willy for nearly three years, nor Harry for two years.

Future letters between Emily and her brothers frequently made reference to plans for a trip to Texas by Emily and her father. Hastings was terribly busy, and their visit was postponed for several months.

Despite Granny Hughes' stabilizing influence on Rugby, 1881 was not a good year for the new British settlement. There were cost over-runs and problems with land titles. The summer was hot and dry, and within two months after the arrival of Mrs. Hughes and her followers, a typhoid fever epidemic descended upon the colony. Several young men died. A large number of residents became dreadfully ill--including Emily Hughes. Many residents became disenchanted and left the colony. A few went back to England.

Willy and Harry were terribly busy at the ranche, but they regularly wrote long, newsy, and cheerful letters to Emily and their father and grandmother. They also kept in touch with Gerard (Chico), who was still in England. It was this series of letters--

---

[22] DeBruyn, John R., DISSIPATIONS AT UFFINGTON HOUSE, Memphis State University, Memphis, Tennessee, 1975

[23]    Ibid.

some of which were selected for GONE TO TEXAS--that give such vivid insight into the life and daily activities of Willy Hughes as a pioneer Texas rancher.

### THE DOCTOR TO MADGE IN TENNESSEE   June 5, 1881

I suppose that you have by this time got settled down a bit in your new house. I hope you appreciate the wood fires, and wooden fences and houses, which are far better than coals and bricks.

The flock is in the Schultz field today, and I am down at the house baking, as we find that we can bake better bread in a stove than in a skillet. I presume you have everything handsome in the "stove and cooking tricks" line, and have not had to bake in a skillet, nor fry your bacon on a toasting-fork, nor even been reduced to boiling your eggs in the coffee?

All our cows have calved now, including Gentle (the cow we were milking till March). Our cats are not so fat as they used to be, so we are obliged to feed them two or three times a week. You should just see them after being fed on beef! The flock is beginning to look fat again, and the lambs are so big that I have to count them all together now, or I should make mistakes.

My red mare will be just the animal for you to ride when you come down to visit us, as she is "gentle as a dawg," and both fast and sure-footed. I rode eighty miles on her in two days last week, but she played out after seventy miles of it; and it must have been 11 p.m before I reached camp. Next day I kept losing the sheep all the morning by dropping off to sleep unawares....

### THE DOCTOR TO MADGE IN TENNESSEE   The Ranche
                          June 30, 1881

...Are you going to set up by yourself when you have bought your piece of land, or are you only going to buy it as a speculation? I have the right to preempt 80 acres of State land for nothing; but I have not done so yet, as I cannot do it twice, and I may find a piece some day which cannot be got in any other way, except by buying it at a dollar an acre. I took a photo of the ranche last Sunday, and I am going to mettle up and get some papers prepared for taking positives next Sunday. If I succeed I'll send you one.

All the stock are doing well, and so are your affectionate brothers; but we are dreadfully in want of rain. A watery new moon has just come, so I expect there will be a big storm in a day or two, and I keep one eye on the sky, and the other on my mackintosh to be ready for it....

NOTE--About this time Willy sold his original ranche, and he and the Doctor went into camp within the rock-fenced 60 acre pasture, "the Schultz field" (which had been planted in part with cotton in 1880), in the centre of their new purchase. Here they pitched their two tents, and put up sheds, &c. for the sheep. Lenny Windale had left them, and his place had been taken by Mr. Colton, a young Pennsylvanian, who went to them to learn the sheep business. --Tom Hughes

FROM WILLY TO MADGE                                        July 14, 1881

...Have you got your donkey or mule yet? Thunder! It would be as good as a circus to see you prancing about on a sprightly pie-balled mule; tail cut short, likewise mane; none of your lanky good-for-nothing mules, but a fat, chirpy chap, ready at a moment's notice to seize the bit in his teeth, and "git" from one end of the avenue to the other before the unsuspecting rider knew he had started; one that would take offence at a neighbouring fence, and kick the last paling of it into sawdust; then throw his ears back somewhere in the neighbourhood of the tip of his tail, and chaw down the nearest pine-tree. Admission free; children in arms half-price.

116

The Gov. says that you say there are several things the Doctor asked about, packed away in the various packages, otherwise I would not summon up courage to ask if that small scrap-book of mine (blue, I believe) is still in the land of the living....

## THE DOCTOR TO HIS FATHER IN TENNESSEE
The Ranche
Sept. 4, 1881

I am shearing some of the lambs just to see how they get on; for it is a very general theory that shearing twice a year is better for sheep. I suppose they never take a "full clip" so far north as Tennessee, as the winter must set in before they could grow enough wool?

We shall have to work like blazes for the next week or two, as we have to finish the fence down the middle of the pasture, and several other jobs, before the middle of this month, and the one who happens to be herding cannot do much with his spare time, as he has to keep in sight the flock even while they are lying down.

I take out a piece of canvas with me, and shear a lamb or two while they lie down, but that is all. A lamb looks awfully queer and angular after shearing, but he feels better.

## THE DOCTOR TO MADGE
Sept. 9, 1881

So I hope that by the time this letter reaches you, you will be able to read to yourself.[24]

While I was herding to-day, a big shower came down, and I took shelter in a hollow tree; but unfortunately for me, it had a small opening on the rainy side, and a small lake began to creep gradually in along the floor of my house. For about ten minutes I kept it out by making a dam

---

[24] Emily was seriously ill with Typhoid Fever from July 14th through August of 1881--Author

117

of the loose earth that lay inside the tree, but at last my materials gave out, and the dam broke, so I had to stand in two inches of water till the rain stopped.

Our division fence is stretching gradually down the pasture, but as yet we have not put any boards on. Willy and I made the water-gate two days ago, and as there was a tree on only one side of the creek, I had to cut a forked post for the other. The tree I cut down to make the post of was unfortunately so bound up with another one, that, although I cut it clear through, it refused to fall, and I had to cut down the other as well; and as the other was a dead pecan, very thick and as hard as rocks, I had a very tough job. When I got my post cut loose, we found it too heavy to haul, so I caught my mare, put the rope round the horn of the saddle, and made her pull it for me, while I kept the rope from cutting her back.

When you come down here you will have to take up the photography business, as I really believe I never shall have time to go in for it much. You can have "the whole bag of tricks," if you find you can manage to work them, though I am afraid I shall be a very poor master.

THE DOCTOR TO MADGE                              The Ranche
                                                Sept. 22, 1881

Our fence is more than half done now, although there are no boards up, for the post-setting is far the worst job. On Tuesday we went out surveying our new land, and had a good lot of walking to do, and not a little of it was pretty tough, as one has to go straight through everything that comes in one's way.

Once we came to a bluff and had to go round, and just guess at the distance, for, as we were only surveying an old tract, it didn't matter if we were 30 or 40 feet out, so long as we found the corners and went straight. We had an awful lot of trouble finding the corners, as many of them were in the brush, and several of them had been destroyed;

118

however, we found the trees (they always "blaze" the nearest tree to a corner), so we made new ones.

Father has written to say that he still intends to come down "some time" this Fall. I don't believe he will come at all if he doesn't make up his mind to come soon, for winter is not far off now.

We are labelling some of our ewes now, and they (the labels) look quite neat, and don't appear to rust al all. Our shorn lambs are growing wool very fast, and eat so much, that they are broader than they are deep; in fact I am afraid lest some member of the "Bergh" society will have us up for "overloading" them!...

WILLY TO MADGE                              The Ranche

                                            Sept. 22, 1881

I have just been, for some days past, blistering up my hands like anything, digging post holes for our new fence; but we have nearly finished it now. I hope the Governor will bring you down here this Fall, as he says he may be able to, and that you will be strong enough to get lots of riding here.

THE DOCTOR TO MADGE                         Oct. 2, 1881

...We are making preparations for winter by buying feed now, and I believe we shall soon erect a sheep shed. We have already got all the fodder and hay we shall need, but have not got any cotton-seed yet.

The acorns are falling thick and fast now, and the sheep are very troublesome when they get among them, as they are so eager about picking them up that they don't look where they are going, and get scattered. I opened an acorn today which had eight separate kernels! I never found one with more than three before, so I expect it is not common, and I almost wish I hadn't pitched it away.

119

WILLY TO MADGE                                    San Antonio
                                                  October 11, 1881

...I hope you have quite recovered now, and are getting lots of riding and other exercise. I am now down in San Antonio, buying such little winter clothing and sheep shed material as we shall need for winter, as we may get some cold weather this month, although it doesn't generally come till November.


THE DOCTOR TO HIS FATHER IN TENNESSEE          Oct. 14, 1881

I am glad to hear that Madge is getting so strong and heavy, though 93 lbs. seems awfully light.

I am beginning to put on my winter coat of flesh, though I haven't weighed myself lately. I measured myself the other day and found that I was 5 ft. 9 ins., which is about what I expected. We are all thriving, and so are the stock. Rain has been so plentiful that the screw-worms have got into one or two head of stock, but nothing much, and they are soon going to disappear for the winter... Colton seems to like the country pretty well now, but he freely confesses that if we had been stoveless and big-tentless (as we were not long before he came), he might have gone back to Pennsylvania without giving the place a fair trial.

We have had to make a new sheep pen on the side of the hill since the rain commenced, as the old one was too sloshy, and might have given them foot rot. The new one must be nearly half an acre, and holds them very nicely, giving them plenty of room to scatter. At a pinch it would accommodate over 2000, but we don't like to crowd them.

We are going to make a house soon, I believe, but as for **out**-houses, such an idea has never entered our heads! It takes one of us all day to herd, another to cook and do odd jobs, and Willy is always busy up to his eyes, without any extra work of that kind. Even the division fence (which we found we could do without for the present) remains half finished, and we nearly run out of fire wood occasionally. Why don't some of you come down and help us do work that pays?

THE DOCTOR TO MADGE                                    The Ranche
                                                      Oct. 26, 1881

Willy has bought our winter clothing, and I am supplied with a huge overcoat with a cape, which completely swallows me up, and the collar of which touches the rim of my hat when I put it up. It will be A 1 for herding in, during a Norther. Willy has one too, but it doesn't possess a cape.

We have had one or two touches of north wind lately, but no **Northers**, so I hope we shall not have a very severe winter, as some of the prophets say. If we **do** though, you had better all of you come down here, for it will be far worse in Tennessee!...

THE DOCTOR TO MADGE                                    The Ranche
                                                      November 6, 1881

As one of the "events" of our not-too-over-exciting life has just occurred, I think you would like to hear all about it. I refer to the San Antonio fair. I will begin at the beginning by saying that on Monday last Willy went down with a buck and ewe of the Oxford Downs, and five half-breed yearlings. On Wednesday morning I saddled the mare and rode down myself. I got down by 2:30 p.m., and found Willy and the sheep all right. There were very few sheep on view except our own, but they **were** beauties. All of them belonged to one man, one pen of Merino bucks, and one of ewes. They were all wool, from their noses to their hoofs... Alas! one cannot say "to the tips of their tails." There were only five or six goats, but they were likewise beauties. The show of pigs was even worse--only four! I can't say whether they were good or bad, as I don't know anything about pigs. Chickens were more numerous, but

121

I am no judge of them either. There were very few bulls, but a quantity of cows--from the San Antonio dairies I believe, so they looked rather poor... The best show was of horses, but there again I am no judge....There were a great many wagons, farm implements, and produce, on view, but they didn't interest me much. Next day I came back, so that is all the adventure.

Nov. 10, 1881

....Having put this away and forgotten to post it, I will just add that Willy and the sheep have arrived safe, and everything is going on as usual. Our next job will be the erection of a kitchen to put the stove in, as it has occasionally been impossible to light fires out of doors at all.

Willy and Colton are at present employed making a cotton quilt. I expect the cold won't have a chance against us this Fall, as we have been buying all sorts of overcoats, underclothes, and bedclothes, and cutting up a lot of wood. In any case, I hope to survive till you come!...

THE DOCTOR TO HIS FATHER                    Nov. 10, 1881

Willy seems to think that Madge had better lodge at the Stephenson's, and I am not sure that (supposing it can be arranged) he isn't right. In the first place, even if we could put her up in a room near the tents, it would be pretty difficult to make things as comfortable for her as they ought to be; and after all it would be easy enough for her to come up everyday on horse-back, or for us to go down in the evenings; and if, when you come down, you should wish to arrange it differently, I reckon Madge could monopolize the kitchen till we got a new room added on.

We are soon going to build a kitchen, and turn the big tent round so that they will join.

I do hope you will really be able to come down this time, as it is over two years since you left, and it is high time that we had a spice of

122

civilization in this camp. Just think of "batching" for two years without intermission! The wonder is that we haven't married!!!

...When you come down, you should bring all the too awfully disreputable clothing you can raise, and leave them for the use of the camp; but I suppose that you yourself go in rather strong for that kind of thing, now that you live in the "backwoods"?

WILLY TO HIS GRANDMOTHER IN TENNESSEE    Nov. 12, 1881

We are having glorious weather, and have not had a frost yet, so the grass and foliage are still green, and stock and sheep get lots to eat; in fact, the grass is running to seed in many places through not being eaten down enough. We have had good rains lately, and I think there is every promise of lots of grazing during winter.

Very few sheep men feed an ounce to their sheep during winter, but as we only have a few (comparatively) we are able to feed them a little. I gave them some cotton seed this morning, for the first time this winter, and I expect to feed them some about every three days; this will keep them fat.

There was a fair in San Antonio all last week, and I was down there all the week. There were classes for Down buck, Down ewe, and pen of five young ewes, results of cross between long and fine wools, all of which classes I entered for, and took down seven sheep in the wagon accordingly. There was no competition in either of the classes, so of course I took all three premiums. There were some very fine Merino sheep on exhibition, and also some very fair cattle and horses.

We have just been manufacturing a quilt, and it is the most gorgeous thing you ever saw. We have two more to make, and then we shall each have one, and can defy any cold we may have this winter. I bought, for the one made, fourteen yards of a very pretty dark-coloured cotton print, and sewed three widths together for each side. It's seven feet long and six wide. We made a frame, and stretched one side to it; then laid on seven pounds of cotton, and then put the lid, or whatever you call it, on, and then sewed through a piece of knitting cotton all over it, every four inches, each way, and then hemmed the edges; and it looks just as if it had come out of a shop in Bond Street, only rather better if anything!

We have begun to feed our two milch cows. We feed them each half a bucket-full of cotton-seed, night and morning, so we have enough milk to supply a regiment, or should have if we took all the milk; but as we don't need it, we let the calves have most of it. Our cows that have heifer calves we let run out, so that the calves have all the milk; we sometimes don't see them for a week or ten days, as they go some distance off this time of year, and only come up occasionally for salt...

WILLY TO MADGE                                    Dec. 8, 1881

I suppose you have got your chicken-house, &c., pretty well finished now. Chickens in this part of the world are not so luxurious as up there, but then we don't get such cold weather here, nor is it continuous. To-day it was 80° in the shade. Fine Christmas weather isn't it?

The sheep are just doing splendidly. They are herded all day, and brought within sight of the pen about sundown, and then left, and they gradually graze towards the pen, and go in by themselves when it is dark.

We have been so busy lately that we have only just begun our sheep-shed; but I hope we shall have it up in lots of time before lambing in February.

By the way, mind you don't let the Guvnor let that trip business fall through. I want you to see all our stock, &c., and have lots of riding down here; so bring your riding dress, or, if you haven't got one, I'll get you one down here when you come, as I expect lots of riding will do you good. We've got six horses, so we'll be able to make a big turn-out all together.

I think it will be better for you to sleep up at the Stephenson's, if we can arrange it so, as when we do get a few days cold weather our camp arrangements are draughty, and not altogether the place I should like you to be in. The Stephensons are within a mile of here, and one of us can come over every morning and bring you down here.

You're a brave little girl to want to come and rough it with us, but you don't know your brothers if you think they're going to let you. Try and get the Guvnor to come down as early in January as possible, as we shall have lots of time to give up to recreation (comparatively) in January; but about the 10th of February we begin lambing, and from the 15th on we shall be at it in earnest, and shall be kept busy.

We have bachelor feasts around here now and then. Sometimes the chap that bought my other ranche gives them, and sometimes we give them. The last was given by him, when we had a wild turkey that he had shot. He is a very good cook, and he cooked and stuffed that turkey in a way that would shame a Soyer.[25] He shot another last night, and so to-morrow night we go over there again, and if you want to see a turkey "fly," you'd better be there.

I hope you will have a jolly Christmas up there. I suppose people are beginning to think about preparations now. Our next bachelor lay-out (after to-morrow) is going to be spread by this ranche, on Christmas day-- plum puddings, &c....


### Emily Visits Her Brothers

At the end of 1881, Hastings Hughes finally scheduled a business trip to Texas.

---

[25] An oriental chef who specializes in cooking meat with a fermented sauce made from soybeans.

He had strong reservations, however, about letting his only daughter "rough it" at the boys' make-shift camp in middle of winter. But Emily would have no part of the scheme to have her stay with the Stephensons. She chose to stay with her brothers, even if their camp was archaic and terribly uncomfortable.

G.T.T. gives Emily's lively and colorful diary account of the harsh conditions under which Willy Hughes and his associates existed during their early days in pioneer Texas. She wrote about rugged frontier life, as seen through the eyes of a cultured young English lady. Her love for her brothers was obvious in her diary entries. Later, after she returned to her home at Rugby on the remote Cumberland Plateau of Eastern Tennessee, the letters exchanged between her and her Texas family would be spiced with good humor and reminders of shared adventures. Sometimes Willy sent Emily advice on technical points and skills in gardening or improving the quality of her chickens and livestock.

EMILY'S VISIT TO "THE BOYS" IN TEXAS      East Tennessee,
March 1882

We were really starting at last, to pay that long promised visit to the boys; and very glad I was at the prospect of seeing my two brothers again. Willy I had not seen for over three years, and the Doctor for two years and a-half. I came out with my grandmother last year to live in Tennessee, and as soon as I had recovered my strength, after a serious illness, which I had soon after our arrival, my father and I had settled when we should take our journey to see "our boys." We started on the 5th of January last, and, after staying a few days at different places on the route, we arrived at San Antonio at 8 p.m. on the 11th.

On the 13th we took places in a lumbering old coach, with room for six passengers, which was to take us to Boerne, the little town three and a half miles from my brother's ranche. The distance was thirty miles, and we took seven hours and a-half to do it, for there had been a good deal of rain, which had made the roads very heavy.

The next day Willy (my eldest brother) came over to town in his wagon to take us and our luggage to the ranche. It was drizzling nearly all the way, and we were rather damp when we alighted just outside a rock fence with a small gate in it, and found ourselves at the long-wished-for goal.

The "house" consisted of a good-sized tent, and a little board kitchen, which was to be my bedroom during my stay. This kitchen was just large enough to hold a small cot bedstead, the stove, a chair, some shelves, and two rough boards that answered as a kitchen table, and also as dressing table for me. It was very roughly built of boards, which had shrunk from exposure to the weather, leaving about half an inch of space between each board. The roof was by no means weather-tight, of which I was uncomfortably reminded sometimes, by waking up to find a steady cold drip coming into my ear or down my neck.

During the day the cot had to be folded up and carried into the tent, to make room for the cooking arrangements. My wardrobe was a small rough wooden box without a lid, and, as it stood just underneath the kitchen "table," it used often to be the receptacle of the greasy drops which found their way, from time to time, between the two boards which composed that article of furniture.

The "family" consisted of five members; my father, my two brothers, and myself, and Mr. Colton, a young man who had been staying there about six months, working for his board. The first sound I heard every morning was a shout from the tent of "Oh Madge!" which, if I did not immediately answer, was repeated until I was wide awake enough to reply. I then lit a lamp (for it was generally before sunrise, or "sun-up" as it is called there), and hustled on my clothes, and called out that I was ready.

Then the business of the day would begin. The cot was stowed away in the tent, and the fire lit, and then breakfast had to be got ready.

On my first morning Willy initiated me into the mysteries of making "slapjacks." These flabby, indigestible things are made of flour and water made into a batter, and fried on skillets in bacon grease. They are pretty good when hot, but after they get cold it requires a good deal of courage to bury one's teeth in them. We had our meals on a small table in the tent, and as there was no table-cloth, we used to bring the pots and pans straight from the fire, and stand them on the table wherever a corner could be found.

I forgot to say that there was no floor to either kitchen or tent, but only the bare ground, and one morning, after a particularly heavy rain, I stepped into half-an-inch of mud on getting out of bed. Directly after breakfast, my younger brother, the Doctor, or Mr. Colton, whosever turn it was, started off with the sheep, and was not seen again till tea-time, at sundown. They never took any dinner with them, as they said it was more trouble to carry it than it was worth, as they have to walk all day during the winter. In summer the sheep lie down during the heat of the day, and the shepherd has time to go home and get his dinner.

The country in that part of Texas is hilly, and the grass is green all winter. The principal trees being live oaks, which are evergreen, takes away the desolate look in winter, and makes it almost appear like summer.

Three days after our arrival at the ranche, we had our first experience of a Texas "Norther." It had been comfortably warm all day, but looked threatening. We were hard at work making a quilt, of which there were already three, when suddenly Willy appeared at the door, and exclaiming "Here it comes!" slammed the door to after him. The next minute a gale of wind began, which seemed to shrivel us up, and make us tuck our feet under us, as we hurried on with the quilt. It rained at the same time, and during the night the rain froze as it fell on the tent, and made it as hard as a board before morning.

128

We went to bed early, after trying in vain to get warm over the tiny cooking-stove; and after pinching my feet for some minutes, and putting every available article of clothing on my bed, I fell asleep. There were only three cots in the tent, and, as there were four people to sleep in them, my two brother slept together in one, and I think they had the best of it that night. The next morning there was not much washing done, I am afraid, for the wind and rain still continued, and all we could do was to try to keep warm. The poor shepherd had to trudge out as usual, after being laden with all the great coats he could carry.

I used sometimes to ride with one or other of my brothers when they went to hunt up the horses or cattle on the hills. The day after we arrived Willy and I rode out on two of the work horses, to see if we could find a little sorrel mare belonging to the Doctor, who with her colt had been running out on the hills for some months. We soon found her, and I dismounted whilst Willy took off my saddle and put it on Polly, the mare. I then mounted again, and we continued our ride, the colt following. As soon as I wanted to go a little faster than a walk, Polly set off at a tearing gallop and kept on just as long as she chose, for I had not the slightest control over her.

Willy enjoyed the way we were racing across country, and shouted every now and then at Polly to make her go faster. I was not much of a rider, having had very little practice, but by a miracle I kept on, though I had several narrow escapes as Polly swerved round corners at a gallop. When I next rode her, I made Willy put on a strong curb, and with that I could just manage to stop her when I wished.

Towards the end of our stay at the ranche, Willy went away for a few days to buy some more sheep, and came back with a nice flock of 207 very fine Merino ewes and bucks which he had bought about 30 miles off. The next day he, and father, and I, were hard at work cataloguing, ear-labelling, and branding them. The ear-labels are small slips of metal,

129

one of which is slipped through a hole made in the ear of each sheep, and then the ends pinched together to prevent them coming out. Each label had my brother's name and a number on it; and as he labelled each sheep, I wrote down on a piece of paper the number, age, and quality of wool of the sheep, and any other particular characteristic, as he told me them.

As each sheep was being labelled my father branded them with an iron made on purpose, and dipped in tar. Before beginning to label the sheep, we had driven them into a good-sized pen, and sprinkled sulphur on them; and then we drove them into a very small pen, where there was just room for them to stand, so that they could be easily taken hold of.

We finished them at about 3 p.m., after working since breakfast; and then the Doctor came home with the other sheep and had his dinner, as he was to take the new sheep out in the afternoon.. When Willy and father and I went in to our dinner, we found that all the food in the house consisted of a scrap of bacon, a small piece of bread, and some cold slapjacks and porridge. There was no fire, so we ate what there was, and washed it down with cold coffee; and I don't think I ever enjoyed a meal more. We never allowed ourselves more than one plate each at a meal, to save washing up, so I always considered carefully, before beginning to eat, which thing to eat first, so as not to spoil the taste of those which came after. My brothers had been so long used to this sort of thing, that they generally put everything in together, and made what I considered the most disgusting mixtures, such as--porridge, milk, slapjacks, molasses, and bacon, all at once.

They had to fetch all their water, except rain-water, from a creek some distance off; and they generally took a large barrel in the wagon, and filled it at the stream, and then brought it to the camp and set it on a stand, and we drew out the water as it was wanted. The barrel-full lasted us about a week; and once, when we were all very busy, the water gave out, and we had to use nothing but rain-water for everything, cooking included, for several days.

Whenever the weather was warm enough, my brothers bathed in one of the streams; in summer they wash their clothes at the same time; they have nothing but shirts and socks to wash, as sheets, pillow-cases, table-cloths, and such-like luxuries, they do not indulge in. Their beds consist of sheep-skins, blankets, and home-made quilts.

They had made me a mattress, and stuffed it with hay from the stack in the yard, and they had also made me a pillow filled with wool; and Willy had purchased a curtain, piece of carpet, and two cane chairs, besides the necessary bed-clothes. There were no chairs before we came, and the boys sat on boxes set up on end, which were always tipping over with them, or coming to pieces.

Willy had intended to build me a small room before our arrival, as I had insisted on living in camp, but, the roads being so bad, he could not get anyone to haul the lumber from San Antonio. It did arrive, however, about two days before we left. Willy had begun the room with a few boards which were already there, and had finished one end of it, and put a window in it before we left, but unfortunately he had no time for more.

The room was finished after we had left, and is now known as "Madge's room." Our whole visit only lasted about five weeks, but it showed me what "roughing it" means; and I was very sorry indeed to have to leave the ranche.

Madge

## Merino Sheep

Willy Hughes heard of the very popular Merino breed of sheep soon after he reached San Antonio in September, 1878. But he thought it best to procure his own breeding stock from England.

Then Willy saw the Merinos on display at the San Antonio Fair in the fall of

1880.  Both breeds won blue ribbons, but the Merinos really caught his attention.  After talking with his father while Emily and Hastings were still at the ranch, Willy went away for a couple of days and brought back a beautiful herd of 207 Merinos.  It's possible that these sheep were from the top-of-the-line George W. Kendall stock at Post Oak Springs Ranch.  He drove the new flock back to Uffington Ranch by horseback in one day.

The Merino breed of sheep originated in Spain.  One vigorous strain of the breed made its way to England, from which several shipments of choice breeding stock made their way to the American New England states--principally Vermont and New Hampshire--during the mid 19th century.

While Willy Hughes did not liquidate his Oxfordshire Downs sheep operation, he did place major emphasis on raising Merino sheep and saved the best of his Oxfordshire Downs stock for breeding purposes.  In his January 10, 1886 letter to his sister Emily, Willy used the following ranch letterhead stationary.

"Doc's" roll as chief herdsman and sheep caretaker was invaluable to Willy. This gave him more time to study and evaluate different approaches for increasing the size of his ranch. Growth in land and livestock production was imperative if the ranching enterprise was to succeed. Another requirement Willy had was for at least one additional reliable and dedicated ranch hand. That extra person was on his way.

### Partnership Established

Emily Hughes wrote to her friend Lucy Taylor in London on March 9, 1882,[1] saying that her second oldest brother, Gerard, had arrived at Rugby just as she and Hastings were returning from their visit with "The Boys" in Texas. Gerard or "Chico" stayed with his family for a few days before traveling to Texas by train to join Willy and Doc. He arrived at the ranch around March 20th.

As soon as the excitement of their reunion and the exchange of latest news from England was finished, Willy had a serious talk with his siblings about their becoming partners in his ranching venture. They agreed to work as a team for one year before making a final decision on the partnership agreement. Also, in one year the youngest brother Harry would have reached his 21st birthday. Their father of course, had been approached previously about the possibility of the boys entering into a partnership arrangement.[2]

At the end of their one-year trial of working together, the three Hughes brothers concluded that forming a business partnership was in order. They set the time for

---

[1] DeBruyn, John R., DISSIPATIONS AT UFFINGTON HOUSE, The letters of Emily Hughes, Rugby, Tennessee, 1881-1887, Memphis State University, Memphis, Tenn., 1976

[2] G.T.T. - Willy's letters to father, March 21, 1880; Hastings' Introduction to Part VI, pg. 173

formalizing this agreement on Harry Hughes' 21st birthday, March 28, 1883.[3] There is no remaining record of the partnership document, but it is logically assumed that Willy was the General Partner and that their father, Hastings Hughes, carefully scrutinized the details of the agreement in order to insure that proper administrative practices were followed and to allow for equitable dissolution of the enterprise if it became necessary.

## Gaining Ground

With both of his brothers on board, Willy Hughes began expanding his ranch operation in earnest. He had tested the waters of land acquisition in 1879 and 1880, when he bought and preempted 1,600 acres of land three-and-one-half miles west of Boerne. In 1881, he acquired 624.5 more acres, but sold 800 acres at a handsome profit. So at the end of his third year at the ranch, Willy still owned 1,424.5 total acres. When his brothers agreed to a one-year partnership test period in March 1882, Willy took aggressive action to further increase the size of Uffington Ranche. In seven land transactions, he purchased 1,829.5 acres and sold 160 acres, increasing his total ownership to 3,094 acres. He also leased another large tract[4] seven-and-a-half miles east of Boerne on the Guadalupe River, describing it as "a place large enough to accommodate a very large flock of sheep." Using the previous analogy of one shepherd per 1,000 head, and three acres per animal unit, the leased property was as much as 3,000 to 4,000 acres, but again there are no records of the exact size of the lease. The G.T.T. letters do show that Harry Hughes and one of the neighboring Howard boys were dispatched to the rental property with a flock of sheep. Willy later bought an old wagon and built a rectangular box-type wood structure and mounted it on the wagon frame for the boys to use as a camp shelter.

In 1883, Willy purchased an additional 3,110 acres of land adjoining Uffington

---

[3] Hughes, Thomas, G.T.T.--GONE TO TEXAS, MacMillan Co., London, 1884, (Hastings Hughes' Introduction, Part VI, pg. 173)

[4] G.T.T. - Harry Hughes' letter of July 18, 1882, and Willy's letter of June 8, 1882.

Ranch, and he sold 26.5 acres, leaving a balance of 6,177.5 accumulated acres of ranch land at the end of that year.

## Letters From The Boys

### (April, 1882--Nov. 12, 1883)

This segment of letters from Willy Hughes and his brothers to their father and other members of their family concludes the correspondence that formed the basis for the popular 1884 book G.T.T.-GONE TO TEXAS. By closer scrutiny, the reader will notice slight changes in the tenor and substance of their messages. The thrill and romance of ranching had diminished somewhat, and instead there was a trend toward more discussion of business matters, livestock management and ranch growth. Nevertheless, the boys still showed their delightful sense of British humor, and continued to write interesting descriptive details of their day-to-day activities.

The reader will also notice a gradual change in the lifestyle and quality of life that Willy and his brothers were beginning to enjoy. One thing of major personal importance was their move to a real house in October, 1882--this, versus sleeping on the ground or living in a tent for three years. Also, it is noted that the Hughes boys were beginning to participate in some of the social and recreational events in their community. But there is no evidence that Willy Hughes ever once deviated from his goal of becoming a successful rancher.

FROM CHICO TO MADGE                     The Ranche

                                        April, 1882

....We began shearing the beginning of last week, and it lasted three and a half days. There were seven men at it.

I was cooking for the crowd, which proved rather warm work, especially as we ran out of water the second day, and I had to haul it up from the creek in buckets. We killed a sheep and fed on the fat of the land. I found it rather difficult to keep ten men in bread, and was baking all one day from sunrise till a quarter past twelve at night. We were generally up till about half past eleven, so you see we had a cheerful time.

We began the day by driving up a lot of sheep from the pasture, where the whole flock was, and penning them under the shed, in front of which was the shearing table, about two feet high, for the shearers to rest the sheep on.  By the time this was done I had breakfast ready, after which the shearing began.

Willy tied up the fleeces as they were cut, and Doctor stamped them into the sacks, which were hung up to the rafters of the shed.  Each man was given a card-board check after he had finished a sheep, and these were counted at the end of the day, as the men are paid by the number of sheep they shear, and not by the day.

About mid-day we had dinner, after which Willy, the Doctor, and I, had another round up in the pasture, while the men rested a bit, and then shearing again till dusk.  Then supper was ready, and after that we sat and confabbed a bit, and at about half past nine or so we took the tables out of "your room," for the men to turn in on the floor.

The room is finished all but the end next to the kitchen, which is not boarded up yet.  We had meals in it, and the men slept in it, which was a pretty tight fit I can tell you.  Seven rather large men, one of them pretty fat, had to lie in a row on the floor.  The end man overhung the edge of the flooring, and rocked himself to sleep!  However, the room was quite large enough for feeding purposes, with the two tables.

One of the shearers was very talkative, and rather monopolised the conversation.  He talked and smoked all day while he was shearing, and all the meal-times, and as I heard some one perpetually talking, and groaning, and snorting in his sleep, I put that down to him too.

All the men left before dinner last Thursday, and probably went straight off to another ranche where shearing was going to begin...

The fleas are an awful plague here; at least they devour **me**, though they hardly touch the other two.  They run up from the floor up

136

my legs by scores, whenever I'm in the tent. I remember one night they wouldn't let me go to bed. I had taken off all my clothes and was going to the head of my bed to get my night shirt, when I felt two of them bounding up my legs; so I had to go back to the lamp on the table to crack them: then went for the night-shirt again with the same result. This joke was repeated five times that night, but I oddsed it at last by climbing up on to the table to kill the fleas, and then getting to bed over the chairs and barrels without touching the floor. I don't think they are quite so plentiful, now that we've tied Dip up in the corner of the sheep-shed.

The kitten is much tamer than he used to be, and will take food out of your hand. It's wonderful what a lot of bullying that cat will take from Dip. She could easily keep out of his way if she liked, now Dip is tied up; but she comes up smiling, to be hauled about by the scruff of the neck. I don't suppose it hurts though.

There will only be one or two more lambs this year, I fancy. Some of those which were born first are so big now, that they look nearly as big as their mothers, since shearing. You ought to see them in the evening, when it's beginning to get cool. They get frisky, and go tearing about in bunches of about fifty, down the road as hard as they can pelt, every now and then giving tremendous sidelong jumps, sending their hind legs into the air.

Sometimes two lots will charge into each other at full speed, and pile up on to one another in the middle, quite like a foot-ball scrimmage. It's a wonder they don't break any bones.

Why, the other day, Doctor found a lamb down that big hole among the bushes in front of the tent, which I suppose you have seen. It must be 18 ft. deep in the shallowest place. Yet this lamb had jumped down, and hadn't hurt himself a bit.

A new-born lamb is a most clumsy animal, very nearly all leg, and the essence of stupidity. It was only yesterday I saw one trying to suck

137

a wheel-barrow; and they will occasionally follow a hen about in preference to their mother.

FROM WILLY TO HIS GRANDMOTHER          May 21, 1882

....We sheared a little over 3,100 lbs. of wool, and it sold for 26½ cents per lb. in San Antonio.

Isn't there a saying, that one "is never so happy as when working hard"?  It's a very true one I think, for we enjoy ourselves immensely, although we put in just about as much work between daylight and dark, as we can well squeeze in, and by the time we've eaten supper, we feel that we've just done as much as it's possible to do.

I'm afraid that suggestion of yours about some one to cook for us, wouldn't work.  We are more independent you see, as we are, and one of us can always be spared to do the cooking, which is not a very scientific affair, in a sheep camp.

Bread is the hardest job; but Chico has hit that off splendidly, and turns out "a first class article!"  Dewberries are about over; but San Antonio is full of the lower country wild plums, a most delicious little fruit, and very soon our hill plums will be ripe, as also the grapes.

The cherry crop will be short this year I think, but I expect we shall get lots of fruit without them....I gave Dip away as he was such a nuisance to have to look after, and was too fond of making playthings of lambs' ears.

FROM WILLY          June 8, 1882

...We have not reached our new (rented) range yet.  The Doctor and young Howard are with the sheep, about seven miles off, and I have just run back to the ranche to see that the calves &c. are all right.

We are having some downright camping out, going up; a wagon and an 8 feet by 8 feet tent, are our houses, and we do not pen the sheep

138

at night, but let them lie down about 100 yards from the wagon. Sometimes they start off in the night, and then we have to go out and round them back. They bleat when they start off, which wakes us up...

FROM WILLY                                                    July 18, 1882

The Doctor and I are just back from our Guadalupe exile,[5] and very glad to get back. The sheep are looking first-rate, the change having done them a great deal of good; and our own range is looking splendid. We have now lots of range, and so can make all our arrangements complete, for taking every care of a large flock.

We had a big rain-storm the last night that we had to camp out. We got a thorough soaking all night, but are none the worse for it. It began to rain hard just as we were turning in, and it poured through our blankets, and a stream ran underneath us. Next morning, the firewood was so wet it was no use waiting for a fire, so we had bread and water in a hurry, as the restless sheep wouldn't stay.

....We have one cow, with her first calf, that is very fond of chewing up blankets and things. She came into the pen to-day, and chawed up an old shirt that was on the fence. She evidently enjoyed it, as she stayed around outside all the afternoon, after being driven away, trying to get in--to devour more shirts I suppose!

THE DOCTOR TO MADGE                                          Aug. 5, 1882

....What put it into your head that we live on bacon and slapjacks all the year round? Slapjacks and molasses are all very well in winter, but we never touch them in summer. Our **menu** consists chiefly of beans, porridge, meat, bread, and butter, eggs, bacon, tomatoes, and milk.

We have lately varied it with fish, as Sam, the darkie herder, has

---

[5] The hired ranche was on the Guadalupe River.--Author

discovered some small perch and cat-fish in our biggest water-hole.

We have become possessors of the finest bucks within fifty miles. They are real beauties, as you may imagine, and if one touches their skin, one's finger disappears up to the second joint.

FROM WILLY                                                    Aug. 20, 1882

...We can now sympathise with you on the goat question. We have five of them, regular brutes. They are always up on the rock fence, knocking it down. We bought them to eat out the underbush in the pasture. To-day I caught and "side-lined" them, i.e. tied the two side legs of each one together; and I think this will keep them from being able to jump the fence and get out, as they have been doing.

We still have to keep ten or fifteen head of cattle in the pasture, to keep the grass from getting too rank for the sheep. We have a tremendous amount of work to get through between now and November, but one feels able to do lots of work when things go on prosperously.

FROM THE DOCTOR TO MADGE                              Aug. 27, 1882

...We have got a large oat-bin under the shed next to the rock fence, and have 130 bushels or so in it, besides a hut full of oats in straw; and we shall probably put a great deal of cotton-seed as soon as the fresh crop comes in, so there will be no lack of feed this winter, and I expect we shall not have a pasture full of scarecrows, like those you saw when you were down here last Spring... We have got two patches of Bermuda grass started, and one of them is about the size of a table already.

FROM CHICO TO MADGE                                    Sept. 10, 1882

A load of lumber arrived here this morning, and we shall be moving over the frame house from the lately-bought land in a few days; so you can come and see us as soon as you like. We have made a new

140

pen, too, for the hay-ricks, and the place is getting quite a farmy look about it. I suppose you have heard of Willy's upset in Boerne the other night. He drove over a cow in the dark, and it got up with the buckboard on its back, and tilted it right over. The buckboard is as light as a feather, and is very useful to get about in. It just holds two people comfortably, and has plenty of spring in it, as the fore and hind wheels are only connected by the flooring of boards, without any iron bar to stop the springiness.

FROM THE DOCTOR                                    Sept. 13, 1882

. . .The Jones' house is "bein tore downd," and a large portion of the more fragile parts have already arrived. The new cow-pen is finished, all but one string, and we shall have rails enough cut for **it** before long. It ranges from 5 ft. 4 in. to 6 ft. high all round; and we shall be able to rope wild stock in it, and brand. If one begins to rope in the present cow-pen, they break out.

FROM WILLY                                         Sept. 23, 1882

The house we've just moved from the new range is going up rapidly, and we hope to get it finished before the 1st of October; and then we shall be able to get our clothes into a decent place before winter. Up till now everything has kicked about on the ground in the tent; and it will be a tremendous relief to get into a decent habitation. Miss Klemme plays the piano, and sings. She has just got a new instrument, and plays my accompaniments very well, so I have a little music again occasionally.

FROM THE DOCTOR TO MADGE                           Sept. 30, 1882

I don't know how you got into the habit of it, but you call everything a "shanty" now. A tent is a tent, and a shanty is a shanty; but an 'ouse is an 'ouse, and should be called so. You have inflicted a deep and ragged wound in our pride by asking whether we live in the new shanty yet...

FROM CHICO TO MADGE                                    Oct. 1, 1882

The Doctor and I have just come up from our Sunday bathe. We can't get much of a swim without barking our knees, but the water flows quickly, and it's very pleasant to lie and bask in the shallow water; only take care the sun doesn't skin you alive!

The chief drawback is the minnows, which come swarming round one, and nibbling wherever they can find a sore, which is excessively ill-natured of them to my mind. Then there are some leeches, which stick on to one in the most tenacious way; they will pull out to about a yard in length, and stick on at both ends. In fact, all the inhabitants of the water (cray-fish included) seem determined one shan't bathe in peace; so we lie on the rock bed, where the water flows quickest, and flummux them that way.

I've been going about barefoot for the last three weeks or so, and I've serious thoughts of giving up boots altogether as remnants of barbarism. You've no notion how comfortable it is, when there are no thorns about; but my feet are getting so hard now that even they don't hurt much.

We had Bob down here, for one night only. He had come from New York for a car-load of ponies, which he bought in San Antonio, I think, and then paid us a flying visit before going back. He bought a wonderful chair in San Antonio; it is made entirely of cows' horns, excepting the seat I hope. They are very cleverly fitted together, and seem to sell here as fast as they can be made. You'd scarcely think they would be comfortable, but I believe they are...

We have had a wonderful lot of people here lately. I shouldn't notice it so much if I wasn't cook; one seems to be in a perpetual state of

142

killing the fatted calf. There have been the two carpenters and the herder of course, regularly, and also the men who hauled the house over; and two or three extra are sure to turn up when you're pretty nearly full already. However it's rather pleasant to have a crowd now and then.

I spend all my spare time now looking out of the windows in the new house. It gives the country quite a new aspect somehow, looking at it through a window; and makes one feel respectable, not to say grand. I must really invest in a top hat now, to be in keeping with the ranche...

## FROM WILLY                                        Oct. 8, 1882

...We got our cots into our new room last night for the first time; and it seemed quite strange, after having slept in a tent with no floor for so long. The house didn't seem to suffer at all from being moved, very little of the wood having to be replaced by new stuff. There was a kitchen behind the house where it stood before, a sort of small detached room; this we are going to move down to the creek about half-a-mile from here, to serve as a shepherd's hut and room to put cotton-seed in for the sheep.

## FROM WILLY TO MADGE

I am sorry you have been having bad luck with your chickens this summer. I wish you were all down here, so that you could run our chicken ranche. Ours are all doing splendidly. It's no good perpetually selling off and buying more, with a view to getting strong healthy stock.

The way to have it is this; make up your mind as to what breed you intend to have; then buy roosters of that breed, and kill or sell all your present ones. Then, when your young chickens grow up and are old enough to lay, kill or sell your roosters and buy others of the same breed, but if possible, from a different poultry-yard than that from which the last came, and continue this rooster renewing part of the business every time

143

the chickens are old enough to lay, which of course won't necessitate a selling off of the roosters more than once a year.

You ought to have a few packages of "Condition powders" for stock and chickens (cost 25 cents each down here), and, once a week regularly, mix a **tea-spoonful of the powder to a pint of corn-meal for every ten chickens**, and then put in water enough to make it as thick as pretty thick porridge, and feed it to the chickens. Follow all the above instructions, which are not difficult, and you may blame me if you don't have fine healthy chickens all the time. Of course, I presume you feed your chickens regularly every day.

THE DOCTOR TO MADGE                                    Oct. 15, 1882

We have finished changing our little house from the old place to the creek. It used to be the kitchen, but now contains a ton and a half of cotton-seed. The sheep are camped there to-night, and I am going down there presently, to sleep on the cotton-seed.

FROM WILLY                                             Nov. 6, 1882

We are looking forward to the Guvnor's visit, which we hope will occur in the order of things, although we don't "bank" very much on it. "There's always a contingency," as our friend Howard said to his son the other day, when the latter was averring that a certain steer must be dead because they'd found its bones!...

I had a most charming parting present from _____ in the shape of a corn shuck hat. They are the prettiest hats that are made, to my notion. Shucks are torn up and plaited, and then sewn up into broad-brimmed hats. I believe they are very easily made, and are very becoming, especially on a lady, when plainly and prettily trimmed.

144

Nov. 20, 1882

....The two Howard girls and one of the boys came down to supper two evenings ago. It was a regular bachelors' spread, no table-cloth but plenty of sausages and soup, and coffee and bread; and afterwards we had some kind of romping game, and then blind man's buff, in which we pretty nearly shook the place down, but didn't break anything.

There was nothing to break for that matter, except the things on the table, which were stowed away in one corner, the "blind-man" being warned of his proximity to it by a chorus of Ware, Soup!" So you see we've not grown so everlastingly old yet.

## FROM THE DOCTOR TO MADGE          Dec. 6, 1882

Miss Howard has mixed a plum pudding for us, and to-night we all helped stir it, and put it on the fire, and I've got to keep it boiling till 2 a.m. tomorrow. I had a real genuine four penny bit, which we have mixed in with the pudding, but not one of us could raise a wedding-ring, so we had to leave that part of the ceremony out.

I have begun herding again, and find I am rather out of practice, but I shall soon get into swing again. Chico and I each herd four days a week, which sounds impossible; but on Wednesday he herds bucks just to give them a change of grass, and only herds the flock three days.

Willy has gone to bed in the cotton-seed house, and Chico has gone to see Miss Howard home, so I am quite alone with the pudding, which would be a frightful temptation if it was only cooked; but I don't think it would be worth opening in its present state...

## FROM WILLY TO MADGE          Dec. 20, 1882

A merry Christmas and all the rest of it. Thanks for the socks. They turned up loose at San Antonio, the parcel having busted somehow.

145

They will be very welcome and useful I expect before winter is over, as, when we do have bad weather, of course we have to be out in it, and we haven't come to the extravagance of investing in anything but cotton socks as yet. The Plymouth Rocks are doing finely, the laying hen having begun to sit after laying about two dozen eggs.

FROM WILLY TO MADGE                                    January 1, 1883
Dear Madge,

I hope you had a jolly Christmas up there. We celebrated the day by putting a blast in the well, which resulted in blowing out what I hope will prove to be the last of the rock for some time. We are now on hard clay, which is a tremendous relief after the rock, although the latter was for only three feet or so.

On Christmas afternoon, or rather at dinner-time, I went down to King's and had a very jolly Christmas dinner with them and the Whitworth's[6] who were staying there, preparatory to going away in the afternoon. In spite of my remonstrances, the girls made me go out riding with them, and not only that, but insisted on coming up here to "spy out the land" or something, and "went through" camp as though they were bossing the lay-out.

You should have heard the burst of applause when they looked into the tent and saw Chico with sleeves tucked up, washing up some plates, &c. One exclaimed "Oh how cute!" Whether she referred to the dishes, or Chico, or the mess the tent was in, I don't know.

We are now enjoying a bit of a freeze by way of relieving the monotony, for this is the first really cold weather we've had. But it isn't disagreeable as it keeps dry. Any way, it makes one fully appreciate your

---

[6] Presumably the Robert Whitworths who lived on a farm at Pleasant Valley, west of Bergheim--Author

146

socks and mittens.

By the way, many thanks for the latter: I forgot about them till I turned out the Guv.'s valise, since I last wrote. Christmas night we had a supper, and **the** plum pudding, which turned out to be a decided success. The two Howard girls and their brother came down, and we had supper first, and then we filled in the cracks with socks--no, songs! My hand is cold, so my pen has the bulge on it rather. I started in with the intention of writing about half a page, so you can credit my correspondence with the balance.

CHICO TO MADGE                               Sunday, Jan. 14, 1883

My dear Madge,

If it's not too late to thank you for the socks and the cuffs, and to wish you a merry Christmas and also a happy New Year, and many happy returns of your birthday, allow me to do now. Of course I ought to have done so before, and would be very much ashamed of myself for not doing so, were I not such a hardened sinner.

I always feel pretty chirpy now on Sunday, as it's my first day off herding. Doctor herds from Sunday till Wednesday, and I from Thursday till Saturday; but I get four days a week altogether, as I herd the bucks (about forty) every Wednesday.

It's pretty hard work herding in such weather as we've had this last week. Last Sunday, Monday, and I think, Tuesday, it froze hard, and has been thawing and drizzling ever since; but to-day it's beautiful out of doors. The sheep will travel and scatter so in the bad weather, that one has to be pounding about all day without a moment's rest. I remember last Monday night, I had an overcoat which had been damp, spread over my bed, and in the night it fell off; but it was frozen so hard that it stood up on its side against the bed.

I suppose father has told you we're digging a well now. We've

147

only gone down two or three feet since he went, but we've got through the layer of rock, which was about three feet thick. Old Stephenson is coming again as soon as he has got his crops in, some this week I think. There is still a good deal of rock-picking for him to do, as the well tapers off towards the bottom rather, and he'll have to enlarge it.

The well is nine feet deep at present, and it's nearly as much as one can do now to pitch the earth out with a spade; we shall have to fix a windlass. It isn't pleasant to pitch up a spade full, and have it come down on you, and get inside your shirt: however, on most days, when there's no norther blowing, it's so warm that I work down the well with nothing but a pair of breeches on--so it can't. The last time I was working in the well, I nearly shut myself in. I had shoved the ladder up to the top, and then picked down about a foot, and couldn't reach the ladder afterwards, and nobody was within call; but I managed to get it down at last by jumping as high as I could, and hooking it with the spade.

The Howards were down here on the evening of Christmas, and after supper we had singing. I thumped the wall by way of accompaniment, and we had enough noise to fill the Albert Hall. The wall of a wooden house, which is double, and has a space between, makes a first-rate drum. Our former musician, the nigger-boy Jeff, is gone. His music used to be rather trying to the nerves. His instrument was what he called a mouth organ. You blow into holes in the top, and it makes a noise something like a broken-winded concertina...

We have still got our piece of mistletoe hanging to the beams, but it's beginning to look bilious. I expect it's rather indignant at the very small amount of slobbering that was gone through under it.

Has Granny painted her house yet? We've been talking of painting this one, but it has never been quite finished yet, as the carpenter has been sick.

We shall be getting lambs now in a short time, as I hope we're not

148

going to have much more bad weather.  I'm afraid we shall though, as we've had no winter to speak of yet, and it was prophesied we were to have a very hard one, I believe.

THE DOCTOR TO MADGE                              Jan. 19, 1883

The well is getting deep, but not damp, and we are in rock again, about fifteen or more feet deep.  Old Stephenson is reduced to blasting again, and to-day he put in a blast which went off apparently without the least effect, and, although the well was filled with smoke, he could not discover where it came from, till at last he found it oozing out of a crack in the side of the well, nearly a third of the way round.

I am to have my first day on the roads to-morrow,[7] for I have never been called out before, so I hope the weather will continue fine.

WILLY TO MADGE                                      The Ranche,
                                                    Feb. 28, 1883

The Doctor got all the photos, and we all think they are great successes, except that of yourself.  You look as though you'd just been told that a rival photographer had set up in Rugby, and were in doubt whether to believe it or not.

We don't wind up lambing till the beginning of April, but we're pretty far advanced I think.  There are about eighty lambs or so.

Spring has set in I think, though we need a few more hot days, and then some rain, before the grass will get as good as I want it.

A few wild flowers are opening, and the twigs are threatening to.  I'm dropping off to sleep, so good night.

---

[7] Public roads were worked by citizens selected at random from tax rolls.--Author

WILLY TO HIS GRANDMOTHER                     April 4, 1883

We are well into spring now, and everything is brightening up again.  We have come through a pretty hard winter, which has burst up a good many sheepmen; but we came through about as well as the best, as we had a good shed and plenty of hay.

An Englishman below us bought 900 head last fall, 700 died during the winter, and he sold the rest for 85 cts. per head (having given $2.50 cts. for them).  He came off better than some fellows though.

One man went into winter with 1800 head, and expected about 1000 lambs this spring.  He only has 595 grown sheep, and six lambs now, and is about through with lambing.  He had considerably overstocked his range.

One of our neighbours lost over 300 grown sheep, and only saved about sixty lambs: he expected to raise about 350.

The losses in cattle also were heavy.  I don't believe we lost more than one or two head; but our stock were raised on this range....We shear on 16th inst.  I don't expect you'll hear much from the boys till then.


CHICO TO HIS FATHER IN NEW YORK

                              Easter Sunday (I believe), 1883

Dear father,

This being my first loose Sunday this year, I've taken it into my head to be a good boy for once in a way, and actually write a letter...

Thank goodness we're about through the winter at last.  We haven't had a norther now for some days, but, my gracious, we did have one or two stingers!  Food froze almost before we could get it down.  This winter I experienced, for the first time, the unutterable bliss of getting into a frozen boot in the mornings.  It's scrumptious.  One can laugh at the winter now its back's turned: next year I hope we'll flummux it with a fireplace.

We've had some pretty good rains lately, and the well must have several feet, though we haven't measured it lately. The night before last there was a thunderstorm, with rain in deluges, and the wind rocked the house about, so that I lay awake and considered which window I should make for if it tipped over. However, she's standing still.

There are two of us with the flock all the time now. I have been herding for the last few weeks with young darkie Jeff, and Dr. is herding now with Jeff's brother. At present I'm trying to get things a bit straight about camp. The place gets confoundedly messed-up during the winter. However, with the help of a spade and broom, I've cleared out the tent, and kitchen, and dining-room, and am now on the pen.

We've got a lot of excellent muck, which would delight your heart. I'm making a big pile of it, and we shall spread it on the pasture some time. We put down some of the pen-clearings on a patch of ground, which we marked out (shortly before you came) to try the effect, and now there is twice as much grass there as there is round about. You can see the square patch of green quite plainly marked out. I just put enough stuff down to hide the ground...

We haven't put up our books yet, as the carpenter hasn't come out to fix the shelves; but we shall soon be pretty straight. Willy has ordered two more wardrobes like the last, so when you next come down, by Jove you'll have to come in a topper and white weskit.

The old tent pretty well came to grief this winter. It all wore away at the top, and we had to tie it up with rope, but the fly-sheet kept the rain out pretty well. We had it full of sheep most of the time, when it was cold. One night we had some up in the house, which made a pleasant concert.

The lambs are much tamer this year than they were last, as we have had to feed most of them from the bottle. They're beginning to look fat now, and began to dance a week ago; but before that they didn't seem to be enjoying life much.

One has to go through a winter like the last, to be able to enjoy the spring properly. The green is coming on finely now, and the flowers are beginning to show up too; but it strikes me everything is much later than it was last year. Things were looking a good deal greener when I arrived here, which must have been almost the beginning of March.

Devilish little news to chronicle at present, as I've been doing nothing but run after sheep and howl, for the deuce of a while. I might tell you what I said to the sheep, but it was not as a rule parliamentary. I tell you, it just knocks the stuffing out of you, herding in winter, as the sheep don't get much to eat, and, in consequence, run like the deuce; which wouldn't matter if they all ran the same way--but they don't. However, they're better now, and begin to lie down for a bit in the middle of the day. I begin to feel faint.

I must drink a glass of water. I've been writing too many letters lately, I fear, and it's telling on my constitution; can't write any more, or I shall collapse.


THE DOCTOR TO HIS FATHER IN NEW YORK

Sunday, April 29, 1883

It is with a delightful sense of rest that I sit down to write to you to-day. It is, I believe, the first real day of rest I have had since the beginning of January, and feels, in consequence, more than usually pleasant. It is a lovely day, with just sufficient cloud to make it cool.

I started a letter to you and also one to Granny, out herding, but being in pencil they both came to untimely ends, though getting chafed into illegibility.

Willy and Chico have gone down to San Antonio with a second load of wool, so I am quite alone. The clip this year is probably lighter than last, owing partly to a late spring, and consequent lack of grease; but

152

the wool is in greater quantity, as we have filled thirteen sacks, and have over half-a-sack of tags besides. This is more than we had last year, although the number of sheep shorn is smaller.

The fruit-salt arrived all right, and was a very seasonable gift, as Chico was beginning to be more than usually irritated by tick and flea bites, but he is all right now, and one bottle has nearly disappeared under our frequent attacks.

I don't think that Texas has been visited by such severe northers for many years as those we had last January and February. Old H_____ (the German) says he can remember a far worse winter--"before the war"!! and Billy A_____, who was raised here, cannot remember one at all. Stock of all kinds suffered fearfully, though not so much during, as after, the norther. We ourselves came off remarkably well: which was mainly owing to Willy's foresight in weaning the calves (an unheard-of thing here), and providing unlimited feed for the sheep.

I don't believe we lost a single cow, and very few sheep; but some poor fellows, who had scabby sheep, and not sufficient shelter or feed, lost all the way from thirty to seventy-five per cent. of their sheep; and Capt. Turquand and others, who started into winter with poor cattle, lost tremendous quantities of them.

Everything that isn't dead already is now on the fair way to recovery, as the grass is splendid; and if the winter has done nothing else, it has given the old-method stock-raisers a lesson that will probably last a considerable time.

Some one's theory concerning Texas northers is, that they occur on the same day, or very nearly so, every year; and as I have on various occasions noticed this to be the case, I should like very much to have additional proof, which I believe that Madge can supply, as it would be very useful to us if we could put any faith in the idea. I wish you would ask her to look into her diaries and old letters, and tell me the dates of--

153

i.  The ice-norther which occurred during your stay here, in January, February, 1882.

ii.  The March norther, 1882, in which Willy and I were reduced to sardines.

iii.  The November (?) 1880 norther, when the icicles hung from the sheep's ears, and we had a Mexican herder.

iv.  The norther which occurred during Willy's stay in Tennessee, January 7, 1881.

v.  The one which occurred during Bob's stay with us, in March, 1880, about the middle of the month, I fancy.  Dave was also at the ranche, breaking horses.

If Madge could give me the dates of the above-mentioned northers, it would, with those I already know, satisfy me that the theory is or is not to be relied on.


WILLY TO HIS GRANDMOTHER                    May 1, 1883

I believe the last time I wrote was before shearing.  We have now finished that business, and the wool is all in San Antonio, except four bags, which I expect to take down in a few days.  We had very fine weather during shearing, only a little windy.  We began with two hands, then a third came, so, as this was slow going, I sent to Boerne and got four more (Mexicans) out.  That made seven shearers, so with ourselves and a herder we were a big crowd here for a few days.

Our Plymouth Rock hen is raising her second lot of chickens; she has nine, and they are doing well.  We had a late frost, which killed nearly all the plums on our only large plum-tree; but there will be a tremendous crop of fruit this year, I expect.  The mulberries and dewberries are nearly ripe, and there will, I think, be lots of wild cherries, and I believe the peach-crop is all right.

We have got several young calves, but I really don't know how

154

many, as I've been so busy with other things that I have "lost the run" of them.

The people in Boerne have just begun some improvements there, by mending the road, which hitherto in rainy weather has been a sort of mud pond. The citizens subscribed $500 or $600 I believe, and the last time I was in there, they were ploughing the sides of the streets from end to end, preparatory to ditching, I suppose. Our neighbour Shultz and his family have moved down to his father's, on the other side of Boerne, so the old place I first settled on is now unoccupied, and again for sale.

I bought up some Bermuda grass from San Antonio yesterday, and planted it after a very heavy shower, which came just after I got back, so I hope the grass will grow. The well still continues to be as full as ever, so the water-question does not trouble us as it used to, and the water in the well is very good.

THE DOCTOR TO MADGE                Sunday, May 27, 1883

Chico and I went to see the polo-playing on the 13th. It was rather pretty, though I should think they have a great deal of room for improvement, as there is hardly one of them who can carry the ball with him for more than two strokes without missing it, even when there is no one else in the way. We have been having rather a drought lately, but a timely thunderstorm on Friday made everything fresh again.

I think I have already told you that I camp with the herder, on the other side of the creek, during the greater part of the time. As we have no stove, we cook all our food on the ground. I soon found out that it did not pay to leave things on the fire all night, as something used to come and eat them; but it was only a few days ago that I discovered the thief.

It was a 'possum, and at last got so bold that it used to come out of the brush, and stand on the other side of the fire while we were having supper. So I tried to poison it by leaving little bits of poisoned bread and

155

bacon for it, next to the fire; but, though the stuff had always disappeared by morning, he was always around in the evening as well as ever, and I had to change my plans and lie in wait for him with the axe, and jump up and hit at him when he came close enough.

But he was too quick for me, so, as a last resource, I went for the shot-gun, which I didn't much like using, as it was sure to frighten the sheep. But even then I missed him, as it was too dark to aim properly, and I had to fire a bit of paper on the sight the next time, before firing. He is dead now, for I nearly smashed his head to pieces with the second cartridge, and we shall be able to cook our beans at night without any fear of having the lid pulled off and half of them stolen.

The sheep are doing excellently, and so are the cattle, and several of the nannie-goats are going to have kids very soon. There are only two of the last batch of kids left now, as we killed all the males to eat.

I have been engaged lately in making a road between the mineral spring and the creek, so as to connect the two camps, as it is awkward having to go right round by Klemme's; but the earth was so dry, and the rain so sudden and hard, that a great deal of it was washed away before it had time to get sodden. The way it is made is, to cut away part of the bank, and build a little rock wall up on the lower side of the road, and fill up the gap with the loose earth and rocks, taken out from the upper part of the bank. Of course it is only a small portion of the road that needs making in that way, or the job would hardly be worth doing...

WILLY TO MADGE                                    June 3, 1883

Many thanks for your letter. Of course I get all the news from your letters to the Dr.; so it's just as well to write to him, as I know you feel like unburthening photographic lore when you write, and I'm not sufficiently initiated in the business to understand anything about it. I hope the photography progresses favorably.

The next time you are here you must bring the machine down, and "take off" the ranche...I had a letter from Colton the other day. They had a pretty tough time of it through winter, lost 600 head from death and straying off, and lost a good deal of wool from the scab, which was pretty bad in their flock, and had to pay $150 damages for letting some scabby sheep get on a man's clean range, &c.

Colton says he expects to buy a ranche that he knows of, and thinks his brother is going to join him. I hope he will have better luck in future.

THE DOCTOR TO HIS GRANDMOTHER                    June 17, 1883

We are having very hot weather now, and rather a drought, but not enough to hurt the stock, although people say there will be very little corn raised in this part of the country. All the little springs and creeks are dry, and we have to water the sheep at the cotton-seed house, although they are at present penned at "the chimney" (where our house used to be before we moved it). And, as we do not like to take them over the same grass more than we can help, we only water them every two days, but they are doing very well all the same.

They lie down a very long time during the day now, and have to be turned out very early and kept out very late, in order to get sufficient time to feed in; so I go out at sundown and take the flock from the herder, and keep them out for a couple of hours or so, while the herder has supper (I take mine beforehand), and take a nap during the day, to make up for it.

Willy has just returned from San Antonio with the book-case, which looks large enough to hold all our books, and has a large cupboard underneath as well, for newspapers, and so on. Now at last we shall be able to unpack our books and put them where they can be got at.

Willy has traded some muttons for an old wagon, which is to be

157

made into a permanent sheep-camp, that is to say, it will be fitted up instead of a tent, and have all the bed-clothes, salt, &c., in it, and will be moved whenever the flock is. This will be very handy, as it is not always convenient to use our other wagon, and it takes a lot of time and trouble to move the things on a horse.

I am afraid you will find this letter very full of sheep, but I am with them nearly all the time, and so it comes more natural to write about them than anything else.

I am writing fearfully badly to-day, and, if it isn't the heat, it must be the want of practice, which is a judgment on me for not writing oftener.


WILLY TO HIS FATHER                                June 20, 1883

Stock of all kinds doing finely. So much biz. on hand to think about, that I shan't give you any news now; in fact I don't think there is any. Shall be glad to see Bob. He will make himself at home here, and very likely see Colton, who expects to go through, **en route** for San Antonio, about 1st proximo.


THE DOCTOR TO HIS GRANDMOTHER                     July 15, 1883

Bob has been staying with us lately, and has improved a good deal; he was badly in need of rest when he arrived. Colton turned up almost the same day, and stayed with us some time also, before going on to San Antonio. He passed here again on his way up country, with his younger brother, but I did not see him, as I was out all day.

Bob and Colton went on a fishing excursion while they were here, and, as they were fishing with a net, they had to leave their clothes on the bank; and the cattle came up and chewed them, and one of the cows almost destroyed Colton's watch, by chewing at it till the covers were flat and the glass broken. However, I believe the works remained uninjured.

158

Bob has arranged a partnership with Colton, and will soon start on a prospecting tour through New Mexico, where he expects to buy land and raise cattle.

Our cotton-seed house was getting almost uninhabitable, from the quantity of hornets which infested it, and built their nests on the roof. They used to drop on the blankets in a semi-torpid state, and sting as soon as they were touched, so I cleaned all the nests off with the crook the other day, and then fled till the excitement was over, and now I believe they have deserted the place.

The flock is looking extremely well, and will not feed much after sun-down, although the moon is half full, so it shows they get plenty to eat.

I went to get up Molly the other day (the bay mare that was here when we first came out), and had no end of a run before I could catch her. She is a very clever animal, and tried hard to throw me off her trail by dodging round the clumps of brush; but I managed somehow or other to come round one side just as she was disappearing round another, and never lost sight of her till she gave in, and allowed herself to be caught.

She has got a black mule colt this year, which is a very absurd-looking creature, with ears like a thoroughbred jackass, and tremendous joints.

WILLY TO HIS GRANDMOTHER                    The Ranche,
                                        July, 16, 1883

We only settled in here just in time to secure a decent ranche. Now, buying land is a far different thing round here to what it was three years ago, and respectable locations don't go begging long for a solid business-meaning tenant and purchaser.

Up to quite recently the owners and purchasers of real estate round here consisted of the old original settlers (mostly Germans), and incoming

159

immigrants and their families. Now, the generation that was born round here, of the first settlers, is growing up, and marrying and settling down; and a very industrious and prosperous generation it is too.

Having been brought up sometimes within a few miles of where they have now settled down, the young farmers go to work in the way which they have learnt is the most practical and best, right from the start; the result of which will be that the annual advancement and prosperity in these parts will be, during the next ten years, three times as great as it has been during the last ten. I am moralising to an extent that I don't often give way to, but it will show you that we have a contented and hopeful view of the future.

About Bermuda grass: the first root generally mats before sending out shoots to any extent, and then, after a good rain, when the matted starting-place is well rooted, it will send out shoots from three or four sides; the joints when matured rooting in their turn, down into the ground. Perhaps this will be sufficient for you to be able to satisfy yourself as to whether your Bermuda has started or not. Certainly the roots I sent were Bermuda; but if they did not start, I will send some more.

CHICO TO HIS GRANDMOTHER                    Sunday, July 22, 1883

We've been quite lively here lately with visitors. Bob has been staying at the ranche since he came from New York, except when he has been in San Antonio, and Colton was here too about a week. He came down from his ranche, which is about 125 miles off, principally, I fancy, to go to the Boerne ball on the 4th of July, and was very nearly prevented from going by the rain. However, he rode in enveloped in a macintosh of Bob's, and got there at last, after having been brought back to camp once by the horse just as he thought he was at his destination; it was so dark he couldn't see his horse's head and the horse didn't see the force of a three-mile ride in a deluge.

160

The 4th and 5th were both miserable days in this country. We had had a drought for some time previously, and when the rain did come it came in buckets. It disappointed a lot of pleasure-seekers, no doubt, but it did a wonderful lot of good to the country. Our well was just running dry, we got a quart of gravel up with each bucket; but now we have about three feet of water...

Bob started off two or three days ago for New Mexico with the two Coltons, looking for a good place to run cattle. They were going all the way in an ambulance, and will have a very jolly trip if they have fine weather.

Bob brought three dogs down from New York with him, a Scotch deer-hound and a couple of fox-terriers, one of which went mad and ran off as he was walking down from San Antonio here, when he first arrived--the sun was too much for it, I suppose. The hound he has taken with him on the trip, and the little fox-terrier bitch he has left here till he comes back.

It's rather stupid at present, it will sit and look at rabbits; however, it's young, and will know better in time. Bob has grown awfully "high-toned" since he's been in New York, shaves every week, and so on! He started on the trip fully equipped.

I hope the Coltons didn't each take as much, or I pity the horses. He had a couple of rifles (one of which fired explosive bullets), a full-sized shot gun, a gigantic six-shooter, about a million rounds of ammunition, a handkerchief, and a pair of socks.

The Boerne polo club returned last week from their trip to Austin and San Antonio. They had terribly bad luck, but luckily, they only lost a dollar or two out of pocket. They were to play two or three days in Austin, and expended hundreds of dollars in getting the ground (which was full of weeds) into order, and then it rained incessantly, so that I believe they only had one day's play there; and at San Antonio they had the same kind of luck.

The 4th and 5th, as I mentioned before, were flooded, and of course they would have been their best days had they been fine, as everybody would have been out sight-seeing.

They are making arrangements to play at the State fairs of Omaha, and some other capitals up North, in September and October, out of which they'll probably make a good thing.

We've been having such hot weather lately that we always sleep on the gallery. Last night it was full moon, and I read in bed for some time by moonlight, it was so bright.

I'm so glad to hear your 4th July celebration was a success. Madge says you rode the mare up town: we shall hear of your breaking in the colt next. What swells you must be now that the floors are varnished; I hope you've put an adequate shoe-scraper outside.

We haven't stained our floor all over yet; but there are some good-sized blotches...

We have an Englishman herding for us now, so we get plenty of time for jobs about camp. I have been painting all the wagon wheels lately, and the buckboard I painted all over, as the sun plays the dickens with them as soon as the paint wears off. I began writing just now sitting in a chair like a Christian, but I've gradually subsided on to the floor-- such is the heat.

### THE DOCTOR TO HIS GRANDMOTHER                    July 22, 1883

Whenever I sleep on the ground now I use Chico's Spanish rug instead of a blanket, as it doesn't pick up any dirt; but, as it is striped with all colours of the rainbow, it makes me look like a Mexican.

I believe we shall have another calf before long, from one of our best milch-cows. We have had more calves this year than ever before, and more than half of them are heifers, which of course are more valuable than bulls.

Several of the calves, whose mothers do not run near here, are not yet marked, and I am going to get them up as soon as possible, and mark them, as it is not safe to run stock out here with neither mark nor brand. I suppose that both those barbarous customs are pretty nearly obsolete in Tennessee, where there are few cattle.

The only animals here that are left unmarked are horses, as it disfigures them so; but several people mark their mares (my mare is marked) in the less settled counties.

THE DOCTOR TO MADGE                                                        July 29, 1883

Everything is doing well here, and the crops are going to turn out pretty fairly after all; but we are needing some more rain, as we have had none since the 4th of the month.

Polly cracked a piece out of her hoof the other day, so we turned her out of the pasture to give her a rest; but she has been so long inside the fence now, that she wouldn't go away, and just hung round the gate till we let her in again.

I ride the colt now whenever I need a horse, but he is not fast enough, nor strong enough yet, to hunt cattle with. I have just begun to quarry rocks for the back of the new shed. We intend to build a large sheep-shed down on the creek, where the present sheep camp is, and shall make the back out of rocks; but I am not quite sure yet what kind of roof it is to have. It will be a great deal handier to have a shed down there in winter, because last winter, whenever there came a big norther, we had to take the sheep up to the house; and that interfered with the cattle and bucks and everything else.

It is odd that I should be writing about winter with the thermometer at heaven-knows-where in the shade; but we always begin preparing for winter now, so as not to be crowded at the last moment.

163

Willy has told me that I shall probably be able to go up to you for a short while in September, but of course nothing can be certain as yet. He and I had a day's branding last week, near Boerne. There are six head of cattle out there of ours, that do not come up to our pen; so we took the rope and iron down to a pen near Boerne, and branded them there. One of them was a large two-year-old heifer that was very wild, and made our hands sore by rushing round the pen after she was roped, and eventually jumped over the side; but we got the brand on at last in spite of that...

### APPENDIX

When the Dr. was staying in Tennessee last month, with his grandmother and Madge, I suggested that he should write me a letter summing up the pros and cons of ranche life in Texas for English public-school men; and at the same time I wrote to Willy at the ranche, asking him if he had anything to add to the selections from his letters, which I had by his leave made. The following were the replies.--Hastings Hughes

New York, Nov. 21, 1883

FROM THE DOCTOR                                           Tennessee
                                                          Oct. 20, 1883

Dear Father,

Thanks for your letter of the 17th; but why can't you let me alone on G.T.T. business?  I am perfectly willing to have all such extracts as you think fit taken from my letters, but I don't want to stop immigration to Kendall County, Texas, by stating what I believe to be the chances of a young fellow (without any capital) who settles there. You see, unskilled labour is very cheap; and I know very little about the profits of teaming (which requires only a small capital), by which most of the young men seem to make a start in life; and owing to my entire ignorance of all

164

money matters connected with our own business (except price of sheep, wool, herding, &c.), I should be a very bad authority even on the very subject which I ought to know best. I am not quite clear as to whether your question refers to money-making at all; but if not, what would you wish me to write about-- climate, society, or what? I don't want to be disobliging, but I don't want to write about that of which I know but little, or to send you a letter which would be of no use. And I think a fellow would have to be very steady and economical to save $100 a year out of his wages as herder or farm hand; which is scarcely an encouraging prospect. Kelly, who has worked pretty steadily with us for six months at $15 a month and his grub, and been economical, had saved about $45 when I left. If you want a climatic, &c., letter, please say so, and I shall be only too happy to write one. You know, your question was a little indefinite, "What can you say about your part of Texas as a country for an English public-school boy to settle in, assuming, &c.?"

Ever your affectionate but puzzled son.

FROM WILLY                         Boerne, Kendall Co., Texas
                                              Nov. 12, 1883

Dear Gov.,

I have just returned from a trip to Kendalia with Mr. Vogel, who, as you know, is the founder of the new town by that name which is growing up in the eastern part of this county; and as you are always interested in matters appertaining to Texas in general, and this county in particular, I will give you an account of what was to me an exceedingly interesting trip.

Kendalia is about 23 miles N.E. of Boerne, on the road to Austin. We crossed the Guadalupe about 15 miles from here, and then, after leaving the cedar brake, had a very pleasant drive of some miles through a very pretty piece of country, passing several farms, and through as good

165

a stock range as can be found anywhere. One of our most successful sheepmen has his ranche a few miles east of Kendalia; and horses, cattle, and goats are all raised in the neighbourhood.

We reached Kendalia about sundown, and so hadn't any time that evening to see much, as of course the horses had to be attended to, and we had to look after getting supper in Mr. Vogel's house, which stands a short distance from the road on a slight elevation above the cotton gin and mill, and almost within a stone's throw of the store and post-office.

It speaks a great deal for the intellectual attainments of the folks in the neighbourhood that they have a debating society in full blast, with weekly meetings at the schoolhouse: they held a meeting the night we got there; the subject, so we were told, being "The relative profits on sheep and cattle raising;" but my thirst for the fray was so far quenched by the drive we had had, and the prospective walks and return drive next day, that, acting upon the precept that discretion is the better part of valour, I very ignominiously "turned in"--to bed. Next day we heard that the cattle stumpers had routed us poor sheepmen bag and baggage. Great Scott! where were the sheepboys?

Next morning, after a good night's rest and a hearty breakfast, we sallied forth to "take in" the place and surroundings, and, running the gauntlet of a host of Kendalians and others, we went down to the lake, which is a very beautiful piece of water not far from the town. Mr. Vogel has stocked it with German carp, and has ordered two rowing-boats, which he intends to place at the disposal of pleasure-seekers. The water is in many places over 14 feet deep and beautifully clear, and I had the first good plunge that I have had for some years; as here in Texas, water that is deep enough to plunge into, except so far from the edge as to render it impossible to take a header off the bank, is a scarcity.

After returning to the town, I amused myself examining the machinery in the mill (which consists of a very fine engine, the power of which is utilized in running a cotton gin and press, grist mill and flouring mill), and strolling out amongst the timber, which is exceedingly fine--live oak, and post oak, and all the other smaller varieties of trees and shrubs that grow in these parts, including abundance of wild grape-vines, wild cherries, and plums, &c.; and admiring the view of the distant mountains, which are very fine, whilst Mr. Vogel was being besieged by his miller and fence-builders and other men who had business with him, and a crowd of others the chief intent of most of whom seemed to be to become the possessors of town lots. These, he tells me, he is at present selling at from $10 to $20 according to location, it being a significant fact that most of those tackling him for town lots were old settlers in the neighbourhood, which shows that those who have the best facilities for judging, have perfect confidence in the future success of the town.

Mr. Vogel watches the growth of the town with an interest almost akin to enthusiasm, and not (as do so many of the inaugurators of similar projects) as a speculative venture; and he is therefore of course always ready to assist any individual enterprise on the part of the settlers which may tend towards the general advancement and prosperity of the town and community. By the way, Mr. Vogel has so many details to attend to in connection with Kendalia, and also the UNION LAND REGISTER, of which, I believe you know, he is editor, that he intends to sell the cotton gin and mill which he built and has been running himself. So if you know of any one coming to these parts with some capital, whom such an investment would suit, send him along to Mr. Vogel at Boerne. I think it a first-rate opening for an energetic go-ahead man, standing as it does in the centre of a very good farming district, the acreage of which is being annually increased, and in a young town surrounded by a fine stock-raising country, which, coupled with the farming interests, ensures for it a steady growth and future success. Added to this I think it has a great future as a health resort, lying as it does at an altitude of 1400 feet above

167

the sea-level, and having so many varied natural attractions.  Mr. Vogel intends as soon as practicable to build a hotel there for pleasure and health seekers.  During my trip to and from Kendalia I came across some very fine specimens of mesquite grass, one of which I had not noticed before, and which I as usual took specimens of, and have been busy planting out in the pasture to-day.

All the stock is doing well, and a good rain last night promises to help the range immensely.


## More Land

The ranch fluctuated for several years from 5,000 to 7,000 acres of land owned by Willy Hughes.  This was augmented by open-range grazing land and leased pasture space.  Unfortunately, there is no way to determine the exact size of the ranch with its leased land included.  But we do know about additional leased space on the Guadalupe in 1882 and later ranching facilities near Pipe Creek in Bandera County.[8]  A nephew of Willy's, Professor John W. Stout, wrote in 1978 that "Uncle Willy Hughes had hundreds of pieces of school land leased at turn of the century."

A search of Kendall County deed records indicated that Willy Hughes bought practically all of the ranch land in his own name.  His brother Gerard obtained a land patent from the State on two seventeen-acre tracts adjoining the ranch.  He later sold the 34 acres to Willy.  Harry, on the other hand, found one 80-acre tract that he contemplated buying, but he was hesitant to buy it for fear of finding another place he'd like better.[9]

On January 23, 1887, Emily Hughes wrote to her friend Lucy Taylor from Rugby, Tennessee, "As I think I told you, Harry has settled that he will stay with us, and

---

[8] Norris, Vernon, Interview, July, 1993, Boerne, Texas--Norris said his father, Sam Norris, was managing a large herd of Angora goats for W. G. Hughes near Pipe Creek in Bandera County before he became manager of Hughes Ranch in the 1890s.

[9] G.T.T.--Harry's letter to his sister dated June 30, 1881

has already more work than he can get through."[10]  This was the first inkling that the youngest Hughes brother was thinking of giving up ranching, although as noted earlier, he had not purchased any land in Kendall County.  Then, too, his decision might have been related to his aging grandmother's declining health and Emily's difficulty in caring for her alone.  It must have been a hard decision, though, to leave Willy and Gerard after having been affiliated with them in the Texas ranch operation for six-and-a-half years.  Also,  Harry had not seen his grandmother and sister in three years, so the excitement of having spent a joyous Christmas (1886) with them might have been a factor in his making this monumental pronouncement.  Another revelation was that his father had become engaged to marry Miss Sarah Forbes of Milton, Massachusetts in February, 1887.[11]  This was the same Miss Forbes whom Hastings had known in London some twelve years earlier.  Obviously, Harry wanted to stay around for that special occasion.

Gerard Hughes stayed on at the ranch until sometime after January 30, 1890.[12] Kendall County Deed Records, dated 12-28-1889, show that W. G. Hughes and Lucy C. Hughes conveyed to Gerard Hughes by Warranty Deed 1,100 acres of land, or one-half undivided interest in the Hamilton Ranch.  The reason for this transfer of property is not indicated in the records, and Willy's settlement with Harry on his equity in the ranch operation is not clear.  It is noted, however, that Willy sold 1,728 acres of land in 1888.[13]  He also bought 640 acres, while realizing a net reduction in land holdings of approximately 1,000 acres that year.  This might have been a settlement with the younger brother, or Harry might have taken a leave of absence in order to help with Granny.  Whatever the arrangements were, it was an amicable agreement, and Harry visited the

---

[10] DeBruyn, John R., DISSIPATIONS AT UFFINGTON HOUSE, Memphis State University Press, 1976

[11] Ibid Emily's letter to Lucy, page 68

[12] Kendall County Probate Record, Case #214, Vol. 3, pages 316-432, Will of John M. Forbes, Codicil #8, dated 1-30-1890, (Gerard Hughes was identified as Step-grandson in Boerne, Texas.)

[13] Kendall County Deed Records, Vol. 11, pages 33, 57, 311.

ranch several times in the early 1890s.

More than a century later, in 1992, Gerard H. Hughes, youngest son of Willy Hughes, said that it was the romance and adventure of living on the "wild-and-wooly" Texas frontier that enticed Harry and Gerard to join their big brother at the ranch near Boerne. He said that Gerard was basically an artist at heart and, in his opinion, neither Gerard nor Harry was as dedicated and determined in pursuit of ranching as Willy. Nevertheless, they gave ranch life their very best effort, each devoting approximately seven years of his life to ranching. Most of that time was filled with hard work, fun, excitement, and a few disappointments.

## Polo In Boerne

Some old timers in Boerne say that polo was first played in the United States at Boerne, Texas. They point toward the level field on the north side of Upper Balcones Road just before crossing into Bexar County where, more than 100 years ago, English immigrants played polo, soccer, rugby, and cricket. Mr. and Mrs. A. T. Wendler are longtime owners of the pasture where the Boerne polo team played.

GALLOPING OFF IN ALL DIRECTIONS, published in 1978, says that polo originated in Persia (Iran) approximately 600 years B.C.[14] British Cavalry units returning home from India in 1869 first introduced polo to the Western World.[15] James Bennett Gordon, Publisher of the NEW YORK HERALD, became infatuated with this very popular game while visiting in London in 1875.[16] He brought polo balls and mallets back to New York and immediately immersed himself in the study of the rules, skills, and techniques of playing polo.

---

[14] GALLOPING OFF IN ALL DIRECTIONS, Angus & Robertson, U.K.,Ltd., 16 Ship St., LONDON, 1978

[15] Ibid

[16] WORLD BOOK ENCYCLOPEDIA

According to GALLOPING OFF IN ALL DIRECTIONS, American indoor polo was first played at Dickels Riding Academy, an indoor arena, in New York City in 1876. The same reference says that **outdoor** polo was first played at New York's Jerome Park in 1880. (Other places listed later were Belmont Park, named for August Belmont, and the Polo Grounds at 110th Street.) What does polo in New York City have to do with Boerne and Willy Hughes? There is a connection.

A colony of mostly young middle- to upper-middle-class British subjects settled in and around the German populated hamlet of Boerne between 1870 and 1885. They located in an area south to southwest and west of town at a distance of two to five miles. A few became merchants in town or engaged in other businesses, but most English settlers who came to Boerne during this period became ranchers and farmers.

In an October 1993 interview with Mr. A. T. Wendler, he recalls his father--who was born in 1869--having said that as a teenager he rode out from Boerne on horseback to the Balcones and watched the English gentry play their exciting game of polo. He noted that the players were a happy lot and played with great enthusiasm. Willy Hughes' younger brothers' letters made reference to polo being played in Boerne. Doc wrote to Madge on May 27, 1882, saying, "Chico and I went to see polo-playing on the 13th. It was rather pretty, though I should think they have a great deal of room for improvement....."

On July 22, 1883, Chico wrote to his grandmother, "The Boerne Polo Club returned last week from their trip to Austin and San Antonio. They had terribly bad luck (it rained incessantly), but luckily they lost only a dollar or two out of pocket." He wrote, "They are making arrangements to play at State fairs of Omaha, and some other capitals up North, in September and October, out of which they'll probably make a good thing."

The Hughes family involvement with Texas cow ponies--some later to be identified as "polo ponies"--dates back to 1874. In that year James, or "Jim" Hughes, son of Thomas Hughes, emigrated to Canada and immediately crossed over the United

171

States border, making his way first to Colorado, then on to Texas.[17] He participated in cattle drives up the Western trails and quickly recognized the many excellent qualities of Texas cow ponies. These ponies were mostly of mustang blood crossed with short distance race horses, like "Steeldust," a stallion brought to Texas from Illinois by Middleton Perry and his brother-in-law, Jones Greene. They settled near Lancaster, in Dallas County in 1854. Another famous sire of that period was "Shiloh," bred in Tennessee and owned by Jack Batchler, near Ferris in Ellis County.[18] These blood lines and those from other quality horses, crossed with the native horses, produced the popular Texas cow ponies. They were intelligent, agile, quick and fleet of foot, and they also had tremendous endurance and stamina. Both as cow ponies and race horses, they were great favorites with cowboys and the Mexican population of South Texas and Mexico. Races were usually arranged in **matched** or **challenged** short-distance races, often run on straight dirt roads near the center of a settlement.

Prior to their early acceptance as polo ponies, Jim Hughes was making shipments of the wild mustangs and mixed breed Texas cow ponies to New York as race horses. His father, as noted previously, was in New York during late 1870s making final arrangements for his Rugby, Tennessee, English colonization experiment, and had already leased the O'Brian pasture on North Central Avenue as a holding place for horses that Jim was shipping to that area. It seems logical that Bennett Gordon, publisher of THE NEW YORK HERALD, would have sought the aid of Jim Hughes when ordering a carload of Texas polo quality horses for delivery to New York. He knew Jim Hughes and his father, Thomas, well, and Gordon's paper published one of the 1880 stories about the mustang polo horses from Texas.

Another cousin, Robert Francis "Bob" Hobson, brother of Edward "Ted" Hobson who brought Willy's registered Oxfordshire Downs sheep to Texas, came to Boerne with

---

[17] DeBruyn, John R., LETTERS TO OCTAVIUS WILKINSON: TOM HUGHES' LOST UNCLE

[18] THE HANDBOOK OF TEXAS, Walter Prescott Webb, Editor-in-Chief, The Texas State Historical Association, Austin, Texas, 1952, Vol. 1, page 838

Hastings Hughes and his son Harry in July 1879. At about this time, Jim Hughes moved to Mexico and established a major ranching operation there. Bob took over the practice of shipping Texas cow ponies to New York, first as race horses, then as polo ponies when the price of polo ponies became much more lucrative.[19] Bob used Willy Hughes' place outside of Boerne as a collecting facility for prime ponies he bought throughout Southwest Texas and Mexico. There, the animals were fed and given preliminary training and closer observation to determine their potential performance as polo ponies before they were shipped to New York.

A 1983 book by Hugh Best, DeBRETT'S TEXAS PEERAGE, gives credit to a retired British Army officer for organizing the Boerne polo team. William Glynn Tourquant[20] was said to have served most of his military career as a cavalry officer in India. He immigrated to Texas in the 1860s and established a large ranch in western Bexar County that extended into Kendall County. "Tourquant" recruited a polo team that started playing polo in 1872 on the same Kendall County property that is now owned by Mr. and Mrs. Wendler.

Other compelling evidence in support of local claims that American polo was first played in Boerne is a statement made by Mrs. Edith Gilliat Gray. In a pamphlet published in 1949 (Boerne's 100th anniversary), advertising the upcoming sale of her book on Boerne history, she wrote, "The first American polo games were played in Boerne, Texas."[21]

Mrs. Gray was 38 years old when her father, Alfred Gordon Gilliat, died in 1936.

---

[19] TEXAS ALMANAC, 1904, p. 128 --"Prices vary from $60 for doubtful or otherwise risky purchases to $300 and even $400 for what they call **cracker-jacks**. A top pony with up to six months polo training sold at major polo centers back East for as high as $2,500."

[20] Name possibly in error. A. T. Wendler's deed abstract shows that Augustin Toutant changed his name to Toutant Beauregard in 1867, then to William Glynn Turquand in 1878. Additional information from Howard C. Calder, a leading historian of Boerne, and part owner of old Turquand Ranch.

[21] Copy of pamphlet in author's files

He was born in London, England, November 18, 1860, and immigrated to Texas in 1880, one year after Willy Hughes came to Kendall County. Alfred Gilliat was knowledgeable about polo and other popular English sports of that period. He played on the Boerne cricket team, along with Willy Hughes and a group of other young Englishmen, including three Howard brothers and two sons of Edmond King. Mrs. Gray grew up knowing many of the polo players of 1880 in their middle years. She was repeating first-hand information that American Polo was first played in Kendall County at least three years before it was played in New York City in 1876. Were the editors of GALLOPING OFF IN ALL DIRECTIONS and several encyclopedias in error by claiming that American polo was first played in New York City? A few knowledgeable citizens in Kendall County think so.

In the meantime, Bob Hobson grew weary of "beating the brush" in Southwest Texas and Mexico for ponies to ship back East. He gave up this practice and became a "fashionable riding master" in New York.[22] Later (about 1885), he moved to Virginia and established a horse raising operation near Castle Rock on the James River.[23]

Willy Hughes was assisting Bob Hobson with selecting and training horses at the Hughes Ranch beginning in 1879. With Bob's departure from the Texas scene, Willy began providing polo ponies to polo clubs in major cities on the East Coast.

Jerry Hughes tells a story about his father Willy's flair for showmanship. On one shipment of ponies to New York, he recruited his father Hastings to help drive this herd of horses from lower Manhattan up 5th Avenue to their pasturing destination North of the city. Hastings was dressed in formal English attire--riding boots and pants, black coat and derby hat--and rode a beautiful, high stepping saddle horse. Cowboy outriders hopscotched ahead of the herd to keep them from going down side streets. Excited spectators and news reporters gaped at the unusual equestrian parade through their city.

---

[22] DeBruyn, John R., LETTERS TO OCTAVIUS WILKINSON: TOM HUGHES' LOST UNCLE - Thomas Hughes' letter of Dec. 9, 1880, to his Uncle Octavius, regarding his grandson.

[23] Ibid, page 51

According to the 1904 edition of the Texas Almanac, Texas monopolized the earlier market for polo ponies. When the United States Polo Association (USPA) was organized in New York City in 1890, their adopted standards for a polo pony pretty much described the Texas cow pony: "Not over 14½ hands in height; must be handsome; must be as swift as a race horse, courageous and high strung, and withal possess a docility and amenity to the bridle demanded in no other class of horse."

## Annoying Problems

Pioneer ranchers not only suffered livestock losses because of weather, disease, parasitic infestation, and predators; but thievery, fence cutters, and other man-made problems often proved to be a great nuisance to Texas ranchers.

Willy obviously received excellent counseling from his advisors on such matters, because he took necessary measures to protect his land and property. On July 8, 1879, he recorded his livestock earmark and brand in Marks and Brands Book No. E-1, page 167, at the Kendall County Clerk's Office. That was just three months after he bought his original 160-acre tract of land west of Boerne. The earmark designation was changed April 29, 1882, as shown.

*No. 825.*
*W. G. Hughes, — Kendall Co.*
*Brand thus: (H) on left shoulder.*
*Earmarks : ⊂⊃ half upper. crop in each ear.*
*Recorded July 8, 1879. Earmark changed April*
*29, 1882, as follows: ⊂⊃ a swallow fork in each ear,*

With wood poles, boards, and rock materials, Willy promptly built corrals and pens for his livestock at the newly acquired Kendall County ranch. He also built shelters to protect his animals from severe weather.

Upon purchasing his first small flock of sheep, he followed an old George Kendall practice by using herdsmen, or shepherds, to look after the sheep. This safety precaution and close observation of individual sheep reduced losses to a minimum, only one to three percent annually, while some ranchers suffered 30 to 70% losses. Winter ice storms were extremely devastating.

Many farmers and ranchers preferred to let their stock run free on thousands of acres of unfenced state, railroad, and speculators' land. Willy even let some of his common stock horses and cattle graze on open range, but he was not comfortable letting his best quality livestock run on unfenced land. Consequently, he started fencing all of his land at an early date. Willy also continued branding his horses on their lower left shoulder with his circle H brand.

Barbed-wire was invented in 1873, and fencing land with wire was common practice by 1880.[24] This caused major problems between ranchers and small land holders throughout Texas, but particularly along a belt running north and south across the center of the State.[25] Hostility intensified between ranch owners and fence-cutters until several men were killed in open clashes between the aggrieved parties. Competition for grass and livestock watering places intensified in the fall of 1883. It was a dry year, and fence cutting damage was estimated at $20,000,000 ($1,000,000 in Brown County alone) forcing politicians to take action. Governor John Ireland convened a special session of the state legislature on January 8, 1884. The legislature passed a law making fence cutting and malicious pasture burning a felony offense punishable by one to five years in prison.[26]

Texas Rangers were assigned the task of dealing with extreme cases of fence cutting, but they abhorred such duty. One Ranger complained that fence cutters carried no evidence--unlike cattle and horse thieves who were usually found in possession of

---

[24] Webb, Walter Prescott, THE TEXAS RANGERS, University of Texas Press, Austin, Texas, 1965

[25] THE HANDBOOK OF TEXAS, Walter Prescott Webb, Editor-in-Chief, The Texas State Historical Association, Austin, Texas 1952

[26] Ibid, Vol. 1, page 590

their prey.

Fortunately, Willy Hughes had settled in a friendlier environment where German and English immigrants were generally better educated and of temperaments that made them more inclined to settle their disputes through judicial means.[27] This, and the fact that Willy kept close surveillance on his property and livestock, helped him avoid most of the frontier hazards of fence cutting and thievery.

But Willy didn't get off scot-free. On the night of August 5, 1889, someone cut the fence on Hughes' Hamilton Ranch pasture. Outraged, Willy's offer of a $100.00 reward for apprehension and conviction of the culprit was prominently displayed in the next issue of local newspapers. A copy of Hughes' notice appears on page 428 of Prescott Webb's 1935 book, THE TEXAS RANGERS.


$100
## REWARD

I WILL PAY THE ABOVE REWARD FOR INFORMATION WHICH WILL LEAD TO THE CONVICTION AND INCARCERATION IN THE PENITENTIARY OF THE FELON WHO MALICIOUSLY CUT THE HAMILTON PASTURE ON THE BANDERA ROAD LAST NIGHT

W. G. HUGHES


A number of letters from Willy and his brothers to family members made reference to neighbors' hogs rooting up the vegetable garden and wild turkeys scratching up a whole field of freshly planted corn. The bobcats, mountain lions, cougars, black bear, coyotes, and domestic dogs, some still the bane of ranchers today, were Willy Hughes' enemies as well.

Hughes used diplomacy in dealing with neighbors about damage to his property by their domestic animals. In the case of wild creatures, he used a six-shooter, a shotgun, or his 44 rifle, depending on the size or threat of the animal or varmint

---

[27] TEXAS ALMANAC, 1904, page 304--District Attorney's annual report called attention to freedom from crime in Kendall and surrounding counties.

troubling him. When dealing with wild animals of the cat family, and destructive pack hunters like dogs, wolves, and coyotes, he often baited the carcass of sheep and goats with strychnine. Using lethal agents such as strychnine risked accidental killings and liability consequences, but Willy was not alone in resorting to these extreme measures. Sheep and goat ranchers have used and continue using such methods today on a limited basis.

In 1978, Willy's ninety-four-year-old nephew John W. Stout, professor emeritus of California Polytechnic Institute at San Luis Obispo, dictated for his family a series of historical events that occurred during his early lifetime in and around Hughes ranch. One of the hair-raising stories concerned one T. E. Hicks, who came to the Hughes' home to kill Willy Hughes. Actors in this exciting drama, besides Hicks and Hughes, were John Stout, brother-in-law of Willy Hughes, Stout's two oldest sons, Perry and John, Sheriff Albert Bodemann, and Mrs. Hughes, her three children, and the maid. The professor's story:

"When I was about 10 years old this incident took place.

We were living in Hastings,[28] Kendall County, which is about one fourth of a mile from the Hughes' place. I used to work for Uncle Billy Hughes quite a bit. He seemed to think I was the kind of a fellow that he liked. Some of the rest of them, why, he didn't care much about and he let them know that he didn't care much about them.

I was working in the barn fixing a broken harness for him when he came in there and told me that he wanted me to come with him. He had something important he wanted to tell me. Instead of going around between the barn and the house he took me the other way and went right through the barn and came out the other side of the barn and up to where his house was. He had an office up in the barn right where it faced the house and not very far from the house. He took me up there to his office

_____

[28] Hastings, Texas was name of Post Office at Hughes Ranch, named for Hastings Hughes.

and then he told me that I might be witnessing a very important thing, because there was a man there who was gonna kill him.

I said, 'What! Gonna kill you!'

He said, 'Yes. T. E. Hicks has got a shotgun and he said he was going to kill me. He told the hired girl. And so I've sent my wife and three children upstairs.' The stairs there went up the outside of the house to a 'gallery' that really was a porch that was out from the house. To go 'upstairs' you had to go up these stairs to the porch above. And at this level were the bedrooms. This was where he had sent his family.

Up there in the barn in his office he took me by the hand, and he said Hicks would have to go up the steps to the gallery in order to get to his family, and if Hicks did that - - why - - he'd have to shoot him. He had his 44 rifle there with him.

He said, 'If he starts up there I'll start shooting him - - shooting for the legs and if that doesn't stop him I'll shoot up higher. Til I get clear up to his body. But then you'll be a witness to it. When you're a witness just don't tell a thing that isn't true, and don't make up anything. If somebody says something to you, or asks you a question such as, 'do you think it was that way?' - why, you stick to the truth, because this is going to be very important.'

Well, I felt very elated to think I was going to be the one that the whole country, pretty near, would be dependent on what I said.

So we were up there in the barn in his office. And he could see the stairs and the 'gallery' from the window.

When T. E. Hicks came there Perry saw him. He asked Perry where Billy Hughes was. Perry said he didn't know, that he was around some place. Perry knew there was something wrong, with him having that gun with him and he was pretty drunk anyway. So Perry ran out to get Papa who was out in the field with the mowing machine getting some green hay for the cattle.

179

Papa told Perry, 'Alright. You hold the horses here.' Papa ran up to the house and asked if anybody saw T. E. Hicks. Somebody, the maid, said she thought maybe he went in the house. Papa ran in and there was T. E. Hicks sitting there with a shotgun in his hand. He was waiting to see Billy Hughes. He was right in the sitting room. Papa said, 'You don't want to do anything like that. You'll get put in jail for it.'

But Hicks said he was going to get him. Papa said, 'What did he do?'

'Well, he poisoned one of my dogs.'

Papa said, 'Let's see that gun.' and he took the shotgun. He said, 'I'm gonna unload this gun. You've been drinking too much. You might shoot somebody and then be sorry for it.' They argued about it, but Papa took the gun away from him anyway and unloaded it. Then he said, 'Now I'm gonna take you back home.'

Hicks didn't like that much, but he thought he'd better do it anyway, because he didn't have any ammunition in his gun anymore. Papa had taken it away from him. So Papa started off with him to take him home.

Billy Hughes got word that Hicks was taken away now, taken home. He said, 'Well, Johnny, guess nothing's going to happen. So you'd best go back to your job of fixing the harness.'

He got the cart--that one-horse cart of his--and hitched up a horse and off he went to Boerne to get the sheriff. He swore out a warrant for T. E. Hicks. Came back. The sheriff came out there and he went on down to Hicks' house. Hicks hadn't gotten home yet. After Papa left him there he laid down under the shade of a tree and went off to sleep.

So the sheriff thought he'd hunt for him around the place there, but he didn't find him. When he started back--why--here Hicks came. He'd woken up and he was coming down the road. The sheriff said he was under arrest. And Hicks said, no, he didn't do anything. The sheriff bound him over then -- to keep the peace.  And he told Hicks he'd have to come in and make a record of this thing.

Well, that was about the most exciting thing that had happened around there for some time.  I felt very much as though I was an important individual in the whole affair if it ever came to the court house.  But nothing ever happened about it." [29]


## Railroad To Hill Country

Probably the greatest single event that occurred in Kendall County, and the Hill Country, for that matter, was the arrival in 1887 of the San Antonio and Aransas Pass (SAAP) Railroad.

The SAN ANTONIO DAILY EXPRESS reported the event in its Friday Morning, March 18, 1887, edition:


### THE BOERNE EXCURSION

A jolly crowd and a jolly day, when six hundred or more San Antonians boarded seven bright red coaches for a trip to the Kendall County Capitol and one big picnic celebration.

The Lone Star and city breweries had a good supply of fresh, cool beer aboard, according to the reporters story.  There was lots of laughter and singing during the entire trip, and upon arrival at the make-shift depot, the Boerne brass band struck up a lively air.  A welcoming committeeman, seated on a prancing horse, cried as loud as his lungs would permit:  "The ladies will please take the hacks, and the gentlemen can walk." -- The place to go was a grove of live oaks in back of the

---

[29] Stout, John Willard, Memoirs, AS I REMEMBER IT, 1978. Use authorized by Dr. John Willard Stout, Jr., March 8, 1994, and Mrs. Beatrice S. Dooley, April 25, 1994.

famous, historic Phillip Manor House at the corner of Hosack and South Main Street in Boerne.

Dr. W. G. Kingsbury, erstwhile State Commissioner of Immigration, welcomed the visitors on behalf of Boerne citizens. He was the same Dr. Kingsbury who persuaded many of the Boerne English Colony to settle in Kendall County. His speech was glowing and colorful. The first paragraph set the tone for his address.

"LADIES AND GENTLEMAN: The pleasing duty of giving a welcome to our little hamlet of Boerne has been assigned to me, and never in my life have I undertaken to perform a public duty that afforded me so much pleasure. My only trouble is to find words that will express the joy of this people, both of the town and country; words that will make you understand how very welcome you are here today. The approach of the first railroad is an important event in the history of any town in any country, but when it is driven through a mountain region it borders on the mysterious, and is all the more valued because of the difficulties it has encountered and overcome. We welcome you today, not only because you bring the iron horse of commerce harnessed with iron traces, but because it will give you an opportunity to breathe our pure air and see our picturesque country, dotted with little mountains, interspersed with valleys as fertile as the famed Scotia. We have a climate and a country here unsurpassed; in fact, unapproachable by any in the broad state of Texas-- and that means by any on the face of the earth."[30]

Willy Hughes did not attend the train celebration. At least there is no record of his having participated in the festivities. He likely worked at the ranch that day, but there is no doubt in the minds of those who have spent years researching the life of Willy

---

[30] Perry, Garland, HISTORIC IMAGES OF BOERNE, LEBCO Graphics, Boerne, Texas, 1982

Hughes that he fully understood the impact the railroad would have on business, commerce, and economic growth of the Boerne-Kendall County area, just as he had predicted in his letter to his grandmother on July 16, 1883.

The train meant mass transportation of people and goods from San Antonio to Boerne in a smooth, fast mode that was tremendously efficient and cost effective.[31] Time for this trip was reduced from seven-and-one-half hours by stage coach to two-and-one-half hours by train. A one-way ticket cost $1.00 by train, while a ticket by stage could be as much as $3.75, if the weather was bad. People would not miss the bumpy, lurching, cramped, and terribly uncomfortable ride by stagecoach.

In a short time, Willy was transporting his prized breeding stock of sheep and goats to state fairs and livestock shows in the Midwest and Northern states. Vernon Norris, son of Sam Norris and Hughes' ranch foreman in the 1890s, said Mr. Hughes got a permit and always rode in the caboose during long trips so he could be near his animals.

### A Switch To Goats

The U.S. House of Representatives passed its version of the Mills Bill in 1886, a bill which pertained to a part of President Grover Cleveland's election platform of 1884, seeking tariff reform on a number of import commodities, including comparatively deep cuts in the tariff on imported cotton and woolen goods.[32] By the end of 1887, Willy Hughes had dramatically switched from sheep ranching to raising Angora goats.

The National Wool Growers Association had fought long and tenaciously against any tariff reductions in their industry. This was especially true during the reign of Henry S. Randall as president of the Association in the 1860s and until his death in 1876. Not only was he the foremost American authority on sheep husbandry, but he also wrote two

---

[31] Perry, Garland, HISTORIC IMAGES OF BOERNE, LEBCO Graphics, Boerne, Texas, 1982

[32] Welch, Richard Jr., THE PRESIDENCY of GROVER CLEVELAND, University of Kansas Press, 1988

books and many newspaper and magazine articles on sheep raising and the perils that a reduction of import tariffs would have on the expanding sheep and wool industry.[33]

Obviously Willy, with his magnificent business sense and foresight, was keeping abreast of economic and political trends of his day. His monumental decision to change from sheep to Angora goats was no "fly by night" decision. It was carefully researched and calculated. While the Mills Bill was said to have triggered Willy's action to give up sheep as his primary ranching interest,[34] there were several other practical reasons that influenced him in making this determination.

No doubt Hughes had read, or had heard of, Henry Randall's books, WOOL GROWING AND THE TARIFF: A STUDY IN ECONOMIC HISTORY OF THE UNITED STATES, and THE PRACTICAL SHEPHERD, an invaluable management handbook for any aspiring sheep rancher. Also, in the 1868 TEXAS ALMANAC (p. 164), Randall wrote about the "depressed condition of the wool market," and that except in the case of a very few choice "fancy" animals, the price had temporarily lessened the demand for full blood Merinos (Randall specialized in the Merino breed). He went on to say, "If the present wool tariff continues in force, sheep will soon be in more active demand in the North."

But that was not the case. People had been pushing Congress for tariff reform for several years, but not necessarily with the intent to single out the sheep and wool products for deep tariff reduction. There already was plenty of competition from overseas markets like Australia, South Africa, Spain, France, England, Scotland, and other areas, but the American wool industry was growing at a very fast rate. In Texas alone, the total sheep inventory increased from 1,223,000 head in 1870 to 6,024,000 in

---

[33]    Randall, Henry S., WOOL GROWING AND THE TARIFF: "A Study in Economic History of the United States", (2) - THE PRACTICAL SHEPHERD, a popular handbook on sheep raising, and (3) numerous TEXAS ALMANAC articles, (market tariffs on page 164, 1968 edition.)

[34]    Hughes, Gerard Hastings, son of W. G. Hughes. Interview with writer in 1988 and comments by letter.

1880.[35] At the same time the average pounds of wool clipped per animal unit had doubled through improved breeding practices, bringing the annual clip from approximately two lbs. to four pounds per animal unit.

Willy Hughes, as well as other knowledgeable ranchers, was greatly concerned about the future of wool and sheep prices, so he proceeded with a plan to dramatically reduce his sheep inventory. He did, however, keep his most valuable registered animals for an inventory of breeding stock. It is not known just when Willy Hughes first became interested in Angora goats, but we do know he saw them regularly at the Bexar County Fair, and he obviously talked to ranchers who were experimenting with Angoras, such as Col. W. W. Haupt of Hays County and Henry Fink of Leon Springs (Bexar County), ten miles south of Boerne on the San Antonio road.

The fact that Willy operated a diversified ranching operation of sheep, cattle, and horses also influenced his decision to switch to Angora goats. Most of his ranch property was located in the bushy, hilly area west of Boerne and extended into Bandera County. This type of terrain, with its abundance of scrub trees, brush shrubs and a great variety of plant life, made it ideally suited for goats, rather than sheep. Whereas sheep compete with cattle and horses for grass, goats prefer plant forbes and leaves and actually help prune limbs of trees up to four or five feet while destroying smaller bushes and shrubs on land that is best suited for grass.

---

[35] TEXAS ALMANAC, 1986-87 Edition, p.627 (2) TEXAS HANDBOOK, p. 599

Goats Trimming Trees
Hughes Ranch (Circa 1890s)

Also in competition with the common short-hair Spanish goats, Angora goats were receiving considerably more attention from a few ranchers because of the market value of their fleece, or mohair. Tanned hides with one-inch growth of mohair were popular as rugs, buggy robes, and some wearing apparel, with good hides bringing up to $10.00 and $12.00 each.[36]

First introduced to the United States in 1848, Angora goats were a gift from the Sultan of Turkey to Dr. James B. Davis of South Carolina. The Sultan sent nine head of best quality animals to Dr. Davis in appreciation for his having helped Turkey conduct experiments in the culture of cotton, at the request of President Polk. Only eight Angoras reached America--two males and six females.

Several additional purchases were made by other parties between 1848 and 1880. After that, the Sultan issued an edict prohibiting further exportation of Angora goats from

[36] Conwright-Schreiner, S. C., THE ANGORA GOAT, Longmans, Green and Co., 39 Paternoster Row, London, England, 1898

Turkey in 1880.[37]  Approximately 400 best blooded Angoras reached America before the Sultan terminated his exporting venture.[38]

This limited number of purebred Angoras necessitated crossbreeding with the "slick-haired" Spanish goats[39] and upgrading the bloodline through use of purebred Angora bucks.  There were about 70,000 Angora goats in the United States in 1882, and the U.S. Department of Agriculture didn't start keeping statistics on Angora goats and mohair until 1900.  In the late 1880s, the population of Angora goats in the U.S. was estimated to be 247,775; the Texas share was 75,000 head.[40]  Of the 247,775 head of Angoras in the U. S., it was estimated that not more than 100,000 Angoras produced good quality mohair.  Applying the same ratios to 75,000 Texas goats of this breed, only about 30,000 would have clipped four to five pounds of fleece per animal.  So the United States Angora goat and mohair industry was in its infancy when Willy Hughes took what some called a great risk in switching his ranch operation from sheep to Angora goats.

It is not known if Willy had already begun collecting his foundation goat stock before 1887, but we do have compelling evidence that he went to the right place for the best breeding stock and sound advice on goat management and the mohair industry, William M. Landrum.

William M. Landrum was one of the foremost breeders of Angora goats in the United States.  From 1850-1883, he made his base of operation in Joaquin County, California, enjoying phenomenal success in raising and showing some of the highest quality Angora goats in the United States.  His best purebred seed stock came from two sixteen-month-old supreme quality males purchased from Col. Richard Peters of Atlanta,

---

[37]  Conwright-Schreiner, S. C., THE ANGORA GOAT, Longmans, Green and Co., 39 Paternoster Row, London, England, 1898, p. 31

[38]  Ibid, p. 240

[39]  THE TEXAS HANDBOOK, T. C. Richardson, contributor, Texas Historical Association, Austin, Texas 1955

[40]  Conwright-Schreiner, S. C., THE ANGORA GOAT, Longmans, Green, and Co., 39 Paternoster Row, London, England 1898

Georgia in 1861. Shipped to California as wagon freight, they walked the entire distance tethered behind wagons that averaged twenty miles per day. Landrum exhibited his prized Angoras at the State Fair that fall and was awarded a special premium--a large silver goblet--for introduction of the first pure Angora or Cashmere goats to enter California. One of his prime young billies died of snake bite after having sired about thirty kids. The other male, dubbed "Billy Atlanta" won top honors at all state fairs and livestock shows on the west coast for the next nine years, until he died in an accident at ten years of age. He sired about 2,000 offsprings.[41]

Col. Peters, known as one of the most competent authorities on Angora goats in his time, sold another twenty-five choice-bred female goats to Landrum's firm near San Francisco in 1868. Then in 1872, the group acquired the larger portion of Peters' pure-bred herd and removed them to the same state. By 1882, California led the nation with up to 70,000 head of Angora goats of all grades. Landrum was a well-known, popular man when he picked up his share of his firm's outstanding herd of Angora breeding stock in 1883 and moved to the Edwards Plateau area in Southwest Texas, settling in Laguna, a community of English immigrants in Uvalde County.

Landrum's reasons for relocation in Texas probably centered on two factors: the climate and vegetation that is better suited for goats and the economic advantages of cheaper land and being closer to markets. George Kendall and Henry Randall wrote of these advantages for raising sheep in the Texas Hill Country during the 1850s and '60s. The rich farmland around Stockton and Modesto, California, was much more valuable for field crops, truck farming, and orchards than for browsing goats.

By 1890, Texas was leading all states in goat and mohair production. At the end of 1993, ten Texas counties were producing 96% of U.S. raised mohair and Angora goats, and almost 40% of world production (15 million pounds annually).[42] Edwards,

----

[41] Conwright-Schreiner, S. C., THE ANGORA GOAT, Longmans, Green, and Co., 39 Paternoster Row, London, England 1898, p. 237

[42] Texas Agricultural Statistical Service, Uvalde A&M Research & Extension Center, 1994

Val Verde, Uvalde, Sutton, Kimble, Terrell, Crockett, Mills, Kenney, and Mason are the highest mohair producing counties in Texas.

Time has destroyed hard evidence, like receipts and sales journals, supporting the source of Willy Hughes' Angora goat foundation stock in 1887, but Willy's 100 year-old-son, Gerard H. "Jerry" Hughes, remembers the Landrum name being used at his home. While it might have been in reference to Frank O. Landrum, son of W. M. and a **known** breeder of Angoras in his own right at the turn of the century, there is no doubt that Willy knew the famous William Landrum.

When Landrum moved to Texas from California in 1883, he must have received favorable press coverage in local papers and in Angora goat trade circles. It is evident that Hughes soon made the two-day horseback trip over to the Laguna English Colony to seek out Mr. Landrum for help and advice in establishing his foundation stock of Angora goats. In S. C. Conwright-Schreiner's book, THE ANGORA GOAT, W. G. Hughes is credited with having obtained most of the historical and statistical information on Angora goats and mohair production in the U.S. from Mr. W. M. Landrum.

While Willy Hughes remained a diversified rancher--running cattle, horses, and the remainder of his sheep flock at the same time, he also pursued the new goat enterprise with enthusiasm and determination. He kept his choice pure-blood male and female Angora animals at the ranch headquarters property but leased additional State school land and perhaps some privately owned acreage near Pipe Creek in Bandera County, where he ran several hundred goats.[43] Sam Norris, a teenager from Boerne, was put in charge of the Pipe Creek Ranch operation.

Willy utilized many of the tried-and-proven skills and management practices he learned from his sheep operation to perfect controls and procedures in his goat ranching business. From the beginning, Willy was successful. He worked fervently to improve and continuously upgrade and advertise his exciting new industry, and he placed special

---

[43] Texas State Land Board Records, viewed 11-8-93

emphasis on enlightening people about the merits of mohair and Angora goats. He showed his prized animals at state fairs and livestock shows throughout the country. He wrote stories for publication and made significant contributions to at least two popular books that were written about Angora goats and mohair. During the 1890s, W. G. Hughes was a man with a **name** in his trade.

Angora Goat
Hughes Ranch, Boerne, Texas (Circa 1890)

Sixty percent of a goat's diet is made up of leaves from wood plants, briars, and shrubs, referred to as "brouse." Source: Mohair Council of America, San Angelo, Texas, 1994

Chapter VII                **SIGNIFICANT EVENTS**

## "Granny" Hughes Dies

Granny Hughes became progressively more feeble during the hot, dry summer months of 1887. Already in her 90th year, she rallied briefly when her sons Hastings and Tom came to visit her in September. Tom announced after his departure that he didn't expect his mother to live more than a few more weeks.

Margaret Elizabeth "Granny" Hughes died at Rugby, Tennessee, October 5, 1887. With her passing, the Hughes family was in a state of disarray, particularly Hastings and his four children, Willy, Gerard, Harry, and Emily. But it was not only the Hastings Hughes family that was shocked and suffered emotionally at the loss of their grandmother; the entire Hughes family and a host of friends on both sides of the Atlantic were terribly saddened by her death.

Granny had come to America to be closer to members of Hastings' family and to give support and stability to Tom Hughes' ill-conceived socialistic experiment at the English colony of Rugby, Tennessee. She was the very backbone and fiber that held the Rugby project together. There was little doubt that the passing of Granny Hughes would also sound the death knell to Rugby, Thomas Hughes' most outlandish and most expensive dream.

Margaret Elizabeth "Granny" Hughes was buried at Rugby Cemetery on a beautiful wooded hillside plot overlooking the valley below. When her estate matters were settled, her family and some original residents of Rugby began moving away.

Emily Hughes inherited her grandmother's elegant Victorian furniture and her personal possessions. Her problem was, what to do with the furniture? She and her father knew that Willy was planning to build a larger house at the ranch, so they asked if he would like to have Granny's household furnishings on loan until Emily established a home of her own. Willy gladly accepted the offer because he was already making very important plans.

## Willy Takes A Bride

Willy Hughes had hardly noticed little twelve-year-old Lucy Stephenson when he moved to Kendall County as an 18-year-old lad in March, 1879, and met his nearest neighbors, the John Stephenson family. He became more aware of Lucy's presence as she grew up and went away to Normal College to become a schoolmarm. In fact, he must have become quite giddy about Lucy sometime earlier, according to a remark his future sister-in-law, Julia Perrin Stephenson, made in a letter to her sister while she was living temporarily with the Stephensons. She wrote, "Lucy, Ella, and the Hughes boy were cutting up so last night that I couldn't possibly scribble a word, such a boy to talk as I never saw."[1]

Willy completed his two-story ranch house in early 1888 and brought in the borrowed furniture that Emily sent down from Rugby. William George Hughes and Lucy Caroline Stephenson were married in San Antonio at St. Paul's Episcopal Church at 1018 East Grayson Street (across from Fort Sam Houston) on June 28, 1888. The ceremony was performed by Henry Swift, Army Chaplain and Rector of St. Paul's Church. Indications are that this was the social event of the year for Boerne, as a host of relatives and friends from Boerne and San Antonio attended the wedding.

---

[1] Hoch, Margaret Perrin, DANIEL AND EMILY PERRIN: LIVES THAT TELL A STORY, LEBCO Graphics, Boerne, Texas 1992, page 103

Lucy Caroline Hughes
(Circa 1888)

Next day the newlyweds boarded a special train for Corpus Christi, where they attended a highly publicized sailboat regatta. The round trip train fare was the same as a one-way ticket, according to the San Antonio newspapers.

After the festivities were over, the happy young couple caught the train back to Boerne and moved into their beautifully furnished home. Many of their early discussions concerned the business aspects of the ranch and its future growth and activities. Lucy brought up the subject of a dairy operation, and Willy thought it was an excellent idea. They also gave thought to starting a family. Their first child, Jeanie Elizabeth, was born May 8, 1889; George Forbes came September 8, 1892, and the Hughes' second son, Gerard Hastings, arrived January 15, 1895.

The balance of 1888, and into the 1890s, was a very busy time for Willy and Lucy Hughes. Willy was pursuing the trade he knew best to insure a reliable income-- land, horses, cattle, sheep, and Angora goats. He was masterful at buying and selling land and livestock, but not all such transactions produced a profit.

In Willy's letter to his father, November 12, 1883, the last one published in G.T.T.-GONE TO TEXAS, Willy told about making an overnight trip to Kendalia with Mr. C. G. Vogel, who was in the process of developing this new town 23 miles NE of Boerne. Mr. Vogel was primarily a real estate developer and promoter who founded the BOERNE UNION LAND REGISTER newspaper in 1875. He used the paper principally to report land transactions and developments such as Kendalia, which he began in 1882; the plat was filed at the courthouse in 1884. Willy availed himself of only one prized lot in that great future city with Vogel Park; school and church lots; and future Mountain College--all advertising the place to be a great health resort in Kendall County.

The city never quite developed as planned, and Mr. Vogel sold the newspaper and moved on to another promising land deal. Willy kept Lot #9.

Four years later, Willy made another unrewarding investment. In 1887, Mr. H. J. Graham, a Boerne businessman, and Captain D. S. Irons of San Antonio, had announced an exclusive development in central Boerne. The property was enclosed by Hosack Street on the south, School Street on the west, and Cibolo Creek running southeasterly, then along S. Main Street to Hosack. It was scheduled to be a premier subdivision with large spacious homes. Willy moved quickly to buy nine lots before they were all sold. The Irons and Graham Subdivision never materialized.[2]

Hughes appears to have ultimately fared better with Mr. Vogel when the gentleman became overextended and went into receivership or liquidation. Hughes

---

[2] Davis, Harry, Sr., BOERNE STAR, story published 11-17-93

bought 2,682 acres of Vogel's land in Harris County and Lot #1, Blk. 24, Hardcastle Sub-division in Houston;  320 acres in Atascosa County and 200 acres adjacent to the East side of Sisterdale township in Kendall County; and approximately 50 acres of land in the Kendalia Subdivision that had not sold.  In addition, Willy bought 200 acres of subdivision land (not Vogel property) at a Sheriff's sale in Bexar County.[3]

Except for these limited experiences, there are no indications that Willy ever again became involved with subdivision investments.  His expertise was in farm and ranch land.

In the 1890 guide and history book, SAN ANTONIO DeBEXAR by William Corner, Hughes bought a quarter page ad announcing his services as a farm and ranch real estate agent, with properties to sell in Kendall and Bandera Counties.

## The Healthiest and Most Attractive Section of Texas

IS FOUND AMONGST THE HILLS AND FERTILE VALLEYS ON THE LINE OF THE SAN ANTONIO AND ARANSAS PASS RAILWAY, NORTH OF SAN ANTONIO.  SEE S. A. & A. P. RAILWAY MAP.

I have Farms and Ranches for sale in Kendall and Bandera Counties, and City Property in

## ✢ BOERNE ✢

The well known Health Resort and County Seat of Kendall County.  There is a Daily Mail and Stage Line between

## BOERNE AND BANDERA,

A Distance of 25 Miles, the latter Town being the County Seat of Bandera County.

## W. G. HUGHES, Real Estate Agent.

Post Office, Hastings. Kendall County (on border of Kendall and Bandera Counties).

### Ranch Growth Stabilizes

Willy's deeded land holdings stabilized at around 7,000 acres in the later part of the 1890s.[4]  He was known to have leased substantial privately owned grazing land on

---

[3] All of these transactions are recorded in Kendall County Deed Records.

[4] Kendall County Deed Records, reconciliation of annual purchases and sale of land, Hughes owned balance of 7,284 acres as of January 28, 1902 when he purchased 195 acres of State land.

the Guadalupe River at an earlier date, and he leased 960 acres of state school land near Pipe Creek in Bandera County in the early 1890s.[5]

Unfortunately, there are no remaining records of Hughes' land-leasing activities from private property owners, but it's reasonable to believe his ranch reached from 15,000 to 20,000 acres in size at its peak of operation. Professor John Willard Stout had earlier said that Uncle Willy Hughes also had hundreds of pieces of school land leased, besides the ranch he owned.

Willy had employed Sam Norris of Boerne to manage the Pipe Creek portion of the ranch in the early 1890s. Willy was known to be a perfectionist who demanded top quality performance, and Sam was an ideal choice. He was a courteous, hard-working young man who was also extremely knowledgeable in matters relating to livestock. He managed the Pipe Creek ranch to Willy's complete satisfaction. This was fortunate for Willy because it gave him more time to manage his goat and horse breeding programs and to concentrate on his marketing skills.

## Lucy's Dairy Business

Ever a disciple of diversification, Willy strongly supported the idea of Lucy going into the dairy business.

Luckily, Willy had learned a great deal about the dairy industry during his 18 months as junior clerk to the Managing Director of Aylesbury Dairy Company in London. He knew something about record keeping on dairy cows and their milk production. He understood the basic rudiments of the feeding and care of dairy cattle and the marketing of dairy products.

With this background, Willy began building a dairy barn and fences and setting aside pasture land exclusively for Lucy's milk cows. He visited with successful dairy owners and bought her a foundation herd of thirty-five best quality Jersey cows. The dairy business proved to be successful by the time it was in full operation, and at its peak

---

[5] Texas State Land Board Archive Records, viewed by author, 11-8-93.

Lucy was shipping 400 pounds of butter per month to market in San Antonio.[6]

## Nimrod The Stallion

In the mid-1880s, Willy Hughes entered competition with a few pioneer Texas ranchers in trying to develop and improve his own breed of horse to meet special needs-- racing, harness, polo, cow pony, gaited saddle horse--or an all purpose horse to meet most of these requirements. The first horses he purchased in 1879, were used for transportation and basic harness work, plowing and wagon team usage. Then he became infatuated with the wild mustang and its strong features: stamina, endurance, quickness, agility and its ability to survive on native grasses.

Willy was also very much aware of the cross infusion of bloodlines between the Texas mustang--thought to have been left with the Pueblo Indians at Ysleta by Coronado in 1540--and the "Virginia" horse, or similar quality horses from Illinois, Tennessee or Kentucky, that were first brought to Texas in the 1840s and 1850s. These fine horses descended from an earlier cross between standard English horses and Spanish ponies that were abandoned on Chincoteague Island and other islands off the Virginia-North Carolina coast by Spanish ships in distress in the 1500s.[7] The Virginia horses were popular as short distance race horses, often called "short horses." In Texas descendants of the Virginia type horses were quickly adapted as Texas cow ponies, later known as Quarter Horses. They were fast, durable and intelligent animals. Bulky and stout enough to handle cattle in any cutting, roping or branding situations, these mounts were favorites of pioneer stockmen and cowboys. They were also the dominant breed used for short distance races.

When Willy was working with his cousins, Jim Hughes and Bob Hobson, in breaking, training and evaluating horses for the New York racing market, he noticed that they traveled long distances to find hybrid mustang type cow ponies that were more

[6] Brown, John Henry, INDIAN WARS AND PIONEERS OF TEXAS, p. 483

[7] (1) TEXAS ALMANAC, 1904; (2) THE HANDBOOK OF TEXAS, The Texas Historical Assoc., Austin, Texas, 1952, Vol. I, p. 837-838.

slender and leaner than the larger but more popular cow ponies of the 1880s. Presumably they were more competitive on the longer race tracts where they sometimes competed against thoroughbreds.

When polo was becoming a popular sport in the 1880s and the price of good quality polo ponies began to escalate, a number of horsemen modified their breeding programs to meet market requirements. It was about this time that Willy Hughes got into the act and started his own breeding program with the purchase of the young, handsome iron-gray Arabian stallion, Nimrod.[8]

Nimrod, Famous Arabian Stallion

There are no records or personal letters that explain Willy's horse breeding strategies. The mustang was favored as a race horse and later as a polo pony in the Northeast when Willy's cousins, Jim Hughes and Bob Hobson, were shipping horses to the New York area. The mustangs were also crossed with other strains of horses by many pioneer settlers. But Willy Hughes was in the business of raising, buying, and selling these native horses as polo ponies, U. S. Cavalry mounts, and general purpose horses. So it appears that he infused the Arabian bloodline into his breeding program

---

[8] Stout, Donald Hughes, quoted his father as saying that Uncle Willy Hughes imported eight Arabian stallions from Egypt. Telephone interview, Jan. 21, 1995.

198

to capitalize on the finer traits of the Arabian--intelligence, endurance, better riding comfort--that complemented the best qualities of other popular breeds. Although never recognized as a breed, the Hughes horses were in demand and existed in the Boerne-Kendall County area for many years.[9]


### Death of Brothers.

Despite the glowing success and excitement of Hughes Ranch in the 1890s, Willy Hughes and all of the Hastings Hughes family were further saddened and emotionally devastated by the untimely death of not just one but both younger Hughes brothers.

Gerard went to see his father, Hastings, and his family in Boston sometime around 1894. While there he spent considerable time alone sight-seeing and exploring the city. On one occasion he wandered over to the Marblehead seashore resort area and went for a swim. His clothes were later found on the beach, but his body was never recovered.

There were no witnesses, nor evidence to confirm exactly what happened, but family members, knowing that Gerard was an excellent swimmer, think he just underestimated the powerful undertow currents off the coast of Massachusetts and accidentally drowned.

A couple of years later, Harry Hughes went on a six-month trip to Asia and South Africa--perhaps as a courier or messenger in some business deal. He had departed Cape Town on the ship Drummond Castle headed for London, England, when it ran on a reef off the coast of Spain. Hughes received considerable praise for having remained calm while helping women and children into lifeboats. He went down with the ship on June 16, 1896.[10]

---

[9] Shumard, M.A. Jr., former County Judge and lifetime resident of Boerne, Interview, 1991

[10] (1) Cantrell, Pearl, Archivist, Historic Rugby, Tennessee, Telephone interview, 12-4-93; (2) Members of Hughes family

Chapter VIII     **COMMUNITY INVOLVEMENT**

Following the tragic loss of his brother Gerard, Willy appointed Sam Norris foreman of Hughes Ranch.  From that day forward, he dedicated his enormous talents to the management of his livestock breeding and marketing programs.  He spent considerable time traveling to state fairs and livestock exhibitions, showing and publicizing Angora goats throughout the country.  Hughes became a premier merchant of top quality livestock.  Today, 100 years later, livestock production still accounts for a major portion of the Gross Domestic Product of Kendall County.

<u>Civic Accomplishments</u>

As Willy's ranch operation began to stabilize, he became more involved with civic events and community affairs.  A natural leader, he was quickly recognized for his good judgement and ability to get things accomplished.

On May 10, 1886, Hughes joined with ten neighbors in preparing and signing a road petition[1] for the Commissioners' Court to consider at the May term of court.  They asked the Honorable Court to appoint a Jury of View to view and lay out a third-class public road, commencing at the Court House in Boerne and running in a westerly direction on the most practicable route, ending where the northwest line of Sur. No. 873, B.S.& F., C. H. Klemme tract, crosses Frederick Creek.

The petition was signed by Barbara T. Newton, E. R. Newton, W. G. Hughes, C. H. Klemme, John Stephenson, I. Minnich, Bertha Tolsom, Mary Fleming, L. Fabra, and P. D. Saner, and adopted by the Court September 13, 1886.  The land was viewed, surveyed, and staked out October 21, 1886.[2]

A Prospectus of THE BOERNE ACADEMY AND COMMERCIAL COLLEGE[3]

---

[1] Original petition in author's files

[2] Copy of Documents in author's files

[3] A Prospectus of THE BOERNE ACADEMY AND COMMERCIAL COLLEGE is in the author's files.

was published for the 1889-90 school term. Officials of the Academy included T. F. Swanwick, Principal; H. J. Graham, Secretary and Treasurer; and the Board of Directors included John Reinhard, O. M. Brown, and W. G. Hughes.

One interesting aspect of The Boerne Academy and Commercial College is that it addressed a language problem that existed between the English immigrants and earlier German settlers. Paragraph two, page three, of the eight-page prospectus gives a summary of the difficulty in two sentences: "Hitherto Boerne has suffered as regards material progress from the want of academic advantages, and an institute where a sound liberal English education could be obtained at reasonable rates....The classes are conducted in the English language."

There was no rivalry nor hostility between the German and English immigrants in the Hill Country. Rather it was a matter of time and the conditions under which they immigrated and existed on the Texas frontier. The Germans arrived in the 1840s and 1850s, under contract with a German immigration agency called the "Adelsverein" or "Society of Noblemen." They were isolated in a cluster of remote counties without public transportation to the outside world. The counties of Kendall, Comal, Gillespie, Llano, and Mason retained their population of approximately eighty percent German for many years, speaking and teaching their children exclusively in German private schools until the State of Texas began funding Public Schools in 1857. Even then, public school classes in Boerne were taught in German one-half day and in English the other half day.

The English settlers came to Boerne and Kendall County in the 1870s and 1880s. The SAAP railroad arrived in 1887, bringing an influx of people who spoke languages other than German. Nevertheless, Boerne Academy, with which Willy was associated, appears to have folded after one or two terms. It was, however, superseded by Holy Angel's Academy, an all-grades school operated by Sisters of the Incarnate Word. They taught in the English language but offered elective courses in German.

Another of Willy's significant civic contributions was obtaining a post office for the Mineral Springs area. On February 26, 1890, Willy made application to the U.S. Post Office Department for a Class IV Post Office to be established in this small community located 4 miles southwest of Boerne. He stated that a population of 60 would be served, and he recommended that the post office be called Hastings (in honor of his father), with William George Hughes appointed as postmaster.

Hastings Post Office was approved by the Post Office Department April 17, 1890, with Hughes designated as Post Master.[4] The post office was located in a 6 X 6-foot enclosure inside the Hughes Ranch house.

On April 15, 1891, William George Hughes received his Certificate of U.S. Citizenship[5] at the April term of District Court at the Bandera County, Texas, Court House in Bandera. The certificate acknowledged that Hughes had resided within the limits of the jurisdiction of the United States of America for more than five years last passed, and not less than one year thereof within the State of Texas, and that during this time he had behaved as a man of good moral character. By taking the oath of allegiance and signing the necessary documents, Willy Hughes became a United States citizen.

W. G. and Lucy Hughes deeded 9/10 acre of land to August Seawald, County Judge, for Hastings School,[6] on April 29, 1898. Hughes was the prime instigator in establishing Hastings School No. 1, District #19, in Kendall County.

The one-room wood frame schoolhouse with 10 double desks was located 200 yards northwest of the Hughes Ranch house. School terms were approximately four months long, beginning in November or December and terminating in March. Teachers were usually female, and their pay was budgeted at $25.00 to $35.00 per month. The first term of Hastings School was October 24, 1897 to January 24, 1898. Five of the fifteen students were grandchildren of John and Ann Dover Stephenson, including four Stout children and Jeanie Hughes, age 8. One-hundred-year-old Gerard H. "Jerry" Hughes--a graduate of Harvard University--said he was horrified at having to memorize his ABCs upon entering Hastings School at six years of age in 1901.

---

[4] Copy of documents in author's files

[5] Copy of document in author's files

[6] (1) Kendall County Deed Records, Vol. 16, Pg. 587
(2) Mary Cartwright, School Research paper, February, 1981

Old Hughes Ranch House, 1994
Twice Renovated; Owned by the W. H. Maytum Estate

Gerard, George, and Jeanie Hughes

## A Busy Social Life

The 1890s were active, prosperous years for Willy and Lucy Hughes. Despite being terribly busy with her three children and managing the dairy business, Lucy joined Willy in entertaining a host of local friends and outside business associates whom Willy met during his livestock marketing adventures. In his book INDIAN WARS AND PIONEERS OF TEXAS, John Henry Brown said, "Mr. and Mrs. Hughes are delightful entertainers, genial and cultured, and have a wide circle of friends."

The Hughes family often received favorable comments in the BOERNE POST and other publications. One such article in the Post, dated January 12, 1899, concerned Willy's involvement with Angora goats in Kendall County. The Posts' editor wrote: "The following interesting article appeared in TEXAS FARM AND RANCH MAGAZINE under the pen of Mrs. S. E. Buchanan:

"A visit to the home of Mr. W. G. Hughes at Hastings in Kendall County was somewhat ill timed because that gentleman was absent from home in attendance upon the Omaha Exposition. He had carried a large number of his finest goats to the Exposition for the purpose of exhibition and also taken a car load of Angoras to Kansas City to place them on sale. Mr. Hughes being away from home, Mrs. Hughes kindly gave me such information as she could, showing me around."

The Hugheses also entertained house guests quite frequently. Family members sometimes stayed three or four weeks.

BOERNE POST, 1898: "Mr. and Mrs. W. H. (Hastings) Hughes and children of Milton, Mass., are visiting in home of Mr. and Mrs. W. G. Hughes."

## Willy's Violin

Several references are made to Willy's violin in G.T.T.-GONE TO TEXAS. In his unedited letter to Hastings, dated March 21, 1880, Willy asked his father to bring his violin, music, and thirty-four strings: 12-E, 12-A, 6-D, and 4-G.[7] Unfortunately,

---

[7] The paragraph pertaining to the violin was edited out of the G.T.T. book. Copy of original letter in author's files.

Hastings didn't get back to the ranch until 1882. He was detained at his brother's English Colony at Rugby, Tennessee for more than a year. Willy's violin remained locked up at Hastings' apartment in New York during this time.

Willy traveled to Rugby in December, 1880, at his father's request to "prospect" on moving his sheep operation there, but didn't bring the violin back with him when he returned to Texas. The instrument was not mentioned again until after Hastings and Emily visited the Boerne ranch in January, 1882. In his letter to Emily on September 23, 1882, Willy said, "Miss Klemme plays the piano and sings.[8] She has just got a new piano and plays my accompaniments very well, so I have a little music again occasionally."

In Emily's letter of July 23, 1885, to her friend Lucy Taylor in London, she tells about Willy having brought his violin while on a 10-day visit with the family in Rugby over the Fourth of July. She said, "He plays well and we practiced a good deal during his stay. It was a great treat to me to accompany him, and he enjoyed it very much too."[9]

Emily also told of the Rugby Social Club having entertained on the night of July 3rd--she had a part in the program. Before leaving for Texas, Willy prepared the Club's report for the community newspaper, the RUGBEIN. Hastings and Uncle Tom were in Rugby during this occasion. Emily's letter to Miss Taylor didn't say if Willy played for the family during his visit, but he probably did, at least while practicing with his sister.

In the spring of 1993, Laurabelle Ullrich, Lucy and Willy's 88-year-old great-niece, of San Antonio, spoke of family memories of Willy's musical talent. She said her mother commented several times about Willy's having once played in concert before a

---

[8]  Miss Laura or Miss Clara Klemme who taught school in the Hastings Community before there was a public school.

[9]  DeBruyn, John R., DISSIPATIONS AT UFFINGTON HOUSE, "The Letters of Emily Hughes, Rugby, Tenn., 1881-1887," Memphis State University, 1976

large audience at the Boerne Opera House.

Jerry Hughes, of New Hampshire, said in a recent telephone interview with the writer that his mother often described his father as a very talented musician who played the violin at or near professional level.

Between 1897 and 1900, Willy Hughes reached his peak of success as a rancher. The ranch stabilized at around 7,000 acres of deeded land in 1897 and remained there for several years. With his purchase of 195 acres of State School land nine-and-one-half miles east of Boerne (Survey No. 1097) on January 28, 1902, the Hughes Ranch consisted of 7,281 acres of deeded land. There was also 10,000 acres of leased State School land, plus additional open range.[1]

In livestock production, Hughes was known far and wide for the quality of his Angora goats and for his fine cross-bred Arabian-mustang horses. He also had other top-quality breeding stock--Merino and Oxfordshire Downs sheep; Nimrod, the Arabian stallion, Jersey bulls, and jackasses. All made money in stud service fees, and offsprings of each breed were for sale to other breeders.

### Breaking Horses for the U.S. Cavalry

During the 1898 Spanish-American War, Willy Hughes contracted with the U.S. Government to deliver a consignment of horses to the cavalry staging area on Mustang Island, offshore from Corpus Christi. At this time, future President "Teddy" Roosevelt was in San Antonio recruiting "Rough Riders" for the United States 1st Cavalry Regiment Volunteers, which gained fame for its victory at San Juan Hill in Cuba. Roosevelt actively recruited cowboys and lawmen from the Southwest for his colorful Rough Rider unit. Three young men from Boerne signed up with Company "D" of Teddy Roosevelt's Rough Riders: Gerald W. Calrow, John S. "Jack" Howard, and D. Hadden.[2]

---

[1] Stout, Perry, Letter of 12-27-1914 to his sister, Dorothy Candlish, in which he answered her questions about the size of Hughes Ranch and numbers of livestock when he left the ranch in 1900. At that time Stout said Uncle Billy had five goat camps with 1,000 to 1,500 goats at each site. No remarks about other livestock, except amount paid for some breeding stock.

[2] BOERNE POST, September 29, 1898

Professor John Willard Stout tells about breaking horses for his Uncle Willy Hughes in 1898 when he was 14 years of age and his brother, Perry, was 16.[3] Willy hired outside cowboys to break his younger horses that had not been ridden, and his nephews were given the responsibility of working with horses that were already halter trained.

John and Perry planned a secret system for breaking horses. They mounted a saddle horse and led halter-broken horses one at a time into the pasture for training. When near the creek, the youngsters headed for their favorite swimming hole and led the unbroken horses into the water up to their belly--deep enough so they couldn't buck nor kick. Then they threw their spare saddle on the back of the animal, and one boy mounted him. Next, they rode the two horses around and around until the in-training horse was tired and settled down, after which they leisurely exited the water and headed back to the barn. Professor Stout said they had no trouble breaking two horses per day by handling the unbroken animals calmly and gently.

One horse they broke was a beautiful black mare Uncle Willy had given to Perry and John rather than destroy her. She had never gotten with foal and was rather a nuisance at breeding time and when other broodmares gave birth to foals, but the boys trained her well then turned her back to Uncle Willy to sell for them.

Perry and John were terribly disappointed when they were not permitted to accompany the Hughes Ranch horses to Corpus Christi, but John remembered the story the cowboys told upon their return to Boerne. Uncle Willy was not satisfied with the cost of $1.50 per animal, nor with the loss of time in sending his horses across the waterway on a barge, with a capacity of eight or nine horses each trip. Willy watched the tide ebb and flow, then told his cowboys that they would hit the water at next low tide and swim all the horses across to the island. The boys were told that their black mare led the herd and followed the boat without hesitation. Only one horse became confused and tried to turn back. It drowned.

---

[3] Stout, Prof. John Willard, AS I REMEMBER IT, Stories dictated for his children, 1978, courtesy Dr. John Willard Stout, Jr. and Mrs. Beatrice S. Dooley

Professor Stout, with his vivid memory, said he and Perry often wondered if Teddy Roosevelt was riding their beautiful black mare as he led the Rough Riders in their victorious charge at San Juan Hill.

## Sharing Science and Skills

By end of the 19th Century, Willy Hughes was recognized as a foremost authority on Angora goats and mohair production. He willingly shared his scientific knowledge and technical skills in the breeding and management of this special animal that was getting so much attention in the United States.

Hughes made a major contribution to a book entitled THE ANGORA GOAT, by S. C. Conwright-Schreiner of South Africa, in 1898. The author gave special recognition to him in Chapter XVIII, which dealt with the Angora goat and mohair industry in the United States. The footnote reads:

"I wish to thank Mr. W. G. Hughes, Hastings, Kendall County, Texas,
for the information he has supplied personally, and for assisting me in
obtaining much of the information contained in this chapter."

Mr. Schreiner also credits Hughes with helping to compile a list of Angora goat importations to the U.S. by name of importers and year. He had obtained most of this information from his friend, Wm. M. Landrum of Laguna, Texas.

The U.S. Bureau of Animal Industry did not maintain and publish statistics on Angora goat and mohair production until 1900. But because of rapid growth in this new industry and frequent request for information on the Angora goat, Professor George F. Thompson of the U.S. Bureau of Animal Industry, began soliciting technical papers on the breeding, care, and management of Angora goats from key authorities in the goat and mohair industry.

This material was printed in book form by the U.S. Bureau of Animal Industry (circa 1903) under the title ANGORA GOAT RAISING AND MILCH GOATS. Willy responded to questions in four categories pertaining to technical aspects of Angora goat management. Three excerpts follow.

209

From W. G. Hughes & Co., Hastings, Tex.—"The Angora is much more nutritious than sheep mutton, especially where the meat is grown on underbrush (leaves), as the following compilation of relative values of feed will show:

| Character of Feed. | Protein. | Starch, etc. | Fats. |
|---|---|---|---|
| | Per cent. | Per cent. | Per cent. |
| Good pasture grass............................................ | 3.5 | 9.7 | 0.8 |
| Rich pasture.................................................... | 4.5 | 10.1 | 1.0 |
| Leaves of trees................................................ | 5.2 | 15.2 | 1.5 |
| Red clover...................................................... | 3.3 | 7.0 | 0.7 |

"It is often prescribed by physicians for invalids and children for this reason. The meat is excellent, and not distinguishable from mutton of the same age and condition. It is largely sold as such in many of the larger markets, being regarded as a staple in the districts where it is raised."

Dr. Thompson, under this category on taking care of kid goats at birth, describes a method of keeping the mother goats in a single pen, or in small groups of not over 20 does, until each mother "owns" her offspring.

Once the mothers have accepted their kids, the little ones should then be confined together in larger pens and not allowed to follow the mothers outside for feeding until they are four to six weeks old, or they may be confined to the pen by placing a 12- to-20 inch board on the ground across the gate until the kids can jump the board and go outside to feed with their mothers. He liked the Hughes method that was illustrated by picture:

"W. G. Hughes & Co., of Hastings, Texas, has a device for separating the does from the kids which is better than the board. It has a bridge, either end of which drops to the desired height. This device enables the does to go out and in without injuring their udders, which is apt to occur where they have to jump a board."[4]

---

[4] Hughes family pictures show that Willy Hughes also used the bridge to count goats as they were moved from one pen to another.

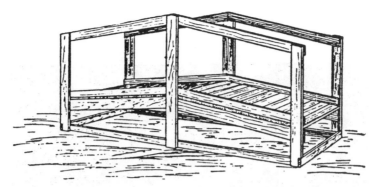

THE HUGHES SEPARATING BRIDGE.

From W. G. Hughes & Co., Hastings, Tex.:  "We keep the nannie and kid to themselves so far as possible for a day or so, and do not allow more than 20 nannies and kids in the same pen until the kids are over a week old, nor more than 50 nannies and kids in the same pen until 2 weeks old.  Kids are kept in the pen day and night until a month old, and are then allowed to run outside the pen during the day to eat a little; the feed may be furnished them in the form of cut branches if there are no bushes near the pen.  They should also have access to water after 4 weeks old.  When 6 weeks old they can go out with the flock for a few hours in the afternoon, the flock being brought in at midday for this purpose.  After 8 weeks they can go regularly all day with the flock. We use a bridge for the purpose of 'cutting back' such kids as should not go out with the flock."

Registered Buck and Three Does

211

Nursery Pens

Counting Bridge

212

## Ranch Employees

The picture below identifies some of the key employees and children at the Hughes Ranch. Two of the men played a vital part in the operation of the ranch; another provided an important service and considerable entertainment.

Back Row, Left to Right: Sam Norris, Ranch Foreman; Olive Claridge, Servant; Francis McNeil, Servant; Rickhoff, Ranch Tanner; Perry E. Stout (Nephew of W. G. Hughes; Julio, Ranch Herder; Alan Stout (Nephew), Ranch Hand; Unknown; John W. Stout (Nephew), Ranch Hand;
Front Row: Esther Stout, Niece; Gerard Hughes; George Hughes and Friend

Sam Norris, the intelligent young man who displayed such unusual savvy in management of livestock and other ranch activities, was appointed foreman before he was twenty-one years of age. His leadership and positive work habits made Norris ideally suited to take over day-to-day ranch supervision while Hughes concentrated on livestock marketing and other business affairs.

Sam Norris (circa 1900)

Julio, a Mexican National whose last name is not known, was an exceptionally reliable goat herder and a fine man. He was greatly admired by the Hughes family and ranch employees.

Julio (circa 1900)

Julio's Houses (The only ranch employee who possessed two homes--one, a dugout near ranch headquarters; the other, a prairie house on wheels that he used while working in remote areas of the ranch).

Rickhoff, the tanner, was one of the most talented and sometimes the most colorful employee on the ranch. He was a "boozer," and as a man of that bent, he was ingenious at devising means for acquiring a bottle of spirits. He knew Mr. Hughes kept whiskey in the house, for medicinal purposes, rare snake bites, and for an occasional celebration, but the ranch house--other than the dining room--was off-limits to ranch workers. This didn't keep Rickhoff from thinking about this one potential source of moonshine.

In early spring, wild turkey gobblers came to the ranch and whipped the domestic toms in ferocious fights then mated with their hens. The resulting offsprings were as wild as March hares. One day while Willy was away attending a livestock show, Mrs. Hughes told Rickhoff that she wanted to catch some of the wild turkey poults but had no idea how to trap them. Rickhoff offered a solution.

Soak shelled corn in whiskey and feed it to the turkeys, Rickhoff suggested. Once they became inebriated, they could be picked up and placed in an enclosed wire pen. Mrs. Hughes thought this was an excellent idea, so she fetched the bottle of corn squeezings from the pantry while Rickhoff shelled a bucket of corn. They put the corn into a stone crock and poured the booze over it. Rickhoff said the container should be placed in the corn crib with a lid over it to soak for a couple of days. He would check on it, he promised.

Of course, Rickhoff checked on the corn frequently--with a small quill made from a joint of switch cane. Within two days he had siphoned off most of the liquor. When time came to demonstrate his technique for catching wild turkeys, he threw small amounts of corn on the ground, and the turkeys quickly gobbled it up.

Rickhoff kept throwing more corn and waiting for the alcohol to take effect, but it was a slow process. Finally, as the supply of feed was almost depleted, the turkeys began acting a little tipsy and coming closer for their feed. It was then that Rickhoff reached down to pick up a young poult. The turkeys instantly flushed like a covey of quail and flew to the top of nearby trees. They appeared to go completely ape--making all kinds of loud, strange noises and flying from one tree top to another before finally flying off in all directions.

216

Rickhoff didn't understand what had happened. But Mrs. Hughes immediately realized she had been victimized by a scheme that only an alcoholic could have concocted.[5]

Since Hughes ranch was in its heyday at the turn-of-the-century it's logical that domestic help would have been a necessity. Willy and Lucy Hughes were great entertainers, and they frequently had house guests. Olive Claridge and Francis McNiel, shown in the employee's group picture, were identified as servants at the Hughes household in the 1900 U. S. Census Report.

The novelty of ranch life and cattle drives caught the fancy of some visitors, particularly their friends and relatives from the Northeast. A. T. Wendler remembers his father having told him about Mr. Hughes stating once that his range cattle were loosing weight for some reason. Mr. Wendler reminded him that his cattle weren't getting enough grazing time due to being penned up too much so the ranch guest could play "cattle driving."[6]

Some senior citizens in Boerne still recall their parents having commented about Mr. Hughes raising Shetland ponies at the ranch. One hundred year old Jerry Hughes said that his father sold some Shetlands. He also kept two or three Shetlands at the ranch--along with a burro or so--for visiting children to ride and for his own children to play with. Jerry remembers one incident when his dad had a small pony in a wooden crate, awaiting shipment at the railroad station. People were stroking and admiring the animal. Then when a local minister came by, the pony stuck his head out and tried to bite him. The people of Boerne got a big laugh as the story spread about town.

---

[5] One of many fond stories memories Gerard H. "Jerry" Hughes remembers from his childhood at Hughes Ranch.

[6] Interview with A. T. Wendler, November, 1993. His father operated a general store in Boerne for many years.

George and Gerard Hughes With Their Burro
(Appraising the value of this high-speed racing animal)

Jerry Hughes told how envious he was when his brother, George, three years older, put on chaps and a cowboy hat and mounted his little pony--with a saddle and a 44 rifle in its scabbard--and rode into the pasture to drive up the milk cows. Jerry said he discovered another way to ride since he didn't have a horse and saddle. One day he sneaked up on a hog sleeping in the sun and climbed on her back. The startled sow jumped up and threw him off on a rock, bruising his knee. That ended his cowboy days.

The Stout children shown in the group picture of ranch personnel were members of a large family of nine children who grew up at or around the Hughes Ranch. Their mother, Jennie Stephenson Stout, was Lucy Hughes' sister, and her parents were Mr. and Mrs. John Stephenson, whose homestead adjoined Willy Hughes' property when he first bought land in Kendall County.

The Stephenson family of three boys and four daughters immigrated to Texas from England in 1872. Upon landing at Galveston, John Stephenson bought a team of horses and a wagon and moved his family inland to Robertson County in East Texas, where they remained for a year. Finding the climate disagreeable because of high humidity, mosquitoes, and malaria, the Stephensons moved on to Kendall County, where the drier climate was more to their liking. Here they homesteaded 160 acres of land and became leading citizens of their community.

Mr. Stephenson was a strict religious fundamentalist who gathered his family around both morning and night for a prayer and reading of scriptures from the Bible. His strong religious belief, his supreme character, and his deep regard for humanity had a great influence on the Stout children.

Professor John Willard Stout, in his story AS I REMEMBER IT, told of his grandfather's concern about young people growing up without knowing how to "read, write and cipher." He even hired one of the neighboring Klemme girls to teach classes for several children three days a week at his home. (This was before his son-in-law, Willy Hughes donated 9/10th acre of land for Hastings school in 1898).[7] Professor Stout said, "I learned a lot during those two months with Grandpa and Aunt Ella seeing that my homework was even a little more than completed."

## The John C. Stout Family

A story about Willy Hughes and the Hughes Ranch wouldn't be complete without a brief commentary on the John Stout family whose children spent most of their formative years at the ranch.

John Calhoun Stout, father of the Stout children, came to Southwest Texas from Missouri in the mid 1870s after having ridden a couple of times with the outlaw Jesse James gang.[8] He worked on the San Antonio and Aransas Pass railroad right-of-way

---

[7] Kendall County Deed Records

[8] Stout, John Willard, Sr., AS I REMEMBER IT, 1978, stories dictated for his children, courtesy Dr. John Willard Stout, Jr. and Mrs. Beatrice S. Dooley

project as it extended a secondary spur to Port Lavaca and Indianola, a thriving saltwater port in Calhoun County east of Victoria. Stout had a boardinghouse address in Port Lavaca in 1877, and while there he met and became friends with James Stephenson who was working for the same railroad company. It was through this connection that he met the John Stephenson family and his future bride in Boerne.

John Stout and Jennie Stephenson married in 1879. Jennie was 24 years of age, and John was 27. The Stout's first child, Perry, was born in 1882, and for the next 18 years Mrs. Stout averaged giving birth to a child every two years: John Willard came in 1884, Dorothy in 1886, and Alan Stephenson in 1889; Claiborne was born in 1891, and Eugene Paul, in 1893. Mr. Stout obviously had many fine qualities--he grew up in a prosperous family in Clay County, Missouri; he was intelligent, handsome, and he fathered a family of nine bright, beautiful children who grew up to be outstanding citizens.

Historical records of 100 years ago do not leave a definitive trail of John Stout's activities, his successes or his failures. There are only bits and pieces of information about his work places and skills. He appears to have been a "Jack-of-all-trades" and was evidently quite good at some things. As a twelve year old, he served as a Confederate spy by swimming his horse across the Missouri River at night and posing as a half-wit orphan while begging for food at Union soldier campsites. Later as a teenager he worked as wagon freighter on the Santa Fe Trail, and in Texas he was said to have served intermittently as a Texas Ranger.[9] Mr. Stout's major problem appears to have been a lack of productive employment, at least enough to provide for the comfort and stability of his family. He is also rumored to have been a compulsive gambler, and a boozer at times.

Prof. John Willard Stout, in his paper, spoke of some of his father's occupations in Texas. He worked as a dirt mover in building a railroad tram (the San Antonio and Aransas Pass extended its line into the Hill Country), he was the stage coach driver from

---

[9] Letters courtesy of his granddaughter, Dorothy Candlish Winke of Modesto, and grandson, Donald Stout of Snelling, California, 1994

Boerne to Bandera, he tried his luck as a wagon freighter, and he farmed for a while without much success. Reference is also made to his father having been away from home a great deal. He spoke of one incident that happened about 1886 when his father went out to the San Angelo area to homestead a tract of land. Instead, he got in a fight over the property he claimed and was locked up for a year. The charge was disturbing the peace.

After the jail time was served, Mr. Stout was permitted to write to his brother-in-law James Stephenson and asked that he come to San Angelo and get him out of jail; the fine portion of his sentence was still unpaid. Stephenson paid it. Professor Stout told about a letter his mother wrote to Dorothy on her first birthday. She explained to Dorothy that her father "is not with us tonight but he is remembered." In her book about Daniel and Emily Perrin,[10] Margaret Perrin Hoch included family letters in which Jennie Stout's name was mentioned. They indicated that Jennie and her children were staying with relatives at least on two occasions. She was with her parents, Mr. and Mrs. John Stephenson, when Dorothy was born in 1886.

Apparently, the Stout family was happy when Mr. Stout was home. The children adored him, but his father-in-law, John Stephenson, and brother-in-law, Willy Hughes, were probably not quite as forgiving.

Jennie Stout and her children were better off when they were near her parents and Hughes Ranch. Mr. and Mrs. Stephenson had patience and time for the children. Mr. Stephenson and the Hugheses were sticklers for education and learning. The ranch, with its large assortment of interesting barnyard fowls and livestock, was an exciting place for youngsters. All the Stout children helped with chores at the ranch from the time they were quite young. Of course, with the Hughes dairy in operation the Stout family had plenty of fresh milk and other produce from the ranch.

With the help of Willy and Lucy Hughes, Jennie Stout was appointed postmistress at Hastings on November 8, 1894. It is not known why Lucy and Willy sought to have

---

[10] Hoch, Margaret Perrin, DANIEL AND EMILY PERRIN: LIVES THAT TELL A STORY, LEBCO Graphics, Boerne, Texas , 1992

Mrs. Stout appointed postmistress, but one of Jennie's granddaughters said there were at least two valid reasons: (1) Her grandmother desperately needed the income, and (2) the Hugheses probably noticed that Jennie was showing signs of stress, and they thought the job might improve her morale and self-esteem. But there were other factors contributing to Jennie's declining health; her father died January 31, 1895, when she desperately needed his counsel and support; then she gave birth to three more children during her tenure as postmistress. They were Esther, born 1895; Alice, 1898; and Marion, 1900.

In the spring of 1900, Jennie became even more depressed and finally lost touch with reality, to the extent she had to be committed to the San Antonio State Hospital. Her baby, Marion, was taken to raise and later adopted by Jennie's brother and sister-in-law, James and Julia Stephenson. She was raised as a Stephenson.

Willy Hughes again had become postmaster at Hastings on June 13, 1900, but his sister-in-law, Ella Stephenson, helped manage the post office as she had done for Jennie since 1895, when she and her mother moved to the Hughes home after the death of John Stephenson. Evidently, Mr. Stout anticipated being appointed postmaster at Hastings when his wife became ill, but according to U. S. postal records, W. G. Hughes was appointed postmaster as Jennie Stout's replacement. An ad appeared in the local paper-- The BOERNE POST, July 26, 1900: "W. G. Hughes, not Mr. Stout, is now postmaster at Hastings."

Later in the summer of 1900, Mr. Stout moved his family to San Antonio. However, school records show that two of the Stout siblings, Alan and Esther, remained at Hughes Ranch and attended Hastings school during the 1901 school term.[11] Their Aunt Ella Stephenson moved near the Stout family in San Antonio to help Mr. Stout take care of the small children. Dorothy had already dropped out of Hastings school in 1899 at age 13 to help her mother with the babies. Prof. Stout noted that his father was still having financial problems in San Antonio.

In late August, 1900, Perry and John Willard Stout departed from San Antonio

---

[11]    Cartwright, Mary R., Research Paper on Hastings School, 1981

in search of a better life somewhere, perhaps California. They worked their way through Kansas, Colorado, and the grain harvest in Eastern Washington. They went to Portland, Oregon and finally landed at Hughson, California, a small settlement southeast of Modesto. Here they found work in construction of an irrigation canal. They bought a team of horses and a dirt-moving implement called a "frisno," not a "scoop," and went into the contracting business.

They bought 40 acres of prime farm land--soon to be irrigated--and started leveling it. This led to more contracts in preparing other properties for irrigation. They bought a surveyor's transom like the one they became familiar with at Hughes Ranch and became quite proficient with its use in their new business.

The older boys encouraged their father to bring the children to California where work was more plentiful. John Stout left San Antonio in the fall of 1905 by covered wagon with five of his children ranging in age from seven to nineteen. Alan, the third son had already gone to California. They headed north through Central Texas and Oklahoma, with intentions of turning west to the location of the older boys in Northern California.

The Stout family was joined by Walter Candlish, a young itinerant horse trader, when they stopped near Lawton, Oklahoma to work in the late fall harvest. During this stop Dorothy and Walter were smitten by a love bug and they eloped. Mr. Stout showed up at the wedding with a shotgun, but the ceremony was already finished. His strange action intimidated the young couple to the extent that they left during the night and made their way to Oklahoma City where they caught a train for Walter's family home in Vermont. This was the straw that broke the camel's back. The loss of his favorite child, the one that he depended upon most, was more than John Stout could endure. He totally freaked out, and committed an unthinkable act. He abandoned his four youngest children by stealing away during the night and vanishing from the scene. Claiborne, his thirteen year old son, sensed his father's extreme depression and feeling of worthlessness and failure. When he could find no trace of his father the next day, Claiborne talked to some local men about his dilemma. A Mr. John Black and his wife of nearby Sentinel offered the Stout children the use of a small dilapidated farm house near their home until they could get help. Claiborne and Gene hauled wood and performed farm chores for the Blacks to earn money for their food and provisions throughout the miserably cold winter.

Claiborne kept in touch with his Aunt Ella Stephenson in San Antonio, until she came to Lawton in the spring to pick up the two little girls, Esther and Alice. When she arrived, the boys sold the horses and wagon for their train fare to California. Ella kept the two small girls in San Antonio until their oldest brother Perry and his new bride, Hazel Beebe, were ready to take them into their home at Ceres (near Modesto) in the fall of 1906. All of John and Jennie Stout's children lived to enjoy very fruitful and productive lives. Perhaps their earlier experiences, work habits, and the encouragement of their own parents, their Stephenson grandparents, their Aunt Ella, and that of Willy and Lucy Hughes had some influence on their future successes.

About a year after their arrival in California, Esther and Alice were walking home from school in Ceres when they encountered their father as he drove through town in a two-wheeled donkey cart. They said he inquired if they were getting along alright without him, and then he headed out of town going south on Highway 99. The older boys scoffed at the girls' revelation, but the kids were able to confirm their story many years later.

Claiborne appears to have been the most devout of the Stout children in searching for their father. Some 20 years later, while he was farming near the Ruddle Ranch at Snelling, California, he came home one evening and announced that a hobo had just arrived in the area and said he knew an old man in Porterville (100 miles south) by the name of John Stout. He said Stout was working at this particular place for his food and lodging.

Donald Stout recalls that his father put his little boys in the back seat of his T-Model Ford early the next morning and headed for Porterville. Upon arriving at the shack where the old man lived, Claiborne told the children to stay in the car, while he went to the door and knocked. Don said it was with great anticipation and excitement that he and his brother watched as someone opened the door and their father stepped inside. It was about 30 minutes before the door opened again and their father came out with their grandfather in tow. Claiborne later said he told his father that if he was going to work for his room and board, he might as well do that for his own son.

John Stout lived another 20 years with Claiborne and his family while Claiborne was farming, running a dairy operation and later was manager of the famous Ruddle Ranch. He milked cows, chopped firewood, and performed numerous other handyman duties. Donald Stout and his brother Clay both said their grandfather had a close and rewarding relationship with his own children and that his grandchildren thought he was the most wonderful grandfather that a child could have. Mr. Stout was living in the home of his daughter Dorothy Candlish at Merced in 1941, when he became terminally ill. He died there in 1942 at age 90. Jennie Stout never saw her grandchildren. She died while still a patient at the San Antonio State Hospital in 1908. She was 53 years of age. Both are buried in the Boerne Cemetery.

Willy Hughes boarded the caboose of the morning train from Boerne to San Antonio on Monday, November 24th, 1902. Up front in a livestock car was a consignment of his prime Angora goats that were to be delivered to a customer in Paducah, Kentucky on Wednesday morning, November 26th. This was a routine procedure for Willy. He knew the railroad people and always obtained a permit to ride in the caboose while transporting livestock so he could check on his animals periodically.

In San Antonio, the car transporting the goats was switched to the Missouri-Kansas-Texas Line, called the "Katy." Traveling on a Katy freight train was a unique adventure, which Hughes had experienced many times before. He knew where regular stops were made--for water, to leave empty cars on side rails, or to pick up cars loaded with freight and ready for delivery to another destination. Willy tossed his sleeping roll on the Katy caboose, grabbed the handrails, and propelled himself up the steps. Recognizing most of the railroad employees, he greeted them when they weren't busy and watched as they attended last minute details before heading north. Some stops along the way allowed Willy time to check on his goats and to replenish water and feed in receptacles provided for them. On other occasions, there was only time to step off the train for a minute to stretch his legs. When the train was moving, Willy often visited with the crew, principally the conductor or the flagman; otherwise, he had time to think, reflecting on his past live, his family, or pending business transactions.

The first part of his trip was uneventful, as he passed through Austin, Waco, and Dallas to Dennison. From there, the train continued on through the Kiamichi Mountains of eastern Oklahoma to Fort Smith, Arkansas, then through the Ozark Mountains of western Arkansas into Missouri. Willy Hughes was always in awe of the beautiful mountain scenery. The train was a novelty to remote mountain people, and they frequently came outside to watch as the engine huffed and puffed as it struggled to negotiate to higher elevations. These friendly people always waved at the engineer and the train crew, who responded with a smile and wave. In summer months, barefoot children often ran with their dog in tow to the tracks for a closer view of a train and to wave at its crew; or sometimes the boys were leading pet goats on a leash.

On this phase of his trip there is no indication of just what Willy observed. But at this time of year, he likely noticed smoke coming from chimneys of rural mountain shacks and no doubt saw freshly cut firewood that was stacked nearby as most natives were preparing for winter. There is a record of weather conditions in St. Louis when the Katy arrived there in the late afternoon of November 25th, 1902. It was a cool, wet, foggy day with drizzling rain setting in before nightfall. By early evening, freight cars that had arrived at the large St. Louis railway transportation hub during the day were sorted out and rerouted to their new destinations.

Willy Hughes and his cargo were towed across the Mississippi bridge by Illinois Central Engine No.275, under control of Engineer G. A. Adams and Conductor Walkub. The flagman was John Moy. They stopped at the Illinois Central switching yard in Bellville, Illinois. There, Engine No. 554, under control of Engineer J. B. Lemon, with Fireman J. S. Thomas, was assembling a second section to be incorporated with No. 275's freight cars to be dispatched south on the Bellville and Southern division of the Illinois Central line.

## Fatal Crash

Willy Hughes was exhausted from the long train ride and bedded down in his makeshift sleeping gear shortly before 9:00 p.m., about the time a message was received at the Bellville yard to clear the main line for the passing of the fast moving "Dixie Flyer" passenger train that was three-and-a-half hours late on its trip from Chicago to New Orleans.

The BELLVILLE NEWS - DEMOCRAT published a news story on Wednesday, November 26, 1902, giving a vivid account of events as they occurred in an accident at the Illinois Central yard the evening of November 25, 1902:[1]

---

[1] BELLVILLE NEWS DEMOCRAT, Bellville, Ill., Story relating to train accident, Wednesday, November 26, 1902, copy provided to author in 1990.

227

Bellville, Ill., Wednesday, November 26, 1902

## REAR END COLLISION

### SECOND SECTION OF ILLINOIS CENTRAL FREIGHT CRASHED INTO FIRST SECTION WITH FATAL RESULTS.

Wreck Occurred at Race Street Crossing
W. G. Hughes of Boerne, Tex. Killed.

W. G. Hughes, a stockman residing at Boerne, the county seat of Kendall County, Texas, was instantly killed, and engineer J. B. Lemon of Pickneyville and Fireman J. S. Thomas of East St. Louis were slightly injured, an engine, three cars and a caboose were demolished and four cars damaged is the summing of the result of a rear-end collision between two Illinois Central trains in the yards in the city last night.

The collision occurred at the intersection of Race Street, in almost the exact place where a similar wreck occurred last January, in which Conductor Wing and Brakeman Ring lost their lives, and was between two sections of southbound freight No. 275 on the Bellville and Southern division of the Illinois Central.

The collision took place at 9:10 o'clock at what is known as the new depot, about half a mile west of the old station. There were two sections of the train. When the first section, which was in charge of Engineer G. A. Adams and Conductor Walkub arrived at Bellville it took the siding under orders to allow the New Orleans "Dixie Flyer" to pass, the Flyer being three and a half hours late. The train had safely sided, with the caboose and a few cars on the main track, awaiting the arrival of the passenger. Flagman John Moy had been sent back to give the signal to the on coming second section.

Moy claims he walked back the required distance and gave the signal, which was seen by the engineer of the second section. Engineer

Lemon declares that he applied the brakes at the proper time, but that they failed to work, and, owing to the slippery condition of the rail from the rain, he was unable to bring his train to a stop.

He also stated at the inquest that the flagman was only about three car lengths from the caboose of the first section when he gave the signal, when he should have been twenty car lengths or more.

He and his fireman and the other members of the crew had only time to jump before the collision came. The engine continued on its course until it had plowed through the caboose and a number of cars on the rear of the first section of the freight, completely demolishing them. The engine was also totally wrecked.

Shortly after the collision the body of the stockman was found with the back of the head crushed to a jelly. He had been asleep when the collision occurred, and death had evidently come instantly.

No one of either train crew was able to give any information as to his identity, but papers found in his pocket bore the name of W. G. Hughes. His body was taken to Gundlach & Co.'s undertaking rooms.

Hughes had charge of a consignment of Rock Mountain goats, which were billed to Paducah, Ky. Further inquiries made by Agent Jule Heidinger brought out the facts that Hughes lived at Boerne, Tex., and a telegram received from that point this morning stated that relatives of the dead man had been notified of the accident, and would wire instructions as to the disposition of the body.

Following quickly upon the wreck came rumors thick and fast that half a dozen trainmen had met their death. This caused Bellville people to flock to the scene of the wreck in large numbers, but, fortunately, the rumor proved false, as every member of the two train crews were soon accounted for after the collision.

Wrecking crews reached the scene of the wreck about midnight, and by 8 o'clock this morning the debris had been cleared away and all

229

trains were running on schedule time.

The wrecked cars were loaded with merchandise and this was practically a total loss. The engine, No. 554, was damaged to the extent of fully $2,500, and in entirety the loss is estimated at from $8,000 to $10,000.

Coroner R. N. McCracken of East St. Louis was notified, and this morning his deputy, Mr. George W. Brichler, arrived and conducted the inquest. The jury comprised W. R. Merker, foreman; Christ Horn, Henry Wolpert, Fred Weinel, Jacob Gauch and Arthur Wirsing. The witnesses examined were members of the crew of the second section, numbering Engineer J. B. Lemon, Fireman J. S. Thomas, Brakeman J. F. Smith, and W. H. Calvard and Conductor John Leeper.

Engineer Lemon's testimony was the most important. He said he saw the signal of the flagman when his engine was in about half a mile of the train, the flagman being about twelve car lengths from the train which was standing on the siding, when he should have been fully twenty-five car lengths distant. Lemon stated he saw the train, but, although he reversed his engine and did all in his power to bring it to a stop, he could not do so, owing to the slippery condition of the tracks and heavy down grade. He declared that his train was running about fifteen miles an hour when he first saw the signal and, was making about ten miles an hour when he and his fireman jumped, which was when his train was within about six car lengths of the train.

The jury returned a verdict of accidental death, and placed no blame on the Illinois Central Company or its employees.

THE DAILY ADVOCATE of Bellville printed essentially the same story about the train accident under the same dateline, but with more accurate information.[2] The

---

[2] Copy of two articles provided to author by Miss Debbie Miller, Librarian for BELLVILLE NEWS-DEMOCRAT, January 7, 1994.

Angora goats were properly identified, and it was reported that all of the goats, outside of a severe shake-up, were unharmed.

Ironically, the inquest jury returned a verdict of accidental death of Mr. Hughes and placed no blame on the Illinois Central Company or its employees for the accident. (Mrs. Hughes received no compensation from the railroad company.)

THE DAILY ADVOCATE further stated that three boxcars and the caboose were demolished and that the second engine (No. 554) was stripped of its stack, bell, whistle and sand, and steam boxes. The total damage was estimated at about $25,000.

A notice appeared in the SAN ANTONIO LIGHT, Sat., Nov. 29th.--Telegraph Brevities: " W. G. Hughes of Hastings, this state, killed in a railroad collision in Missouri."

## Hughes Returned To Texas

The BELLVILLE NEWS-DEMOCRAT article of November 26th said that relatives of W. G. Hughes in Boerne were notified of his death and would wire instructions as to disposition of the body. The DAILY ADVOCATE (evidently an afternoon paper) said "The remains of Hughes will be shipped to Texas."

A note from Dr. John Francis Nooe of Boerne appeared in the DAILY ADVOCATE on December 1, 1902. (The Nooe and Hughes families were neighbors and close friends.)

## Of A Prominent Family

"A communication received by the Advocate today from Dr. J. F. Nooe of Boerne, Texas, conveys the information that Mr. W. G. Hughes, of Boerne, the stockman killed in the rear-end collision in the Illinois Central yards in this city last Tuesday evening, is of a very prominent family.

Mr. Hughes' uncle is Thomas Hughes, the author of the well known 'Tom Brown's School Days' and other books. The remains of Mr. Hughes were shipped to Boerne for interment."

Unfortunately, a 1942 fire at the BOERNE STAR newspaper plant completely destroyed the local newspaper accounts of W. G. Hughes' accidental death and of his burial service at the ranch. Gerard H. "Jerry" Hughes was only seven years old when his father died, but he still remembers a number of things about his father's funeral. He recalls the casket being in the large downstairs living room at the ranch house. He said the funeral service was conducted inside the house because of cold, rainy weather, but he didn't know who was in charge of the service.[3]

Jerry also remembered going with the family to the grave site on the side of a hill overlooking the ranch house and pasture below. There was another brief ceremony there, and the casket was lowered into the ground near a big live oak tree.[4]

## Dissolution of Hughes Ranch

Just as the passing of Granny Hughes sounded the death knell for Rugby, Tennessee, so the death of Willy Hughes signaled the demise of the Hughes Ranch and the quaint little settlement of Hastings, Texas.

When the household had settled down following Willy's burial, Hastings Hughes had a long talk with Lucy about her future plans. He told her it was imperative that she sell the ranch and move her young family to Milton, Massachusetts, where he could help look after the children and they could attend Milton Academy and move on to a suitable Ivy League University to finish their education. Lucy faced a heart-rending decision, but there wasn't another viable choice. She accepted her father-in-law's advice and agreed to move to Milton as soon as she could sell the ranch and settle Willy's estate.

That was a monumental task. Willy died intestate, and Lucy had to petition the

---

[3] St. Mark's Episcopal Church records in Boerne show that Rev. Erastus De Wolfe was Rector of the church in 1902, and all members of the Hughes family were members of that church.

[4] William George Hughes' remains were disinterred and moved to the Boerne Cemetery in 1990 at request of his son, Gerard H. Hughes. Disinterment and reburial was under supervision of then County Judge Garland Perry and M.A. Shumard, former County Judge.

Probate Court to appoint her administratrix of his estate. Then there was the challenging problem of sorting out and trying to comprehend the complexities of numerous land deals in which Willy was involved. The leveraging method Willy used in financing land purchases worked fine for him, but it was a nightmare for Lucy to deal with in selling property. Hastings Hughes talked with his brother-in-law, Malcolm Forbes, about Lucy's dilemma, and they decided to send Cameron Forbes (Malcolm's son)[5] to Boerne to help her sort out the major problems and establish priorities. Forbes stayed in Boerne about two weeks, then left his assistant behind to help Lucy for a longer period of time.

It took Mrs. Hughes one year to dispose of 6,840 acres of land shown on the Inventory and Appraisement list of community property belonging to her and Willy.[6] She had approximately 2000 sheep and goats to dispose of, 127 horses, and ten Jacks and Jennets.

Fortunately, Sam Norris and Julio stayed with the ranch until its final closing. They were of invaluable help to Lucy in caring for and disposing of the livestock. Mrs. Hughes' thirty-five dairy cattle were handled as personal property and were sold separately from the other livestock. Nimrod, the prized Arabian stallion, was one of the last animals to leave the ranch.

Jerry Hughes tells an interesting story about his utopian carefree lifestyle at the ranch as a youngster. On this certain day, he and his brother George were sitting on the rock fence at the breeding enclosure as Sam Norris was preparing Nimrod and a mare for mating. The horses put on quite a show during this phase of their act. They rubbed their noses and necks together, squealed, and at times suddenly ran to another part of the pen, where they continued the courtship by rearing up, as if fighting. Just as the show was getting most interesting, a gentleman whom the boys didn't know--obviously a city slicker--went to the house and told their mother that her sons shouldn't be watching this

---

[5] William Cameron Forbes (1870-1959), Governor General of the Philippines from 1909-1915 and Ambassador to Japan, 1930-32.

[6] Cause No. 262, Probate Court Records, Kendall County, Texas, dated December 22, 1902

event. Mrs. Hughes was courteous and a little embarrassed, but she called the boys to the house, and they missed the matinee performance. Of course, they had watched similar acts of animal life many times before.

Gerard H. Hughes                    George F. Hughes

Lucy Hughes was appointed postmistress at Hastings, April 23, 1903.[7] The Hastings post office was discontinued December 14, 1903, and all letters and documents were taken to the Boerne post office.[8]

It was a sad event the next morning when a host of relatives, friends, and

_____

[7] Moroney, Rita L., U. S. Postal Service, Letter to author, Sept. 19, 1989

[8] Ibid

neighbors gathered at the Boerne railway station to say goodbye to Lucy Hughes and her children.

When the conductor called out, "A-L-L  A-B-O-A-R-D!," the Hugheses made their way up the steps and took their seats in the passenger car. The engineer gave one short blast of the whistle as the train slowly pulled away. It was farewell to a lifetime of dreams and to Willy Hughes, who lay in his grave on the hillside overlooking the Hughes Ranch estate.

No member of the W. G. Hughes family ever returned to Boerne, but Willy's son Gerard Hughes wrote to the author that he almost got back to the ranch during World War I. While stationed at Rich Field near Waco in 1918, where he was a pilot and Flight Instructor, Jerry bought an automobile and took a three-day pass for a drive down to Boerne and the ranch. He said he came up from San Antonio and turned left on the Bandera road. When he got in sight of the ranch house roof, he was overcome with grief and stopped the car. After walking around for a few minutes, he got in the car and drove back to Waco. The emotional trauma was more than he could endure, and he vowed then that he would never return.

Only 43 years of age when he died, Willy Hughes had already been in the ranching business 23 years. In that short span, his accomplishments were more than most successful ranchers would have achieved in a full lifetime. Yet, he had not reached his ultimate goal of financial success; he still had a few more mountains to climb.

Willy was already enjoying considerable success in selling cavalry mounts and polo ponies to the U. S. Army when the Spanish American War broke out in 1898. His order for the delivery of the consignment of horses to the U. S. Cavalry at Mustang Island was followed by the Boar War in South Africa, 1899-1902. At the beginning of that war, British remount officers were dispatched to America to buy horses and mules that would best meet their needs in the African climate and terrain. They first checked the horse and mule markets in Kentucky, Missouri and Tennessee. But it was in Southwest Texas that they found an abundant supply of the type of horses and mules they wanted.[9]  They were the Texas cow pony, a mixture of mustang and quarter horse bloodlines.  The popular Texas mules came from the same cow pony brood mares.

British agents bought 100,000 U.S. horses and 85,000 mules; the Texas share was approximately 35,000 horses and 50,000 mules.[10]

The Texas horses and mules were favorites with British troops during the Boar War, and they also became popular throughout the American southern states, especially Louisiana and Alabama.  The mules were known for "their iron constitution and easy, inexpensive keep."

Nobody knows how many horses Willy Hughes sold to the agents when they were buying in the San Antonio area, but it is reasonable to assume that he got his share of that market.  But most importantly, we learned through his death that the ever astute and pragmatic Mr. Hughes had once again discovered a golden nugget in the livestock industry that could conceivably have insured his ultimate financial security in another 20 years, had he not died prematurely.  Ever a man with 20-20 long-range vision, Willy had already noticed the phenomenal increase in popularity and demand for mules as harness animals; and he acted accordingly.

The Inventory and Appraisement document filed in Kendall County Probate Court records on December 22, 1902, shows that W. G. Hughes owned 10 Jacks and Jennets and 126 head of stock horses (probably brood mares) in his breeding program.

Texas continued leading the nation in mule and horse production, and mules were bringing up to $200 per head shipped in carload lots, according to the 1904 TEXAS ALMANAC.  By 1910, war clouds were collecting over Europe.  At the same time, the U.S. inventory of horses and mules stood at 19,833,000 and 4,210,000 respectively, in 1910.[11]  Texas was still leading all states with approximately 25% of horses and mules raised in the United States.

---

[9]  Anson, William, TEXAS ALMANAC, 1904, pages 123-127

[10]  TEXAS ALMANAC, 1904

[11]  YEARBOOK OF AGRICULTURE, U. S. Department of Agriculture, 1935

With the tremendous demand for American horses and mules during WWI, 1914-1918, Willy Hughes' major goal for success as a rancher-stockman might have been attained. One other thing of interest on the inventory list was a check to be collected from D. Willis for goats sold, $462.00. Did Willy Hughes actually coax his old friend and mentor, or the mentor's son, into becoming a man with a **name**?

On September 9, 1920, Kendall County Commissioners' Court voted to discontinue Hastings School due to insufficient students.[12] Hastings was consolidated with Upper Balcones School.

The school was the last vestige of the once prominent Hughes Ranch and the thriving Hastings community. It remains only a memory to a few old-timers like Jerry Hughes. But the legacy of Willy Hughes endures, living on in the collection of his letters, bearing witness to one man's spirit of adventure and the power and the pleasure of family bond. This is the **life**, the **times** and the **story** of William George "Willy" Hughes--A Pioneer Texas Rancher.

---

[12] Cartwright, Mary, Boerne, Texas, Research papers given to the writer

# BIBLIOGRAPHY

## BOOKS

Best, Hugh, DeBRETT'S TEXAS PEERAGE, Coward-McCann, Inc., New York, N. Y., 1983

Brown, James, LETTERS FROM A TEXAS SHEEP RANCH, University of Illinois Press, Urbana, Ill., 1959

Brown, John Henry, INDIAN WARS AND PIONEERS OF TEXAS, L. E. Daniell, Publisher, Austin, Texas, 1880; Republished by Rev. S. Emmitt Lucas, Jr., Southern  Historical Press, Easley, S. C., 1978

Conwright-Schreiner, S. C., THE ANGORA GOAT, Longmans, Green and Co., 39 Paternoster Row, London, England, 1898

Cuddon, J. A., THE INTERNATIONAL DICTIONARY OF SPORTS AND GAMES, Schocken Books, New York, N.Y., 1980

DeBruyn, John R., DISSIPATIONS AT UFFINGTON HOUSE, Memphis State University, Memphis, Tennessee, 1976

DeBruyn, John R., LETTERS TO OCTAVIUS WILKINSON: TOM HUGHES LOST UNCLE, based on letters in the Morris L. Parrish Collection of Princeton University Library

Egerton, John, VISIONS OF UTOPIA, University of Tennessee Press, Knoxville, Tennessee, 1977

GALLOPING OFF IN ALL DIRECTIONS, Angus & Robertson, U. K., Ltd., 16th Ship St., London, 1978

Herff, Ferdinand Peter, THE DOCTORS HERFF, Vol. I, Trinity University Press, San Antonio, Texas, 1973

Hickok, Ralph, THE ENCYCLOPEDIA OF NORTH AMERICAN SPORTS HISTORY,  Maple-Vail Book Manufacturing Group, New York, N.Y., 1991

Hill, John Moxon, A TEXAS DREAM SHATTERED, edited and published by John Moxon  Hill, 15, Belvedere R., Earlsdon, Coventry. CV5 6PF., England, 1994

Hoch, Margaret Perrin, DANIEL AND EMILY PERRIN: LIVES THAT TELL A STORY, LEBCO Graphics, Boerne, Texas 1992

Hughes, Sarah Forbes, JOHN MURRAY FORBES, LETTERS AND RECOLLECTIONS, Vol. II, Houghton, Mifflin & Company of New York and Boston, 1899

Hughes, Thomas, G.T.T.-GONE TO TEXAS, MacMillan Co., London, 1884

Kendall, George Wilkins, (Articles on sheep raising) TEXAS ALMANAC, published by The Galveston News, 1858, 1859, 1867, 1868

Perry, Garland, HISTORIC IMAGES OF BOERNE, LEBCO Graphics, 1982

Randall, Henry S., WOOL GROWING AND THE TARIFF: "A Study in Economic History of the United States"; THE PRACTICAL SHEPHERD, a popular handbook on sheep raising; SHEEP HUSBANDRY IN THE SOUTH, (Source of Randall's articles for TEXAS ALMANAC, The Galveston News, Willard Richardson, Publisher, 1860, 1861, 1868)

Stout, John Willard, Memoirs, AS I REMEMBER IT, 1978. Use authorized by Dr. John Willard Stout, Jr., and Mrs. Beatrice S. Dooley

TEXAS ALMANAC, Published by The Dallas Morning News, Dallas, Texas, 1904

THE BIG BOOK OF HALLS OF FAME of The U. S. and Canada, Compiled and Edited by Paul Sodenberg, Helen Washington, Jaques Cattell Press, R. R. Bowker Company, New York and London, 1977

THE HANDBOOK OF TEXAS, Prescott Webb, Editor-in-Chief, Texas Historical Association, Austin, Texas 1952

Thompson, George F., ANGORA GOAT RAISING AND MILCH GOATS, U. S. Bureau of Animal Industry, U. S. Dept. of Agriculture, Washington, D. C., 1903

Webb, Walter Prescott, THE TEXAS RANGERS, University of Texas Press, Austin, Texas, 1965

Welch, Richard Jr., THE PRESIDENCY OF GROVER CLEVELAND, University of Kansas Press, 1988

YEARBOOK OF AGRICULTURE, U. S. Department of Agriculture, 1935

NEWSPAPERS

BELLVILLE NEWS DEMOCRAT, Bellville, Ill. Copy of articles provided to author by Miss Debbie Miller, Librarian, January 7, 1994

BOERNE POST, September 29, 1898

BOERNE STAR, Irons and Graham Subdivision story by Harry Davis, Sr., published 11-17-93

SAN ANTONIO DAILY EXPRESS, San Antonio, Texas

MAGAZINES, PERIODICALS

TEXAS FARM AND RANCH MAGAZINE, reprint in BOERNE STAR, January 12, 1899

TEXAS LIBRARIES, Vol.46, No. I, Spring/Summer 1985, Article on Carnegie libraries by Garland Perry

## INTERVIEWS

Calder, Howard C., a leading historian, businessman, and part owner of
    the old Turquand Ranch of Kendall and Bexas Counties.
    Interview, September, 1994
Shumard, M. A. Jr., former County Judge and lifetime resident of
    Boerne, Interview, 1991
Wendler, A. T., Interview, November, 1993.


## PERSONAL

Cartwright, Mary, Research paper on Hastings School, February 1981
Categories of Land Grants in Texas, Reference Sheet #1,
    Texas General Land Office, Archives and Records Division
Deed Records Kendall County Clerks' Office.
Staggs, Barbara, Executive Director, Historic Rugby, Inc.
St. Mark's Episcopal Church records in Boerne, Texas, 1992
Texas State Land Board Records, viewed 11-8-93


## TELEPHONE

Cantrell, Pearl, Archivist, Historic Rugby, Tennessee, Telephone interview, 12-4-93
Machen, Richard V., Texas Agricultural Statistical Service, Uvalde A&M Research &
    Extension Center, September, 1994


## LETTERS

Moroney, Rita L., U. S. Postal Service, Letter to author, Sept. 19, 1989
Spencer, George H., Attorney, San Antonio, ref. 1889-90 Prospectus of THE
    BOERNE ACADEMY AND COMMERCIAL COLLEGE, August 6, 1993

# INDEX

Hughes, Thomas: 3,105,107-109,111,116
Hughes, Walter Scott: 3
Hughes, William George: 2-4,8-32,36-
39,43,47-50,55-59,61-63,65-68,70,71,80
81-95,119,123-125,138-141,
143,147,149,154,156,159,165-168,192,
201-202
Hugman, Horace: 80
Hugman, R. B.: 78
Ireland, John, Governor: 176
Irons, D. S: 194
Julio: 213,215,233
Kendall, George W.: 97-98
Kingsbury, W. G.: 6-7,182-183
Klemme, Chas.: 78,200
Landrum, Frank O.: 189
Landrum, William M.: 187-189,209
Lend, Genny: 3
Lockwood, J. F.: 12,89
McNeil, Francis: 213,217
Merino Sheep: 123,129,131-133,184
Minnich, I.: 78,200
Newton, Barbara T.: 200
Newton, E. R.: 200
Nooe, Dr. John Francis: 78,231
Norris, Sam: 183,196,200,213,214,233
Norris, Vernon: 168,183
O'Grady Inn: 58
Oxfordshire Downs Sheep: 33,39,74,
Perry, Middleton: 172,
Peters, Col. Richard: 187
Phillip House: 58
Polo: 105-109,170,174,175,198
Purdy, Belmont: 106
Railroad, San Antonio & Aransas Pass:
181-183,201
Randall, Henry, S.: 98,183-185
Reinhard, John: 201
Remmick, Jacob: 78
Rickhoff, The Tanner: 213,216-217
Roosevelt, President "Teddy": 207
Rugby Boys School: 3
Rugby, Tennessee: 4,111-114,205
Saner, P. D.: 200

Scarborough, W. W.: 114
Schultz, A.: 78
Schultz, Leopold: 100
Scott, Sir Walter: 3
Seawald, August, County Judge: 202
Senior, Jeanie Elizabeth Hughes: 3,110
Senior, Nassau William: 3
Senior, Nassau John: 3
Spencer, Rad: 78
Stephenson, Ann Dover: 77,202,218
Stephenson, Ella: 78
Stephenson, Frances: 78
Stephenson, Henry: 78
Stephenson, James: 78,222
Stephenson, John: 77,200,202,218,219
Stephenson, Joseph: 78
Stephenson, Julia: 222
Stout, Alan: 213,220-225
Stout, Alice: 222-225
Stout, Claiborne: 220-225
Stout, Donald: 220-225
Stout, Esther: 213,222-225
Stout, Eugene Paul: 220-2254
Stout, Jennie Stevenson: 78,218,220-225
Stout, John Calhoun: 219-225
Stout, Marion: 222-225
Stout, Perry: 208-209,213,220-225
Stout, Proffesor John Willard, Sr.:
168,178-181,208-209,213,220-225
Swanwick, T. F.: 201
Sweeny Hotel: 8
Swift, Henry, Chaplain: 192
Swisher, J. M.: 78
Taylor, Lucy: 133,168,205
Thompson, George F., Prof.: 209-210
Tolson, Bertha: 200
Tourquant, William Glynn: 173
Ullrich, Laurabelle: 205
Vogel, C. G.: 165-168,194-195
Watt, George Frederick: 3,4
Wendler, A. T.: 170.171,173,217
Windale, Lennie: 73,116
Wright, W: 80
Ye Kendall Inn: 58